BLOK:
An Anthology
of Essays and Memoirs

Edited and Translated by
Lucy Vogel

Ardis   Ann Arbor

Library of Congress Cataloging in Publication Data

Main entry under title:

Alexander Blok, an anthology of essays and memoirs.

    Bibliography: p.
    1. Blok, Aleksandr Aleksandrovich, 1880-1921 –
Addresses, essays, lectures. 2. Poets, Russian—20th
century—Biography—Addresses, essays, lectures.
I. Vogel, Lucy E.
PG3453.B6Z5979 1982   891.71'3 [B]   82-8711
ISBN 0-88233-487-5   AACR2
ISBN 0-88233-488-3 (pbk.)

CONTENTS

ILLUSTRATIONS

FOREWORD

Among the great poets of twentieth-century Russia is Alexander Blok, the most celebrated of all Russian Symbolists. In one of the richest and most heterogeneous eras in Russian poetry, Blok's genius captured the lime-light: his poetry attracted and held in its spell disparate audiences from the unsophisticated peasant to the highly discriminating critic. Whether it sang of personal joys or sorrows, the emptiness of life, or Petersburg's cityscape or nightlife, it had the universal quality and the immediacy of experience that touched even those who were foreign to the sophistication of symbolic verse. For many, Blok's appeal went beyond his poetry. His personal charisma, enhanced by his handsome, serious and tormented face, and his notoriously dissipated life made him somewhat of a legend in his time. His lyrics, stirring with dark forebodings of inevitable upheavals and the secret hope of future harmony, reflected the dominant preoccupations and dreams of a generation lost in uncertainties and contradictions. The extensive memoiristic and criti-cal literature on Blok views him not only as an important literary figure but as a symbolic representative of his age. The critic Z. Mints, who believed that a feeling of *vlyublyonnost* (being in love) which Blok generated in his audience contributed to his popularity, wrote that both as man and poet he filled "that perennial need of every epoch to find in the very image of a living artist a live embodiment of its own hopes and expectations."

It is probably because Blok's significance transcends his poetry that the language of acknowledgements and reminiscences is often itself symbolic. Anna Akhmatova called him "the tragic tenor of the epoch"; to the critic P. Medvedev he was the "Virgil of our generation in its hapless wanderings through the 'Inferno' of a barren world and the 'Purgatorio' of budding dreams." Kuzmina-Karavaeva (Mother Maria) saw in him a martyr "burning himself out" in the name of Russia—the conscience of a dying class. Paster-nak, through his hero Yura Zhivago, paid him the greatest tribute of all. "It suddenly occurred to Yura," he wrote, "that Blok reflected the Christmas spirit in all the domains of Russian life—in this northern city and in the new-est Russian literature, under the starry sky of this modern street and around the lighted tree in a twentieth-century drawing room."

Blok's talent and popularity brought him into contact with the out-standing personalities of his time. There was hardly anyone of prominence, whether in literature, theater, or the arts, with whom Blok was not per-sonally acquainted. He maintained a warm friendship with many of his distinguished contemporaries throughout his life. But not only the famous had access to the poet. Young men and women from cities and provinces near and far sent him their verses, which he diligently read and evaluated; many traveled long distances to hear him read his poems and in the hope of exchanging a few words with him. Blok always gave generously of his time, for he felt a deep sense of responsibility and commitment toward those who sought his help. His numerous interests and activities brought him into contact with all sorts of people and aspects of life, enriching his poetic world with vivid and tangible impressions of reality. Conversely, those people he met and who afterwards recalled meeting him left, together with their reminiscences of Blok, important documentaries of the cultural life and literary milieu of this exciting period of Russian letters—this last period of artistic freedom which vanished with the Revolution.

Aside from his unquestionable talent as a poet, what was there so distinctive and yet so familiar about Blok that made him a towering figure among his contemporaries, a symbolic representative of his age and a source of inspiration to his generation and those which followed?

Almost paradoxically, the spirit of this quintessentially twentieth-century poet was deeply rooted in Russia's literary traditions. His verse, like Pushkin's, is highly musical, elusively effortless, and a subtle blend of the rational and emotional. Like Pushkin's, his themes are eclectic and range from the commonplace to the sublime, from quasi-religious contemplation to motifs of harlequinade, from Russian realities to myths of other nations. Blok admitted that he "loved life in all its fleeting trifles," but like Lermontov's "Angel," he found the "songs of this earth hollow and tedious" and yearned for the "sounds of heaven." Like both Pushkin and Lermontov he expressed a profound contempt for the materialistic "mob" and for life's petty concerns. Like Tyutchev, he saw no dichotomy between the mystic and the real and, looking for ultimate meanings, searched for clues in the chaotic and mystic depths of man and nature. In the tradition of Nekrasov, he felt a personal guilt for Russia's social injustices and consequently perceived the Revolution as a just retribution for the evils perpetrated by the tsarist regime and the gentry against the lower classes. Like Fet, the young Blok's favorite poet, he found in the subtle shiftings of the natural world a corollary to the changing perceptions of the human heart.

But despite the influence of the nineteenth-century poetic and humanistic tradition, Blok looked at everyday reality from his own unique perspective: he described himself as a corpse among the living, he perceived life as a masquerade where people hide behind masks; he joyously prophesied the imminent demise of Western civilization and believed that only a total destruction of the old order could herald a new and wholesome life. An inner duality, a tendency to perceive everything of import in life dialectically, is one of Blok's outstanding characteristics. Two antithetical emotions or convictions could coexist in his soul even though, in the last analysis, what mattered were not the emotions or convictions in themselves, but the struggle between them.

Love and hate, the enticements of both spirit and flesh, of good and evil, hope and despair, intertwined in his consciousness and became inseparable in their never-ending confrontation. Already in his late teens, the budding poet, aspiring to harmony and self-transcendence, was struggling with what he thought were inner demonic forces that were leading him into darkness and chaos. He also sensed the antinomies which he felt in himself as universal forces present in all phenomena. Duality dominated his feelings for Russia, which appeared to him simultaneously as an ideal—a country of martyrs and saints—and as an abomination—a drunken Russia wallowing in corruption and debauch. Blok's prose writings were often the battleground where his inner conflicts clashed and burst out in a style rich in antithesis and paradox. In the structural patterns of poetry he sought their resolutions. Blok wrote in his *Notebook* in 1909 that "Form in art is generative spirit, creative order . . . *The good artist* is . . . the one who out of chaos . . . creates a comsos."

The complexity that characterizes Blok's prose is resolved harmoniously in his poetry. As intricate as his thought may appear in the former, the more artless and simple it appears in much of the latter. It was, of course, only an illusory simplicity, but one that gives his poetry such an authority of authenticity that its persona was often taken for the poet himself. In the course of what seemed an attempt at times to escape from his own self, and at others, to retreat into his own self, he touched upon those problems and strivings that are common to all. The human and universal element of his poetry broke through the core of its symbolism and reached out directly to the reader. "Everyone loved Blok," wrote Gorodetsky. It goes without saying that when he welcomed the Revolution and offered his allegiance to the Soviet regime, not everyone continued to love him. But even those who reacted most passionately to what they regarded as a "betrayal" of their values and of the freedom of art—as did Z. Gippius and Bunin—did not doubt the sincerity of his feelings and the integrity of thought that was one of his most distinct characteristics.

Blok's poetry was protean enough to accommodate a wide reading public: for the avant-garde reader there were the "Poems about the Beautiful Lady," with their hazy landscape and intimations of other realities; for the realist—images of urban decadence and squalor; for the nationalist—poems glorifying Russia's past and defying anyone who would dare to oppose her triumphant march ahead; for the romantic—love lyrics replete with surreal and earthly pathos. It was Blok's rebellion against the prose of everyday reality, however, his alienation and refusal to accept the "terrible world"—be it Russia's or the West's—with its materialistic culture and lack of spiritual values—which became his unmistakable hallmark. These feelings and attitudes cast a melancholy and often gloomy shadow upon his art and earned him the reputation of being a poet of pessimism and despair. Such moods particularly appealed to the educated youth and the intelligentsia—the two classes most critically opposed to the social order and which welcomed the poet's prediction that "unheard of changes, rebellions such as were never seen before" were in the offing. Blok's poems captured the disorientation, anger, and sense of hopelessness which so many felt, and by giving them artistic form, may well have enlarged their scope. At least so thought the critic Knyazhnin, who in his monograph on Blok wrote: "The sad part was that in this despair, in this non-acceptance of the world, in this unwillingness to be part of it, to say 'yes' to it and thus find satisfaction in and a reason for one's life and work, the great majority of Russian intellectuals wasted their capacities in negation." Eikhenbaum's judgment was even more severe. Blok, according to him, having become a "dictator of feelings," did not use his power in a positive way: "Summoning us from the 'pale glow of art' to the 'fires of life,' Blok led us away from real art, but did not bring us to real life."

However, it was not only negation that was reflected in Blok's verses, but the whole Petersburg scene: the winters with their whirling snows and bonfires, red dawns and leaden sunsets, dingy taverns at the edge of town and street lights wearily shining on the mirrored surface of the Neva. Pasternak felt that Blok understood the very essence of the city as it existed "both in reality and in the imagination."

Blok is usually referred to as a lyric poet, but an image of him as a poet does not encompass his creative personality. He wrote dramas, critical articles and monographs, essays on art, history and numerous other subjects. As far as word count goes, he wrote more prose than poetry. Contemporary critics and writers, like the rational and democratic Gorky, who did not share Blok's mystic views and, in fact, by his own admission, could not understand them, contributed to the widespread notion that Blok the prose writer and social theoretician was considerably inferior to Blok the poet. Gorky may have approved the fact that Blok wrote and lectured on subjects of social concern, but the poet's theoretical approach and metaphysical insights clashed with his own pragmatic approach to Russia's ills.

And, indeed, their views could not have been further apart. Blok felt that the survival of the human race depended not on economic or political solutions, but on a transcendental understanding of life. To achieve this understanding man must look beneath the surface of reality for those elemental and universal features common to all peoples and all times. He wrote: "In the unfathomable depths of the spirit, in depths beyond the reach of governments and society, which are the products of man's civilization, and where man ceases to be man, sound waves roll that are akin to the waves of ether that surround the earth: there rhythmic vibrations take place that are like those that form mountains, winds, marine currents and the vegetable and animal world" (VI, 163). It is the task of the poet to explore these depths, listen to their musical vibrations, and transmit their meaning through the medium of art: "The poet is the son of harmony and he has a specific role in world culture. He is entrusted with three tasks: first of all, to free the sounds from the native chaos in which they dwell; secondly, to turn these sounds into harmony; and thirdly, to bring this harmony into the outer world" (VI, 161). Without this "harmony" mankind is doomed. It is the obligation of the artist, as Blok saw it, to awaken man to an awareness of this primordial harmony, to create a yearning for it. Art from this viewpoint is essential to the continuation of a life that is human; it is a dynamic force for progress and humanity's ultimate salvation.

The conception of art as related to the "elemental" and of the artist-poet as the instrument which captures its notes and rhythms and through whom the primordial "music" flows is central to Blok's worldview. He referred to this Music with a capital M and, perceiving it as a mystic force governing the course of history and the destiny of mankind, defined it as the "essence of the world." Chukovsky recollects that Blok even used the epithet "musical" in an individual way. Events were for him either "musical," i.e., meaningful and important, or "non-musical"—banal and empty. Only through art can one hear this Music and thus relate to the universe and partake of the universal harmony. The ultimate goal is for all men to reach that stage of sensitivity that now only artists possess. Blok, however, did not have much faith in man's wisdom and did not really believe in the efficacy of his preaching, but he did believe that an apocalypse was in sight and that mankind would pay a high price for its apathy and deafness. His premonitions, which were later interpreted as uncanny prophesies of the Revolution, had little to do with political consciousness, but were, rather, mystical conclusions arrived at intuitively.

Blok's entire output can be seen in the light of his search for deeper meanings and relationships. He is constantly questioning, analyzing, correlating phenomena from outwardly unrelated spheres and finding among them unexpected analogies. His spiritual quest is an elusive, but nonetheless real presence in his poetry. The faith that his art, inwardly illuminated by his theories, had social meaning and purpose kept Blok's spirits up despite his failing health, family problems, and progressively worse material conditions after the Revolution. But his faith collapsed like a house of cards when it became clear that nothing could change the course Russia was taking. "The year 1918," writes Eikhenbaum, "is the year of his maximalism," his last "attempt to listen attentively to the 'music' of the Revolution," and "drown out his 'personal' tragedy in the roar of the world orchestra." In one of his last appearances before an audience, six months before his death, on the occasion of an evening honoring Pushkin, Blok made a symbolic allusion which, in terms of his own life, was prophetic. He said that a "poet dies when he can no longer breathe; life has lost its meaning." The specific reference, of course, was to Pushkin and to the restrictions upon his creative freedom, but Blok was also thinking of his own predicament as well. Physically he was suffering from a lung condition, and emotionally and intellectually from the stifling atmosphere of the post-revolutionary times. But as Chukovsky tells us, most tragic for him was the fact that he could no longer "hear." Sobered by reality after his initial inebriation with the spirit of the Revolution, he discovered that suddenly all inner sounds had ceased. After the exhilarating din of the old world crashing to pieces, which he had felt with all the fibers of his body, he found himself surrounded by silence. Life "lost its meaning." Hopelessness, a sense of futility, and inability to come to terms with reality hastened his end.

Blok died in 1921, disillusioned in his expectations and estranged from many of his former friends, who ostracized him for his support of the Revolution. The fact that once again a great poet had lived among them, had brought an irrefutably new spiritual dimension into their lives, and that his talent had been allowed to wither and die, awakened in his compatriots a belated sense of guilt, not devoid, however, of a good dose of Russian fatalism. For with each premature death of a great poet the specter of other fateful deaths returns to haunt the mind. "Some deaths are especially significant and prophetic," wrote the critic Chulkov, "Pushkin's, Lermontov's, Blok's . . . Pushkin died and we feel that he was the victim who had to be sacrificed for us all. Then Lermontov, then Blok, the disarmed knight . . . ."

The reaction to Blok's death revealed the extent of the affection and high regard that he had inspired even in those who had feuded with him in life. A mass of eulogies, memoirs and articles began to appear immediately after his death and continued for almost a decade. During Stalin's regime, Blok's reputation declined. He was excluded from the Soviet Parnassus, as were many writers both living and dead. Fortunately, Blok's exile to the archives did not end in oblivion. After Stalin's death and with the publication of his *Collected Works* (1960-1963), interest in Blok revived and many new biographical and critical works appeared that incorporated new materials and interpretations.

Evaluations of an artist by those who knew him or belonged to his generation are not necessarily more credible, perceptive, or reliable than those gained through hindsight or scholarly detachment. And yet we go back again and again to the works of those who knew Blok personally and lived in his milieu, for they alone can give us that feeling of context and contact with the poet that can bring his poetry closer to us and more fully explain how Blok stood as a symbol of his epoch, of its contradictions and aspirations. P. Medvedev, in *Alexander Blok's Artistic Path,* states correctly:

New generations will come.... Alexander Blok will rise before them in a new light. Perhaps their eyes will be sharper, the scales of their judgment more accurate. Contemporaries can err—that is true. But contemporaries inevitably perceive more keenly than will future generations that living spark, that intimate note that made the poet's soul vibrate. This perception comes from the sharing of a common experience.

BLOK THE MAN

LYUBOV MENDELEEVA-BLOK
FACTS AND MYTHS ABOUT BLOK AND MYSELF

When a writer is dead we mourn him, but at least we know that his suffering is at an end. For a writer the greatest of sufferings is submitting to someone else's will and thus being broken.

Neither need nor censorship, neither friendship nor love could ever break Blok. Nothing could bend him, he would not give in. But now there he is: helpless, bound by the earth. A heavy stone lies upon him. Critics measure writers according to their own subjective criteria or portray them according to their whims, just as certain artists paint or sculpt whatever trivial or insignificant image their talents enable them to make. Then they say: "This is Pushkin," or "This is Blok." Lies and slander! That's not Pushkin! That's not Blok! First of all, Blok was never resigned to life, nor to some "lecturer's theme" (III, 126)[1] nor "defeated by destiny...."[2]

Should I multiply the number of blasphemies? Should I, with the pen of a craftsman, attempt what the pen of a genius could not always handle? People have been urging me for a long time to write down what I witnessed, and I know that I must, because I did not merely see, I looked. Yet now, in order to describe what I saw, I need a new perspective, because I never was a passive observer, but rather an involved participant. Are the points of view from which I previously looked still valid? No, they are not: they are subjective. I have been waiting all this time for reconciliation, objectivity, historical perspective. One should not attempt to come to terms with one's own past in one's memoirs; one must be severed from it. But such a time has not yet come for me. I am still living with my past, suffering the pain of "unforgettable wrongs" (III, 70), still loving and hating, and if I write what I feel, I will not give the reader what he expects from "Blok's wife." It's been like this all my life.

"The wife of Alexander Alexandrovich," and suddenly people knew what I must be like, because they knew what the function of the term "wife" was equal to in the mathematical expression "the poet and his wife." But I was not a "function," I was a person, and although I often did not know what I myself was equal to, I knew even less what "the wife of a poet" should be equal to in that notorious expression. It often turned out to be equal to zero. And because I did not see myself as a function, I used to plunge head first into my own "private" life.

Exhilarating days, when one walks along the time-worn country bridges of a small provincial town, along the fence beyond which, under a bright blue sky, the buds are already swelling on the apple trees, bathed in the bright sunshine. One walks to the accompaniment of the noisy chirping of the sparrows which greet, with no less delight than I, this springtime and these currents, the sun and the rapid waters of the melting snow—clean, not like the snow in the city. Liberation from gloomy Petersburg, liberation from hardships, from the days full of fruitless attempts to find one's way. It is easy to breathe, and you don't know whether your heart is beating like crazy or has stopped. Freedom, the spring wind and the sun.... These and similar days are the beacons of my life. When I look back they make up for the many gloomy, cruel, and "unjust" things that life dealt out to me.

If it weren't for the blazing spring of 1908,[3] if it weren't for my other theatrical seasons, if it weren't for these and other remnants of willfulness and self-assertion in my life, wouldn't I seem to you, reader, and to myself rather pathetic and frustrated? Would my unshakable optimism have stood up? Had I passively reconciled myself to my fate, what a helpless wreck I would have been at the beginning of the Revolution. Where would I have found the strength to stand beside Blok at those times when he so desperately needed support in his life?

But what does the reader care about me? I suspect he will respond to everything I want to tell about my own life with those same bewilderingly raised eyebrows with which, throughout my life, all the "educated people" used to meet me (the person, not the "function"): "What? Blok's wife? That actress performing at Orenburg?!" My autobiography is not needed; I am not asked for it. What is needed is the life of the poet's wife, the "function" (I beg the typesetter to make a misprint: the "fiction"!) which, I repeat, is perfectly well known to the reader. Besides, the reader also knows very well what Blok is like. Should I tell him about another Blok, Blok as he was in life? First of all, nobody would believe me. Second, everybody would be dissatisified— one must not break the established rules. I considered the path suggested by the tempter in Blok's poem: "To lie blessedly about the past . . ." (III, 35), "I know, oh blessed one, you will forget the evil . . . ." Comfort is a smooth path. It is comfortable to feel magnanimous and all-forgiving—much too comfortable, and not at all like Blok. It would be, in the end, to betray his personal relationship to life and to himself and, in my opinion, also to truth. Either that, or I should have to raise myself to the level of renunciation and of blessedness which humans can reach only in the hour preceding death or in some similar ascetic situation. Perhaps at times Blok depicted me on this plateau in his inspired lines, but perhaps, even in his moments of faith and spiritual freedom, he never really expected me to reach it.

Perhaps I had the ability to follow such a path, but I embarked on another one—bold, Faustian. If there was anything that I learned from Blok on this path it was ruthlessness in facing the truth. I consider this ruthlessness, as he did, the best gift I can give my friends. I want to apply it to myself too, otherwise I shall not be able to write, nor would I want to, since writing would serve no purpose then.

Indeed, dear reader, is it not to your advantage to know what an author is really like and what his attitude to life is? This is absolutely essential for critical purposes, absolutely essential for evaluating the true weight of the writer's words. Could we, perhaps, combine our interests? Let me speak about myself, too; it will give you the opportunity to judge the trustworthiness of my writing. Moreover, I will not be modest, nor will I pretend. In fact, everyone who picks up the pen says by this very act that he considers himself, his thoughts and feelings interesting and important. From the age of twenty, I got second billing from life and for almost twenty years I accepted this second place willingly and unquestioningly. Then, left to my own resources, I gradually got used to thinking independently. In other words, I reverted to my early youth, when I used to search passionately for new paths in ideas and art. Now there is no longer a chasm between me and my youth. Now the person who is reading and writing at this desk is a woman who has returned from a long journey but has not forgotten, who has not lost the fire she took from her paternal home, who has been made wiser by life, who has grown older, but who is still the same L. D. M. of Blok's early diaries. This meeting with my own self in my mature years is a sweet joy. I love myself for this rediscovered young soul, and this love will inform everything I write.

Yes, I have great esteem for myself. The reader will have to accept this if he wants to read through to the end, otherwise it will be better for him to stop right now. I love myself, I like myself, and trust my judgment and taste. Only in the company of my own self do I find a companion who, with proper interest (from my point of view), can follow me through all my winding paths of thought, who can delight in all the same unexpected things that also delight me—the person who has discovered them. Dear reader! Do not indignantly throw this impudent bragging under the table. There is an advantage here for you, too. The fact is that now, having boldly gotten on my own two feet, having permitted myself to think and feel independently, for the first time I see how needlessly I humbled and belittled my own thoughts when confronted with the realm of Blok's ideas, his methods and approach to life. It couldn't have been otherwise, of course. The fire of his spirit illumined everything for me with such a great light, incommensurate with my own, that I lost the ability to direct my own life. I believed in Blok and did not believe in myself; I lost my inner self. It was cowardice, I see it now.

Now, when I find something that I like in my soul or in my mind, the first thing I do is cry out: "Why can't I give this to Sasha?" I find things in myself that he would have liked, that he would have praised, that would have served him as support, since they contained the toughness of my basic quality—unshakable optimism. And optimism was just what Blok did not have enough of. Oh yes, in my life I tried the best I could to dispel with my optimism the darkness into which he would so willingly sink with such masochistic abandon. Oh, if only I could have believed in myself more! If only I had begun to cultivate my thoughts then and had learned to formulate them more clearly, I could have given him not only my light-hearted gaiety but also the antidote against dark thoughts—the darkness which he regarded as an obligation to himself, to his calling as a poet. And there it is—both his mistake and my great sin in life. There was a wellspring of joy and light in Blok, but also one of despair and pessimism. I did not dare, I could not rise up against it, take my stand and fight. Furthermore, difficult circumstances entered into the picture: Blok's mother, who was very dear to him, but who bordered on mental illness, drew Blok into the darkness. It was a feminine weakness in me which kept me from breaking their closeness or splitting them apart: it would have been an evil in everybody's eyes had I been cruel, had I "exploited" my youth, health, and strength against her. I did not believe in myself enough, I did not love Blok maturely enough not to be afraid. Cowardly, I gave vent to my antagonism toward my mother-in-law only in petty everyday complaints. Instead I should have torn Blok away from his mother' pathological moods. I should have done it but did not, because of a lack of self-confidence, because of the loss of my own self.

But now, when all that's left for me is the opportunity to speak about the past, when everything is beyond repair, allow me to speak confidently about myself. Well, it does not matter, for when I write it is as though I am talking to Sasha. I know what he likes and I give him what he needs. O reader! There is much you must forgive me for; there is much you must pay careful attention to. Perhaps here lies the meaning of my "torments." Let this be a new roundabout way to speak of Blok. And here is something else that comes to mind. By my spiritual disposition, by the way I felt about life, and by the inclination of my own thoughts, I was different from Blok's Symbolist contemporaries. Was I less progressive than they? The truth of the matter is that as I see it now, I don't think I was. I even think I will belong in, and will consider as my own, the next era of art yet to come. Perhaps this era already exists in France, with fewer pretensions in literature and more faith in the meaning of each art work taken on its own terms. Perhaps what estranged me from Symbolism was its self-conscious artifice, its truth predetermined by its rebellion against the previous period of tendentiousness. Blok, however, was considerably less free from this tendetiousness than he wanted to be or than the art of a great era demanded. This is what I am grieving about: if I had only awakened earlier (Sasha used to say: "You are always sleeping. You have not awakened..."), if I had only put my thoughts in order and believed in myself as I do now, I could have counteracted both the seductiveness of literary decadence and his mother's Baudelairianism. Perhaps he was even waiting for something from me. He definitely did not want to break up the life we had together. Perhaps what he was waiting for was...but I sense that the reader is already choking with indignation: what conceit!.. No, it is not conceit, but habit. Blok and I were so used to bringing each other all the good things we found in our souls, recognized in art or observed in life or nature, that even now, having discovered a new truth, how could I not want to bring it to him? Since I am now alone, don't you think that I grieve over not having done so before?

Here is yet another difficulty: how can I convince the reader that it is not *cynicism* that compels me to speak about things which are not "proper" to speak of, but rather a profound belief in their ultimate value in delineating the meaning of life? I would never agree that it is cynical to speak about all this, to speak about those dangerous underground reefs on which boats crash and sink. Before Freud people contrived to discard this side of life, to put up screens, to plug their ears, and to close their eyes even in such an enlightened milieu as the one I belonged to. But how can we now hope to give even an approximately truthful analysis of events and motivations if our concern is to abide by the rules of a "proper," pretentious and unrealistic "psychology"?

My reading, which until now has kept up with Western literature, also accounts for my liberation. In these past years people have become so accustomed to reading Western literature with its detailed and candid analyses of the most intimate aspects of sex life that the conventional standards of propriety or impropriety have lost their significance. One of the main reasons for this is that artists who are indisputably great write that way (Jules Romains' splendid novel is a good example[4]) and thus create the style of an era. It now seems sanctimonious and hypocritical not to speak openly about what one sees as the catalyst of the future. I too will be speaking about sides of life that are still not proper to discuss, knowing almost for certain that I will be accused of cynicism, but I am deeply convinced that it is better not to write than to write what one does not believe in. In the present case there is at least a chance of saying something that is close to the truth, in other words, what needs to be said. If one filters what one writes through "propriety," chances are that a useless jumble will result.

* * *

How simple and clear that fateful day was, that warm, sunny June day —all Moscow's flowers in bloom. St. Peter's Day was still far off. The grass stood unmowed and its scent was sweet, as were the little flowers that covered the grass along the entire linden path with their luminous gray petals like a soft snow. It was on this path that Blok first saw the young woman who was for him inseparable from the life of his native hills and meadows, the woman who knew so well how to blend into her blooming surroundings. To carry away from the fields in the folds of one's dress the fragrance of sweet, fragile flowers; to change a city hairdo for a tightly plaited "maiden's golden braid" (I, 515-516); immediately upon one's arrival to transform oneself from a city person into an inseparable part of the woods, fields, and gardens; to possess that instinctive tact, that knowledge how not to offend the eyes with some inappropriate city mannerism or detail of dress—all this is only given to those who from childhood have lived in the countryside. Sixteen-year-old Lyuba had mastered all this to perfection—subconsciously, of course—as, by the way, had her entire family.

After dinner, which in the country used to end at about two o'clock, I went up to my room on the second floor, and no sooner did I get ready to sit down to write a letter—than I hear the trot of a saddle-horse. Someone stops at the gate, opens the wicket, brings in the horse, and asks at the kitchen whether Anna Ivanovna[5] is home. From my window I cannot see the gate and that side of the house. Directly under the window is the gently sloping, green iron roof of the lower terrace; on the right a spreading branch of the lilac tree blocks the gate and the courtyard. Through the leaves and the branches one can only catch glimpses. I walk up to the window, already knowing subconsciously that this is "Sasha Beketov" (as mother used to call him when speaking about her visits to Shakhmatovo). Through the leaves of the lilac I can see a white horse, which is being led to the stable, and fast, heavy, firm but unseen steps resound along the stone floor. The beating of my heart is heavy and hollow. Is this some ominous foreboding or something else? I hear those heartbeats even now, as I hear the sounds of those steps entering my life.

Automatically I walk to the mirror. Automatically I see that I must put on something else. My calico sarafan looks too much like a house dress. I change into what was so fashionable in those days: an English batiste blouse with a hard starched collar and cuffs, a skirt, a leather sash. My blouse is pink. I wear a small black tie, a black skirt, low heel brown leather shoes. (I never took either an umbrella or a hat into the garden, only a light white parasol.)

Musya,[6] my impish younger sister whose favorite pastime in those days was to make fun of my preoccupation with my appearance, comes into my room. "*Mademoiselle* wants you to go to the *Colonie;* she is there with that Sasha from Shakhmatovo. Powder your nose!" This time I don't get angry; I am deep in thought.

Colonie was our little garden at the end of the linden tree path which we children used to tend under the direction of *Mademoiselle,* who, no less than we, used to love the countryside and the soil. I have heard that the path of the lindens is still intact, the trees now thick and shady. In those years the linden trees were young. They had been planted recently, about ten years before, and still had not grown full; they were kept trimmed and did not cast much shade upon the path that was therefore flooded by the sun. Halfway to the *Colonie* there was a wooden bench facing the sun and a vista of the adjacent hills and far horizon. (That far horizon is the beauty of our landscape.) Approaching from behind through the birch grove, I see on this bench our *Mademoiselle* chattering away to someone who is sitting with his back to me. I see that he is dressed in a dark city suit and wearing a dark hat. This immediately alienates me somehow; all the young people I know wear uniforms: the students of the gymnasiums, lyceums, universities, the cadets, the officers. A civiliam? That's something foreign to me, from another world. He is either a civilian or he is already "old." Furthermore, I dislike his face the minute he says hello. Pale eyelashes and thin, barely-delineated eyebrows give a cold expression to his pale eyes. All of us have dark eyelashes; our eyebrows are distinct; our glance is lively and direct. A meticulously shaved face, in those days, gave one a "theatrical" look—an interesting look, but not ours.

Formal and aloof, I directed the conversation toward the theater, toward shows that might be worthwhile putting on. At that time Blok carried himself like an actor, spoke slowly and clearly, smoked with affectation and looked at us as if from above, throwing back his head, lowering his eyelids. When we did not talk about the theater or a show, he would talk nonsense, often with the obvious intention of confusing us with something we would not quite understand, but at which we would inevitably blush. By "we" I mean my cousins the Mendeleev, girls, Sara and Lida,[7] their girlfriend Yulia Kuzmina and I. In those days Blok frequently used to quote Kuzma Prutkov,[8] especially his anecdotes which sometimes have a double meaning, a fact that I caught onto considerably later, of course. He also had at that time a favorite facetious expression in English that he inserted at every occasion: "Oh yes, my kind!" [sic] And since sometimes that phrase was directed straight at people, it embarrassed them with its incorrectness and they did not know how to react.

Soon after, on that first day, my cousins arrived. We spent some time together, made arrangements about the shows, played halma and croquet. Then we went to visit our relatives, the Smirnovs,[9] a large family ranging from young ladies and students to children. Together we played tag and catch. Here a change came over Blok, and he suddenly became natural and simple. He ran and giggled like all of us, children and grownups alike.

In the first two or three days after his arrival it seemed that Blok was paying particular attention to Lida and Yulia Kuzmina. They knew how to make lively conversation, how to flirt, and effortlessly adopted the tone which Blok imparted to the conversation. Both were very cute and light-hearted and I used to envy them. I was clumsy in conversation and at that time I was very unhappy about my looks. My involvement with Blok all started because I was jealous.

What did I want? Why did I want the attention of someone I did not even like, with whom I had little in common, who was immature by comparison with us—clever and well-read young ladies that we were? My sensuality had not yet awakened. Kisses, embraces—all this was somewhere far, far away and unreal. What was it, then, that not so much drew as drove me to him? "It's in the stars," Leonora would have said to Calderón.[10] Indeed, this viewpoint can stand up against the most severe criticism, for when we take "stars" as explanation, everything can be made to work out: there will be strange coincidences, good fortune and impunity in the most daring assignations in plain daylight—you name it! But in the meantime, let's admit that although Blok was not the embodiment of my girlish dreams—a Lermontov or a Byron—he was nonetheless a lot better-looking than all my friends, and he was a talented actor. (At that time there was no evidence of anything else, poetry least of all.) He was a bit affected, but was a gallant escort, and tantalized us with suggestions of some obscure, mysterious, masculine kind of experience in life (what is this—straight out of Tolstoi?), an experience that could not be sensed in either my bearded cousins or the nice and likeable Sum,[11] my brother's tutor.

Anyway, "stars" or "no stars," I soon started to feel jealous and turned on all my charms to attract Blok's attention. Apparently I gave the outward appearance of extreme coldness and restraint. Later on Blok would often mention this to me and write about it. My silent efforts, however, were not lost on him and soon afterwards I started noticing with apprehension that Blok—yes, no question about it—was choosing me and surrounding me with his attention. But how unspoken all this was! How very reserved, unseen, concealed! One could always wonder: was it yes or no? Is it or does it only seem to be?

So what did we speak about? How did we give signals to each other? At this time the two of us were never alone; if we were not among our friends, we were with *Mademoiselle* or in the company of my sister or my brothers. I could not entertain the thought of communicating with my eyes; such communication would have seemed to me more meaningful than words and far more frightening. I used to feign worldliness with my eyes and whenever anyone attempted to meet my glance in some deeper way, I would turn away. This, above all, was what gave the impression of coldness and indifference.

"Innumerable are the paths in the woods..." (I, 124), that is, in the Church woods, where we took all our walks. These were fairy-tale woods, and in those days they were untouched by the axe. Century-old fir trees bowed their hoary branches like canopies; long gray beards of moss hung down to the ground. There were impenetrable thickets of juniper, of wolf-berry, of fern; in places the ground was covered with a carpet of fallen needles, in others, with patches of large and dark-leaved lily-of-the-valley like nowhere else. "The path curves, any minute it will vanish...,"[12] "Innumerable are the paths in the woods...."

All of us, but especially Blok and I, used to love the Church woods. Not many people abreast could walk along those narrow woodland paths, so all our group had to stretch out. "By chance" we used to find ourselves walking together for a few steps in the "fairy-tale woods..." Those were the most eloquent moments in our meetings.

They were even more eloquent than those later on when we left the woods for the meadows of the neighboring Alexandrovka estate. Past the woods we crossed the White Creek, a swift, cold stream that still babbles today as it flows over the multi-colored stones. It is not wide and one can easily jump across it by stepping on one of the boulders in the water. We always managed to do this effortlessly. Blok, however, so maneuvered it that without being impolite to others he would extend his helping hand only to me, leaving the other girls to Sum and my brothers. These outings were celebrations, great and lively fun, but the greatest thing of all was what I came to understand in those woods. In the "fairy-tale woods" I had my first silent encounters with another Blok, one who used to vanish as soon as the "actor" Blok started making small talk and one whom I only got to know three years later.

In those years my first and only step in Blok's direction, and a very bold one for me, was on that evening when we played *Hamlet*.[13] We were already made up and in costume as Hamlet and Ophelia. I felt bolder. A wreath, a sheaf of wild flowers and a cloak of golden hair falling loose below the knees... Blok in a black beret, cape, and sword. We were sitting backstage, half-hidden from view, while the stage was being set. Blok sat at the edge of the platform as if on a bench. He was at my feet, since I was on a stool on the stage itself. We talked about something more personal than usual, but what was more important and even frightening was that I was not running away from him. I looked into his eyes, we were together, we were closer than the words we spoke.

Perhaps this ten-minute talk was all the "romance" we had in those years, yet it went beyond the "actor," beyond the well-reared "young lady," and into the land of black capes, swords, and berets, into a land where Ophelia, demented, bends over the stream where she is fated to perish.

This talk remained the one real bond between Blok and myself when, later on, we would meet in town—already in the roles of "young lady" and "student." And later still, when we started to draw apart, when I began feeling estranged from him and considered my infatuation with the "cold dandy" beneath me, I would still tell myself: "And yet the feeling was there."

There was this one talk and the return home from the "theater" (a hay barn) along the side of the hill through the young birch grove that was barely the height of a man. The August nights are dark in the Moscow region and that night the "stars were unusually large." It so happened that still in our costumes (we used to change at home), we left in the hubbub following the performance and found ourselves—as Ophelia and Hamlet—alone on that starry night. We were still under the spell of that talk, and it did not seem strange when right before us a big meteor, bright with an azure light, slowly traced an arc on the wide vault of the sky. "And suddenly a midnight star fell...."

Blok and I, as we found out afterwards, shared the same feeling about nature, about its life and participation in human destiny. This blue "midnight star" said everything that had been left unsaid. It did not matter that "the answer was silence," because "the child Ophelia"[14] could not have found words for what flashed for a moment before our eyes and in our hearts. Even our hands did not meet: we were looking straight ahead. We were sixteen and seventeen, respectively.

Reminiscences of *Hamlet* In Boblovo, August 1
Shakhmatovo, August 2
Dedicated to L. D. M.

Тоску и грусть, страданье, самый ад,
Все в красоту она преобразила.

Офелия

Я шел во тьме к заботам и веселью
Вверху сверкал незримый мир духов.
За думой вслед длился трель за трелью
Напевы звонкие пернатых соловьев.
"Зачем дитя Ты?" мысли повторяли.
"Зачем дитя"? мне вторил соловей,
Когда в безмолвном, мрачном, темном зале
Предстала тень Офелии моей.
И бедный Гамлет я был очарован,
Я ждал желанный, сладостный ответ.
Ответ немел, и я в душе взволнован,
Спросил: Офелия, честна ты или нет!?!?
И вдруг звезда полночная упала,
И ум опять ужалила змея,
Я шел во тьме и эхо повторяло:
Зачем дитя Ты, дивная моя.

> Longing and sadness, suffering and hell itself—
> She transformed it all into beauty.

I was walking in the darkness towards cares and gaiety.
High above, the invisible world of spirits shone.
With trill after trill, the melodious singing
Of light-winged nightingales pursued my thought.
"Why You, my child?" sang in my thoughts.
"Why, my child?" echoed the nightingale,
As the shadow of my Ophelia rose before me
In the silent, dark and gloomy hall.
A poor Hamlet, I was entranced,
And awaited the sweet, desired answer.
The answer was silence and, with my soul all astir,
I asked: Ophelia, are you or are you not true?!
And suddenly a midnight star fell,
And again the serpent stung my mind,
I was walking in the darkness and the echo was repeating:
Why You, my child, my divine one. (I, 382, 649)

*   *   *

Blok's diary of 1918 treats the events of 1898-1901, but Sasha got everything mixed up. Almost everything is in the wrong place and under the wrong date. I am putting it all in order, placing the paragraphs where they belong.

After Nauheim, Blok resumed his studies at the gymnasium.[15]

"From January (1898) I started composing a fair number of poems. Their subjects were: K. M. S. (Sadovskaya), dreams of passion, my friendship with Koka Gun (which had already cooled), my slight infatuation with Mme. Levitskaya, my illness... In the spring... at the exhibition (of the itinerant artists, I think), I met Anna Ivanovna Mendeleeva, who invited me to her house and, in the summer, to her family estate in Boblovo, adjacent to ours.

"As far as I can remember, my stay at Shakhmatovo began with boredom and melancholy. They almost chased me to Boblovo. (I started wearing the 'white tunic' only the following year in school.) *Mademoiselle* and Lyubov Dmitrievna, who immediately made a strong impression on me, entertained me in the birch grove. It was, I think, the beginning of June.

"I was a dandy and my talk was quite trivial. The Mendeleevs arrived. In Boblovo lived N. E. Sum, a shaggy student (of whom I was jealous). By autumn Maria Ivanovna too came to live there. Often the Smirnovs and the Strelitsa crowd came to visit.

"We played scenes from *Woe from Wit* and *Hamlet* in the barn... We declaimed our roles. I was showing off quite a bit, but was already very much in love. Sirius and Vega.

"I think that aunt and I went to Trubitsino that fall, where Aunt Sonya gave me something gold. When we went back, grandmother was finishing up my Hamlet costume.

"In the fall I had a modish coat made to order (the kind that students wear); entered the Faculty of Law, couldn't understand anything about jurisprudence (envied that babbler, Prince Tenishev); tried, who knows why, to read Tun (?) and about some railroad legislation in Germany (?). I used to see Mme. Sadovskaya, and it was probably then that I started frequenting the Kachalovs (N. N. and O. L).

"('To Fall') . . . Upon my return to Petersburg, Zabalkansky's visits became relatively less frequent (than in Boblovo). Lyubov Dmitrievna was finishing her studies at Shaffe. I was involved with declamation and the stage. I used to visit the Kachalovs at that time, and performed in the dramatic circle with Priotsky (a barrister), Tyumenev (the translator of 'The Ring'), V. V. Pushkaryova, and the leading man, Bernikov, who was the well-known police agent Rataev, a fact that one of my liberal fellow students once caustically called to my attention. The director was N. A. Gorsky and the prompter Zaitsev, a poor fellow whom Rataev treated very rudely.

"In December of that same year I went with *Mademoiselle* and Lyubov Dmitrievna to a gala in honor of L. Tolstoi in Peter Hall (On Konyushna Street?).

"Lyubov Dmitrievna came to one of the plays in Pavel Hall, where I, under the name of Borsky (why) was playing a small part as a banker in *The Mine Worker* (I was wearing L. F. Kublitsky's[16] tail coat)..."[17]

Sasha repeated his second year (VII, 341). I do not remember whether the dates of the students' disorders are correct (VII, 509). Further on in the diary Sasha combines two summers—1899 and 1900—into one. According to him, the summer of 1899, which the Mendeleevs spent in Boblovo as usual, passed almost in the same way as that first romantic summer of 1898, but without its tense atmosphere and deep infatuation. We staged Pushkin's "Fountain Scene,"[18] Chekhov's play *The Proposal*, and *The Bouquet* by Potapenko. The following entries refer to the summer of 1900:

"I started going to Boblovo somewhat less frequently, and furthermore, I had to go by carriage (I was not permitted to ride a horse after my 'illness').

"I remember returning home many a night, the bushes aglow with fireflies, and recall Lyubov Dmitrievna's impenetrability and her severity towards me. (The Mendeleevs did not live there that year; the shows were organized by my cousin, the writer N. Ya. Gubkina[19] as a charity function, and we performed *The Burning Letter* by Gnedich. I don't remember whether I visited the Mendeleevs that year.)

"By the fall (1900) I apparently stopped going to Boblovo because of both Lyubov Dmitrievna's severity and the cart. As I was looking through an old copy of the *Northern Herald*, I found Z. Gippius' 'Mirrors.' When I returned to Petersburg, I did not visit the Mendeleevs, since I presumed that our friendship had come to an   end."

Blok's acquaintance with A. V. Gippius belongs to the spring of 1901.[20]

*   *   *

The fact that we stopped seeing each other in the fall of 1900 did not bother me at all. I had just graduated from the eighth grade of the Gymnasium and had been accepted into the Institute.[21] I entered very passively, following mother's advice and in the hope that being a *kursistka* would give me greater freedom than being one of those young ladies who simply live at home and study something like languages, as was then the norm.

Before the beginning of the school year my mother took me to the International Fair in Paris. I felt the charm of Paris immediately and forever. No one can really define the true nature of this charm. It is as ineffable as the charm of a woman who is not too beautiful but in whose smile are a thousand mysteries and a thousand wonders. Paris presents the centuries-old face of a city superlatively enlightened, replete with art from the Montmartre garrets of the dying Modigliani to the golden halls of the Louvre. All this is in its air, in the lines of its river banks, in its changeable illumination, in the gentle vault of its sky.

"Paris blooms in the rain like a gray rose..."[22] Voloshin said it well, very fittingly. But, of course, my attempts to describe Paris are weak in comparison to what others have said. When people winked at me in answer to my admission of love for Paris, saying, "Well, of course! The boulevards, the fashionable stores, the Montmartre cabarets! Ah, ah!", it all so missed the mark that I did not take offence in the least. Later on I found in books that same love for Paris that can never be fully conveyed in words because what we are dealing with here is not only art, thought, or the intensity of artistic energy in general, but something even beyond all this. So how should I convey it? If one is to impart to the word "taste" a very wide meaning (as did my brother Mendeleev,[23] who thought that the unquestionable excellence of the French mathematicians is rooted in the fact that their formulas and calculations possess, above all, "taste"), then this word is appropriate when speaking about Paris. I shall use it, provided that the reader share this widened meaning, and I trust that he will not replace it with the common meaning of this word.

I returned enamored of Paris,[24] inebriated with its art, but also very much enchanted with its colorful display of life. I was, of course, very, very well-dressed in all kinds of wonderful Parisian creations. As usual, mother and I did not have much money; now I cannot even vaguely recall how much. Without any hesitation, we settled in a small, inexpensive hotel by Madeleine Square (Rue Vignon, Hotel Vignon), a hotel so old that when we came back at night the porter would hand us a candleholder with a lit candle, as in Balzac! There was no light at all on the steep stairs and in the narrow hallways. In spite of all this, we were able to see all that we wanted to see. We bought many small articles that were typically Parisian, and each of us had an elegant outfit made by a good dressmaker, the kind of dress that one would wear in Petersburg to go to the theater, to concerts, etc. Mother's was black, made of the finest wool. Mine was wool also, "blue pastel," as the dressmaker called it. This is a very dull, subdued blue, somewhat green, somewhat gray, neither light nor dark. No other color would have suited my hair or my complexion better. It was so becoming to me that once in the theater one very formal lady looked at me indignantly and exclaimed in a deliberately loud voice: "God, look how made up she is! Such a young girl!" In reality, I had barely powdered my face. I wore this dress through the fall of 1902, during which time it witnessed many important events.

Although I had entered the Institute without great enthusiasm, right from the start I enjoyed many of the lectures and professors, and attended not only my own classes, but some of the advanced ones as well. Platonov, Shlyapkin, Rostovtsev,[25] each in his own way opened before me intellectual perspectives whose appeal, however, was more romantic and artistic than strictly scholarly. Platonov's stories and his arguments were at once passionate yet controlled. Students listened to him with bated breath. Shlyapkin, on the other hand, felt such a familiarity with every writer about whom he lectured (whatever the period) that his presentations held a special fascination: the subject became alive, not bookish. Rostovtsev was eloquent despite his speech defect, and one would listen to him with ease as he spoke of "histowical pewiods," bases and stages, thanks to his intense, sonorous, and penetrating voice. But the one I enjoyed most was A. I. Vvedensky.[26] His answers sustained my search for knowledge. Neo-criticism helped me coordinate my thoughts, liberated the faith that was living in me, and showed me the boundaries and value of "true knowledge." All this was very important to me, it touched upon my deepest concerns. I also used to attend philosophy lectures in the more advanced classes, and enjoyed my psychology class because I was fascinated with the possibility of bringing "psychology" (!) down to the empirical level.

I got to know many students and became involved in the social activities of the school. I was appointed collector of certain student fees, but nothing came of my efforts because I did not know how to squeeze the dues out of people and no one volunteered anything. I liked to attend all the student concerts at the Palace. I used to go to the small hall next to the dressing room where the students, under the pretext of innocent "protest" and "disruption of order," would sing "From a Land, From a Far-Away Land" and then disperse after a polite admonition from the police. For our school concert I was among those who helped out behind the scenes. I drove in the cab that picked up Osarovsky[27] and others, but my job was only to sit in the cab; another student, a theater-goer like myself, was assigned the job of running up the steps. In the dressing room I was in a state of reverence and bliss from being in the same place where Michurina[28] had been, the actress who appeared in the French magazine that we had just received. Here too were Pototskaya, Kuza, Dolina and the ubiquitous Tartakov.[29] Having quickly disposed of my obligations, I would go to the concert with my new school friends, Zina Lineva and later on, with Shura Nikitina, and we would stand somewhere by the posts.

I must say that the level of the performances was very high. The voices of the singers, male and female, were disciplined, polished, pure, exact and rich. The artists were superb and did not hesitate to give their utmost before this audience of students whose appreciation was important to them. Ozarovsky's recital, for instance, was like a multi-faceted museum piece, and it is still preserved in my memory. There was a jubilee polish to it, a sense of proportion, a deft touch in choosing the repertoire and performing it, an unmistakable understanding of the audience and how to reach it. The program was light and included even the lightest of pieces, for example, "How One Falls in Love Because of a Plum," but the performance was truly professional, and its success and the audience's gaiety were enormous.

After the concert there was dancing in the hall and people strolled the side corridors among the colorful stands of champagne and flowers. As soon as the area where we were dancing became crowded we would move to another, and would talk and have fun in spite of the fact that our "student escorts" were so insignificant that I barely remember them.

I used to go to the parties that my provincial classmates held in their crowded student quarters, parties that tried to recapture the sixties, but were not successful. We used to have discussions and sing student songs, but we preferred listening to the conservatory students who would sing or play "I Sing to You, God Hymen. . ." and we flirted very mildly and modestly with the blond provincial technologists or with the mining students.

That's how things went all winter until March. When I recalled Blok, it was with vexation. I remember that in my diary, which was later destroyed in Shakhmatovo, I made sharp statements about him, such as "I feel ashamed when I remember my infatuation with that fop with the fishy temperament and eyes. . . ." I considered myself liberated.

But in March, somewhere near my school, I saw his profile flash by. He did not think that I saw him. The encounter shook me. Why is it that with the return of the bright and sunny spring, Blok's image also reappears? We found ourselves sitting next to one another at a performance by Salvini.[30] By the way, his seat turned out to be next to mine, not to mother's, since she and I were already seated. After he came up to me and said hello, I realized in a flash, even before the first words were spoken, that this was a different Blok: simpler, softer, serious, and, consequently, much improved. (A provocative tone and bold demeanor were unbecoming to Blok.) A respectful gentleness and humility surfaced in his attitude to me, and all his conversation and statements were oh so serious! In other words, this was the Blok who had been writing poems for the last three years and whom the dandy's mask had concealed from us.

Subsequently he started coming to see us again, and his visits followed a pattern for the next two years: Blok would talk to mother, who in her youth was lively and witty company, and who delighted in arguing frequently, and did so in her typical paradoxical style. He would talk about his readings, his views on art, about all that was new in painting and literature. Mother would argue heatedly; I would sit silently, knowing that everything he said was for my sake, that he was trying to convert me and lead me into that newly discovered world that he loved. All this would take place over tea in the dining room. Then we would go into the drawing room and, melodramatically, Blok would read A. Tolstoi's "In the Land of Sunbeams" to the music of *"Quasi una Fantasia"* or some such thing from the sheet music that mother liked to buy.

I now liked his looks. The lack of tension and theatricality in his face gave his features a sculptured look, and his eyes seemed darker from concentration and thought. As Blok read by the grand piano—one hand on the gilded chair piled up with sheet music, the other under the lapel of his student uniform, beautifully crafted by a military tailor—he cut a graceful silhouette of strong and formal lines against the light of the lamp. Of course, this scene was not as clear and distinct to me then as it is now. Now I have learned to observe everything around me sharply—objects, people, and nature, and by the same token I can also look clearly into the past, but at that time everything was in a fog. Before my eyes there was always a "romantic haze," especially when it came to Blok and the objects and space that surrounded him. He used to excite and disturb me; I hesitated to look straight at him. In fact, I could not do that at all.

This is what the ring of fire and the swirling smoke around Brunhilde are all about; their meaning became clear to me at a performance at the Marinsky Theater.[31] They not only protect the Valkyrie, but also separate her from the world and her hero, whom she sees through this fiery, hazy curtain.

On those evenings I would sit on the couch at the far end of the drawing room in the semi-darkness where the lamplight did not reach. At home I would wear a black woolen skirt and a light silk blouse that were among the things I had brought back from Paris. I wore my hair piled up high, and my wavy hair framed my face like a heavy halo and was twisted on top in a tight knot. I loved perfume and wore it more than a young lady was supposed to. At that time I had a strong perfume: *Coeur de Jeannette*. As in the past, I was not talkative. I never learned to make small talk, and all my life I preferred conversation with one person rather than with many.

At that time the people with whom I used to talk seriously were my brother Vanya, his friend Rozvadovsky,[32] and especially his sister Manya, who that winter was studying painting with Shcherbinsky[33] and was very progressive in matters of art. I learned a great deal from my conversations with her. It was through her that I discovered Baudelaire ("Une charogne," for some reason!); more importantly, I learned from her a more serious approach to art than the "populism" that was in vogue at home and which, by the way, was instinctively foreign to me. In Paris I got my fill of looking at all kinds of art, even the extreme works of Scandinavian Symbolists who simplified the art of painting by reducing it to dry, intellectual formulas, but in the process helped people to liberate themselves from the belief that only simple, realistic painting is art.

I don't recall what I had been reading that winter. While still in the gymnasium I had devoured Russian literature. That winter everybody was reading *Thus Spake Zarathustra*.[34] It seems to me it was the French authors whom I read greedily (Maupassant, Bourget, Zola, Loti, Daudet, Marcel Proust—forbidden fruit for gymnasium students),who unveiled the "mysteries of life" until then unknown to me. But here is the simple truth: for the pure everything is pure. A young woman can read absolutely anything, but if she does not know the facts of life she will not understand a thing, and will imagine all sorts of improbable nonsense—this I know for certain. Even the loose girls in my gymnasium hesitated to enlighten a person like me. Even if I did understand a little bit of what they used to talk about, my basic ignorance was so pervasive that they would even give me, and those like me, pornographic pictures stolen from their brothers, thinking that it did not matter, because I would not understand a thing anyway! And in fact I did not see anything except some anatomical "peculiarities," all rather uninteresting.

However, this first winter as an "adult" I matured a great deal. Intellectual pursuits and my love for art were not the only interests that had grown strong and more defined. Impatiently I began awaiting the arrival of Life. All my friends had serious flirtations, with kisses and entreaties for more to come. I alone was backward. No one ever kissed my hand, no one courted me. Young people almost never came to our house. Those whom I saw at the

Botkins'[35] or at their parties were like distant mannequins serving the occasion and nothing more. None of the students I used to meet at my girl-friends' houses interested me in the least, and besides, I was cold and aloof. I am afraid that they thought I was trying to stress the difference in our social standing, although at that time such a thought could not have entered my mind. It would not even have dawned on me because I was always very democratic and spontaneous, and was never conscious of my father's high position. Anyway, I did not make anything of the small incident that occurred that winter, an incident that explains much to me now. At one of the student parties I spent a lot of time with a technology student, one of my "provincial" friends. We had fun talking, we had a pleasant and merry time. He did not leave me for a second, and later he took me home. I asked him to come and visit us sometime, and shortly after he came and I received him, as I received all the "callers," in our large drawing room. I remember how he was sitting as though he had been dunked in water. He left quickly and I never saw him again. I did not think anything of it then and did not inquire why he disappeared, but now I realize that our position in society must have seemed a lot more substantial than it actually was because of our official apartment and the way my mother decorated it with beautiful furniture and gold-framed pictures by well known populist painters. In reality, we lived very simply and were often short of money.

I did not know many young people. In our circle of friends there were only a few families with grown-up children—teenagers, I mean. I never took my many third cousins or all those dear, intelligent, bearded "old students" seriously.

To be sure, my mother had many highly-placed acquaintances. Among her "callers" there were many brilliant young men. But here again is a characteristic I shared with Blok: I did not take seriously those whom he would one day call the "scum" of society, parodying what one normally would call the "cream" of society.[36] In those years I was not able to see the person beyond the social mask. All I saw was soulless mannequins standing before me. Consequently, all these brilliant young men did not interest me. They were "mother's guests" and I almost never went into the living room when they visited. Until my marriage I did not come upon the kind of people with whom I could be close and who would interest me. My school acquaintances were somewhat simpler types.

In the midst of this loneliness life was blossoming in me. I felt that my young body had awakened. Now I was in love with myself in a different way than I had been in my gymnasium years. I would spend hours in front of the mirror. Sometimes, late at night, when everyone was asleep, but I was still lingering by the dressing table, trying different hairdos or letting my hair hang loose, I would take my evening gown, slip it onto my naked body, and walk over to the long mirrors in the dining room. I would then close all the doors, light the chandelier, pose before the mirrors and regret that I could not appear in that fashion at the balls. Afterwards I would take off the gown and admire myself for a long, long time. I had no inclination for sports or business; I was a gentle, well-groomed, old-fashioned girl. My white skin, unblemished by the sun, retained its velvety opaqueness. My underexercised muscles were gentle and supple. The flow of my lines, especially the suppleness of my long legs, the short waist and the small, barely developed breasts—all these I later discovered, at least in part, in Giorgione, although I must say that the Renaissance is not quite my era. It is too sober and artificial. My body was imbued with the spirit, the delicate, secret fire of a white, intoxicating hothouse flower. I remember that I was quite good-looking despite the fact that my figure in no way fulfilled the classical ideal of perfect form. Thus, long before Duncan, I had a dancer's sense of my body, knew how to coordinate my poses harmoniously and how to relate to my body through the arts, through the paintings and sculptures I saw. I did not perceive it as a source of "temptation" and sin the way our grandmothers and even mothers did, but as my own precious possession, my link with the beauty of the world. That is why I so enthusiastically greeted Duncan as someone I had expected and known for a long time.[37]

That's how I was in the spring of 1901; I was waiting for events, was in love with my body and already demanding an answer from life.

And then it came—the "mystic summer." Our meetings took place in the following way: Blok would visit us twice a week and I would always guess when. Here he comes, riding his white horse in his white student tunic. After dinner, at two o'clock, I would sit with a book on the shady lower porch, always with a red verbena in my hand whose gentle scent I especially loved that summer. I no longer wore skirts and blouses, but light batiste dresses, often pink. One of them was my favorite—peach colored with delicate white lace. Soon the clatter of horses' hooves resounded across the cobblestones. Blok would hand in his "Boy" at the gates and quickly run onto the porch. Since we were supposedly meeting "by chance," I felt very much at ease, and we would speak for hours on end until someone came.

Blok was very impressed with "them." This is the way we referred in our conversation to those new poets who were called the "Symbolists." At that time he was acquainted with them only through books. He talked endlessly, recited with great ease poems he had memorized, and brought me books, including the first issue of *Northern Flowers*, which was considered practically a sacred book. Upon his recommendations I read Merezhkovsky's first two novels[38] and his *Eternal Wanderers*.[39] He also brought me Tyutchev, Solovyov, and Fet. At that time he used to speak very complexly, in long, convoluted sentences, as though trying to grasp some thought that he

himself did not fully comprehend. It took concentration to follow his argu-
ments, but by then I was already attuned to his way of thinking and aware of
the pull "they" had on me. Once I asked him in the heat of the conversation:
"But surely you must write. Do you write poetry?" and right there and then
Blok confirmed it, but did not consent to recite his poems. On the following
day, however, he brought me four poems, each on its own piece of paper:
"Agrafa Dogmata" (I, 56), "Servus Reginae" (I, 30), "A New Brightness
Filled the Sky" (I, 456), and "Quietly the Evening Shadows" (I, 77). These
were the first poems of his that I read, and I read them alone.

The first one was very clear and dear to me because "cosmism" is one
of my basic beliefs. I remember that the previous summer, or perhaps earlier, I had felt something like a cosmic ecstasy when a "thick fire" indeed
"enveloped the universe." A dense white fog had risen in the west after a
storm, blanketing the distant horizon and the village. The fiery rays of the
sunset broke through the fog; everything seemed ablaze. "A thick fire enveloped the universe." I saw this primordial chaos, this "universe," from the
window of my room. Taking it all in with my eyes, I sank before it, clutching
at the windowsill, in a state of extreme agitation akin to religious ecstacy, but
without any religiosity, even without God....

Blok's second poem, "Sometimes a Vassal, Sometimes a Friend" (I,
30), made my cheeks burn like fire. "What is he saying?" I thought, "or not
saying yet? Should I try to find hidden meanings in his poems or not?" The
last two poems were a source of torment for me in the months that followed,
for I was not in them, or at least I did not recognize myself either in them or
in others like them. Consequently, that bitter jealousy which is considered so
reproachable, the "jealousy of a woman toward art," began stealing into my
soul. However, I felt the music of his poems and quickly memorized them.

Little by little I entered into this poetic world where I could see myself
one minute and not the next, where everything was melodious and nothing
was explicit, and where I knew that all those wonderful verses were in one
way or another inspired by me. Blok made me understand this indirectly, in
roundabout ways, by innuendo. I surrendered myself to the strange enchantment of our relationship. There may have been love, too, but essentially there
were only literary discussions, poems, and escape from this life into another
one, into the thrill of ideas and melodious images. Later on I often found in
his verses the very things he has said to me in our conversations. But in spite
of all this there was many a time when with a bitter smile I would throw
away my red verbena, wilted, its fine scent wasted like oh so many fragrant
summer days. Blok never asked me for my verbena, nor did we once lose our
way among the flowering shrubs...

In June came the most wonderful day of the summer. All our relatives,
including the Smirnovs, had gotten together for a picnic to gather white

mushrooms in the distant, state-owned fir woods. There would be no one except father left at home, not even a maid. I too decided to stay. I would make Blok come, although it was too early to expect him. I thought it was high time we had a talk. They were all mad at me for not going, but I made all kinds of banal excuses. I tried to find a minute for myself, and I remember how, standing next to the clock, I transported myself with all my soul across the seven *versts* that separated us and mentally asked him to come. At the usual time I sat down in my chair on the terrace with the verbena in my hand. And he did come. I was not surprised. It was inevitable.

We started walking up and down the linden path, as we had done on our first meeting, but our conversation was different. Blok began by telling me that he had been invited to go to Siberia to visit his aunt, but that he did not know whether or not to go. He asked me what to do: he would do whatever I said. Coming from him, that was quite a lot. I could now surmise an earnest desire on his part to let me know how he felt about me. I answered that although I myself loved to travel, visit new places, and although I felt that it would be good for him to go, nevertheless I would be sorry to see him leave, and personally I would prefer that he stay.[40] Well, then, he wouldn't go. We continued walking and talking in a friendly way, feeling, because of two sentences, that the distance separating us had quickly diminished, that many obstacles had fallen.

Giraudoux, in his novel *Bella*,[41] said that there was nothing along his heroes' path that disturbed them in the first two weeks of their acquaintance, that nothing they encountered could disrupt the calm, course of their life and the smoothness of the landscape. It was just the opposite with us. At every dip in the road, and also along the flat roads in between, "omens" disquieted us. Neither Blok nor I ever forgot the dead, bright little goldfinch that lay on the grass at the turn of the sandy road that led into the linden path where we walked. At every turn, any flash of color would disquiet our souls with a plaintive feeling of doom.

Our conversation about Siberia did not change anything outwardly. Everything continued as before; only our feeling of being two conspirators grew stronger. We knew what others did not know. At this time, in our family, as well as elsewhere, there was no receptivity whatsoever to the new emerging art.

In the fall Lida and Sara Mendeleev visited us. I remember our conversation in the dining room. I remember how Blok sat on the windowsill, with his riding crop in his hand, in his white jacket and high boots, and spoke of mirrors in general and Gippius' mirrors[42] in particular and of his own still unwritten "mirror..." "And the spurious phantom will rise, leaving his reflection upon the cold expanse" (I, 211). His words, of course, were addressed only to me. My cousins, mother, and aunt either turned away disapprovingly and indignantly, or simply giggled. He and I were plotting, we were in a conspiracy with "them", whom no one there knew. Later on my cousin said that Blok had become very mature, of course, that he had grown, but what strange things he said—the decadent! For a long time that was the word with which they tried to stifle everything, right and left, without distinction.

In those days this understanding and love of new ideas and the new art instantly united sympathetic people—there were so few of them—even when they met for the very first time. The conversations of that "mystic summer" served as a strong bond, as a reliable trust between us; by the fall it brought us so close that we understood each other almost without words, although in the affairs of daily life we remained very far apart.

*　　*　　*

Winter came and brought many changes. I started attending M. M. Chitau's[43] classes on Gagarin Street. Blok's influence was growing stronger, and unexpectedly I became interested in things religious. This was not typical of me at all.

I lived a very intense spiritual life. I was deeply moved by the sunsets that year, sunsets made so familiar through Blok's and Andrei Belyi's poems. I especially remember those I saw when returning from classes across the Nikolai Bridge. Even the winter before, roaming around Petersburg had been a full, intense experience. Once, walking along the Sadovaya, as I was passing by the clock tower of the Church of the Savior on Sennaya Street, I glanced through the open portals. Icons, the flickering of innumerable candle lights, prostrated praying figures. My heart ached that I was outside that world, outside that ancient truth. Not even a *Gostinny dvor* [department store], the favorite mirage of temptations and inaccessible fantastic bright lights, paints and colors (inaccessible because we had little money) could have distracted me. I walked further on and entered the Kazan Cathedral almost mechanically. I did not go up to the rich, elegant, diamond-encrusted and miraculous icon of the Kazan Madonna that was bathed in light, but walked past it. Beyond the columns, I stopped before another Kazan Madonna, which hung in semi-darkness with two or three candles and before which it was always peaceful and deserted. I fell to my knees, still barely knowing how to pray. Afterwards this icon became my (and our) Kazan Madonna. After Sasha's death I would implore Her for help, but even then, that very first time I prayed to Her, soothing and comforting tears came to my eyes. Later on, when I told Sasha about it, he wrote the following poem [with a female persona]:

Медленно в двери церковные
Шла я душой несвободная . . .
Слышались песни любовные,
Толпы молились народные.
Или в минуту безверия
Он мне послал облегчение?
Часто в церковные двери я
Ныне вхожу без сомнения.
И бесконечно глубокие
Мысли растут и желания,
Вижу я небо далекое
Слышу я Божье дыхание.
Падают розы вечерние,
Падают тихо, медлительно.
Я же молюсь суевернее,
Плачу и каюсь мучительно.

Slowly, my soul in bondage,
I walked through the church portals...
I heard songs of love,
I saw crowds praying.
Or did he send me comfort
In a moment of unbelief?
Now I often enter the church
Without any doubt.
And infinitely deep
Thoughts and longings grow.
I see the distant sky,
I hear God's breathing.
The evening roses fall,
Fall quietly, reluctantly.
I then pray more reverently,
I cry and grieviously repent.

(I, 133, 595)[44]

I started visiting the Cathedral to pray to my Kazan Madonna and light candles before Her. As a student of A. I. Vvedensky, I fortunately understood that both a "simple rite" (I, 232) and the lofty outbursts of the human mind are equally insignificant and worthwhile before the mystery of what is unattainable by rational knowledge. But I had no need either to attend church services or to participate in the rituals. I could never submit to the mediation of a priest, except in the two months after Sasha's death, when it seemed less blasphemous to observe the rites for the dead than to abandon myself to my own individual "beautiful sorrow."

In the early evening of an October day (October 17) I was walking along the Nevsky to the Kazan Cathedral when I met Blok. We walked side by side. I told him where I was going and why and let him come along. We sat on a stone bench under the window next to my Madonna in the already darkened Cathedral.[45] The fact that we were together had a deeper meaning beyond simple explanation. It was clear to me that I was giving my soul to him, opening myself to him.

Thus began our visits to the cathedrals, first the Kazan, then St. Isaac's. In those months Blok used to write a lot and assiduously. We continued to meet on the street and still made believe that it was by chance. But often after Chitau's classes we would take a long walk and talk a good deal—always about the same things. More often than not we talked about his verses. It was already clear that they pertained to me. Blok spoke about Solovyov, about the World Soul, about Sofia Petrovna Khitrovo,[46] about the "Three Meetings,"[47] and about me, placing me on an incomprehensible plateau. We would also talk a lot about prosody, about the double function of rhythm within a poem...[48]

Once as we were crossing the Vvedensky Bridge by the Obukhov Hospital Blok asked me what I thought of his verses. I told him that I thought he was a poet no less talented than Fet. This was a momentous statement for us. We used to mention Fet with every other breath. We both got very excited when I said this, because at that time we never made idle talk and weighed every word that was spoken or heard.

Our meetings at the Botkins' became more frequent. M. P. Botkin was a friend of father's, Ekaterina Nikitina, of mother's, They had three daughters my own age and a younger boy and girl. It was a delightful family and a delightful home. They lived in their own house on the corner of the quay and 18th Lane on Vasily Island. From the first to the last floor it was not a home but a museum, containing the famous Botkin collection of Italian Renaissance art. The stairs leading up to the second floor were flanked by an antique wooden panel; the steps were covered by a thick red rug into which your foot sank. The ballroom was paneled with old carved walnut wood which the furniture matched. There were paintings, huge palms, and two grand pianos—all the daughters were serious musicians. In the ballroom the lights were never too bright even when the balls were held. I liked that very much. On the other hand, the next room, the parlor, was drowned in light and in the shiny silvery silk of the upholstered furniture. Its main attraction was an undraped mirrored window which in the evening opened onto one of the most beautiful views of Petersburg: the Neva, St. Isaac's Cathedral, the bridges and the lights. In this parlor, in the winter of 1901, the Botkin sisters organized readings on various literary themes. I remember one of these themes: Cha- adaev's "Philosophical Letters,"[49] which I don't think had been blacklisted yet at the time. In any case they were not too well known. Lilia Botkin at- tended classes with me. Before that we were childhood friends, and later, in the gymnasium years, I started to attend their balls. My most vivid recollec- tions of social life are these balls. The Botkins had a wide circle of friends that included many officers and society people. Young Somov,[50] who sang old Italian arias, V. V. Maximov, at that time a law student (his real name was Samus[51]), and many other musicians and artists frequented their home. The mother and the three daughters were very much alike and they all possessed that charm that was a family trait. They were tall and portly, beautiful in a typically Russian way. Their gentle, friendly, warm hospitality, the melodi- ous speech peculiar to them all, the interest they displayed in whomever they spoke to, created such an atmosphere of cordiality that they were constantly surrounded by friends and admirers.

Knowing about my friendship with Blok, Ekaterina Nikitina asked me to invite him to one of their balls (to which he did not go) and then to some readings, to which he went a few times.

I am quoting a letter I wrote that winter which clearly shows the outer reserve that existed between us at the very time when we felt an inner close- ness: "Alexander Alexandrovich, on November 29 Mme. Botkin asked me again to extend to you her invitation, only this time not to her ball but to the recitals I spoke to you about. Ekaterina Nikitina asks you to come over about eight. I hope that this time I will carry out her request better than I did the last. L. Mendeleeva."

And here is his answer: "Dear Lyubov Dmitrievna, I thank you very much for your note. I will definitely be at the Botkins' today, that is, if I don't get their address mixed up. Your A. Blok. November 29, 1901. St. Petersburg."

That's how formal we were in those days!

Blok took me home from the Botkins' in a cab. This was not quite cor- rect, strictly speaking, but for a *kursistka* anything was possible. I remember how little it took to satisfy my girlish expectations. It was bitterly cold. We traveled on sleds. Blok, as was the the custom, put his right arm around my waist. I knew that the students' cloaks were cold, and I nonchalantly asked him to hide his hand in my warm fur coat. "I am afraid it will freeze." "Psy- chologically speaking, I know it won't freeze." This answer, more earthy than usual for Blok, was so gratifying to me that it imprinted itself on my mem- ory.

Despite all this, on January 29 I broke with Blok. I still have the letter that I wrote then and carried around and that I intended to give him upon our first chance meeting. I could not do it, however, for then I would have been the one to say the first unequivocal words, and my reserve and pride held me back at the last moment. I simply met him with a cold and distant stare when he came up to me on the Nevsky near the Cathedral, and casually, making it clear that this was just an excuse, I said that I was afraid we had been seen walking together and that this was embarrassing to me. I said good-bye in an icy tone of voice and left. The letter that I had prepared read as follows:

Do not judge me too harshly for writing this letter. Believe me, everything in it is the absolute truth and what compels me to write it is the fear that even for one moment my relationship with you might become insincere. I cannot bear an insincere relationship, and with you it would be particularly hard. This explanation is very difficult and painful for me. Do not judge me or my clumsy style too harshly.

I can no longer maintain the same friendly relationship with you as before. Until now I have been absolutely sincere. I give you my word, but now, in order to maintain our friendship I would have to start pretending. Suddenly, quite unexpectedly, and through no one's fault, it dawned on me how very much we are strangers to each other, how little you understand me. For you look at me as if I were some kind of abstract idea. You have contrived all sorts of wonderful things about me, and because of this fantastic fiction that lives only in your imagination you have overlooked the real me, you have failed to notice the live person with the live soul...

I think that you even loved your fantasy, your philosophical ideal. I was waiting all along for you to notice me, to understand my needs and my readiness to respond with heart and soul... But you continued to fantasize and philosophize... Why, I even gave you a hint about this when I said: "One must translate the abstract into the concrete." You answered with a phrase that clearly characterizes your relationship with me: "A thought once uttered is a lie." Yes, everything was only thought, fantasy; there was no feeling, not even friendship. For a long time and in good faith I waited for a little feeling from you, but upon returning home after our last talk I felt in my soul that something had suddenly snapped and died; I felt that your attitude to me, as it is now, is much too upsetting. Shortcomings and all, I am flesh and blood and want to stay that way. When people look at me as some kind of abstraction, even the most ideal one, I find it unbearable, insulting, alien to my way of thinking... Yes, I see how alien we are to each other. I will never forgive what you have done to me all this time. Why, you have been dragging me away from life and up to some heights where it is cold, frightening, and...boring!

Forgive me if I am writing too sharply or in any way offending you, but it is best to put a stop to everything at once, and not to lie or to make believe. I am sure that you will not regret too much the end of our "friendship"; you will always find consolation in calling it fate, or in your poetry or scholarship... But I still carry in my soul an involuntary sadness, the kind one bears after a disappointement. However, I hope I will be able to forget everything as soon as possible, to forget it in such a way that no offence and no regret will remain...[52]

The Beautiful Lady has rebelled! Well, dear reader, if you condemn her, it can only be because you are no longer twenty, because you have lived your life and now are weary, or else you have never felt your blossoming youth singing joyous hymns to nature. I have already told you what kind of person I was at that time.

But I never gave my letter to Blok. No explanation took place, *nach wie vor*; consequently we remained formal "friends" and Blok resumed his visits to our home. Afterwards he gave me three drafts of the letter that he had intended to send me after we broke up but which he could not bring himself to send.[53] He too had evaded the explanation that he felt was necessary.

*   *   *

Life continued in the same way as before. I kept studying assiduously with Chitau, who was not only very pleased with me, but was already planning to prepare me for a debut at the Alexandrinsky Theater in a role I had already played, the role of a young woman in everyday life. That spring Maria Mikhailovna had shown me to some of her former colleagues (N. I. Pisarev[54] was one of them, I remember) in excerpts from Gogol's *Marriage*. Blok did not attend that performance. I remember sending him a ticket with a note: "The first thing to be presented is *Marriage*. I play in it. If you would like to see me, come on time, for one is kindly requested not to enter during the performance. L. Mendeleeva (March 21)."

Even afterwards I continued to perform very successfully in *Marriage*, but here, probably, is one of my basic mistakes in life: playing realistic roles did not satisfy me. True, I enjoyed putting into them my ability to make fun of things, my powers of observation, and my love for the colorful details of life, but this was not my full range. More important than this and what I needed personally was the grand gesture, the ornamental and picturesque pose, the effect of costumes and impressive declamation—in other words, the heroic plane. No one wanted to cast me on this plane. First of all, I was taller and heavier than a heroine is supposed to be; secondly, I did not have the large, expressive eyes that are an integral part of heroic expression. I thought

I could compensate for these disadvantages with the quality of my voice, which was strong, and with that of my performance, which was painstaking and expressive. I also knew how to wear clothes, how to pose and move. Indeed, when I managed to get the part of the heroine I did well and received good reviews. (I played Klytemnestra in Meyerhold's production, Mme. Chevalier in Auslander's *The Emerald Spider* in Orenburg, Zhanna in *Guilty —Not Guilty*, also Meyerhold's, and Iriada in Sh-ninsky's [sic] *Sin Misleads* in some mediocre theater.) But such roles were seldom found in repertoires and I did not have enough warmth or dramatic realism for more ordinary heroines, like Kruchinina in *Guilty without Fault*, for instance.

If I had only listened to Maria Mikhailovna and followed the path she had recommended I would have met with true success playing ordinary people, for here I was always unanimously recognized. But I was not attracted to such roles, and in the fall I did not return to Chitau. Thus I remained without an enjoyable occupation, and life took its own turn.

That summer in Boblovo I did not associate with Blok, although he used to visit us. I took part in a play (I played Natasha in Ostrovsky's *Earned Bread*) in the neighboring village, Rogachevo. Blok came to see me perform. Then I paid prolonged visits to my cousins, the Mendeleevs, on their new estate near the village of Mozhaisk. There I was hoping to meet their actor cousin, who was very handsome and who sounded very interesting to me from their tales. But there, too, fate either saved or fooled me: instead of him, his sister and her fiancé came. Just for spite I flirted with Misha Mendeleev's friends, boy-realists, as I did in Boblovo with my two Smirnov cousins. I also flirted with some gymnasium students who fell in love, back and forth, with my sister and me. But what kind of flirtations were these? Yes, my readers, when you read in Blok's poems about the "innocence" of the princess, do not hesitate for a moment to believe it!

I was moving in a new direction, pulling away from the past. Blok was still the same, and his behavior showed that as far as he was concerned nothing was changed or lost. He came to visit us as before: here were the signs of our predestined path...[55]

However, there was no explanation of his intentions. This irritated me and I brooded—let me at least have some fun, now that all this no longer touches me deeply. That fall I felt free from any kind of feeling for Blok.

The seventh of November was approaching, the day of our school party at the Gentry Clubhouse, and suddenly I knew that there would be an explanation that evening. It was not excitement that I felt, but rather curiosity and restlessness.

What happened afterwards was very strange, unless one admits some kind of predestination and a complete lack of free will in my actions. Everything I did was perfectly mechanical; I knew what would happen and how.

I was at the party with my school friend Shura Nikitina and Vera Ma-
kotskova. I was wearing the blue woolen dress from Paris. We were sitting in
the gallery in the last rows on randomly placed chairs near the spiral staircase which, if one faced the stage, led to the left side of the entrance. I had
turned in the direction of the staircase and was looking persistently, knowing
that Blok would soon appear.

Blok was mounting the steps, searching for me with his eyes, and then
he headed straight for our group. Later he told me that upon arriving at the
Clubhouse he had immediately headed for the gallery, although in the past
my friends and I had never sat there. From that moment on I no longer re-
sisted my destiny. Looking at Blok's face, I knew that everything would be
resolved that day, and a strange feeling dawned on me that I would not be
asked about anything, that everything would go of its own accord, regardless
of my will. We spent that evening as usual, only the words we exchanged were
spoken in half tones, something like the way people speak of trivial matters
or of matters they agreed upon beforehand. Then, after about two hours, he
asked me whether I was tired and wanted to go home. I immediately con-
sented. Putting on my red cape, I felt feverish, the way I do before every inevitable event. Blok was no less excited than I.

We walked out without speaking, and silently, without prior agreement,
we both turned right and went along the Italyanskaya, to the Mokhovaya, to
the Liteynaya, toward our homes. It was a bitterly cold, snowy night. Swirls of
snow circled in the air. The snow lay in drifts, deep and clean. Blok began to
talk. I don't remember how he began, but when we were approaching the
Fontanka in the direction of the Semenovsky Bridge he was saying that he
loved me and that my answer would determine his fate. I remember saying
that it was too late to talk about this, that I did not love him any more, that
I had been waiting for a long time for his words, and that even if I should forgive his silence, it would hardly solve anything. Blok continued to talk, as
though skirting my answer, and I listened. I listened submissively, with the
usual attention, believing as usual in his words. He said that my response was
a matter of life and death for him and continued speaking for a long time.
I do not remember what he said, but his letters and diaries of that time speak
the same language. I remember that deep inside I was not thawing out, but
was acting independently of my will at that moment, somewhat automatically, as though our past was in control. I do not remember what words I used
to accept his love or the things I said. What I remember is that Blok took a
folded piece of paper out of his pocket and handed it to me, saying that if
my answer had been different, he would not have been alive in the morning.
I crumpled up this piece of paper but saved it. It is all yellowed now and still
bears traces of the snow:

My address: Petersburg Side, Grenadier Guard Regiment Barracks. Apartment 13. Colonel Kublitsky. November 7, 1902. Petersburg. I ask that no one be blamed for my death. The reasons for it are quite "abstract" and have nothing to do with "human" relationships. I believe in the one holy catholic apostolic church. I trust in the resurrection of the dead and in life in the hereafter. Amen. The poet Alexander Blok.[56]

Later on he took me home in a sled. Leaning over, he asked me something. I turned toward him and brought my lips close to his in the proper literary fashion. (I read about these things somewhere in a novel.) It was nothing but sheer curiosity on my part, but the frosty kisses, without teaching us anything, forged our lives.

You would think that happiness had come, but what followed was a confused muddle: layers of true feelings, of my true intoxication with youth, and layers of unspoken words, both mine and his, the interference of others—in other words, a mine field with underground passages that concealed future catastrophes.

We agreed to meet on the ninth in the Kazan Cathedral, but I promised to write without fail on the eighth. Upon awakening the following morning I was still not in control of myself, though I had not yet submitted to the "fire of feelings" that was approaching. My first playful impulse was to tell Shura Nikitina what had happened the day before. She sometimes worked for my father as a proofreader in the paper *The Petersburg Page*. I waited for her to leave work; I accompanied her home and laughingly told her: "Can you guess how the evening ended? Blok and I kissed..."

The little note that I sent Blok was absolutely trivial and false, if for no other reason than that never in my life had I addressed him as Sashura, as did his family. But I no longer had to confide in Shura Nikitina, because by the time Blok and I said good-bye on the ninth I was spellbound, shaken and vanquished. From the Kazan Cathedral we went to St. Isaac's. St. Isaac's, huge, tall and empty, was drowning in the darkness of the winter evening. Here and there in the distance lights and candles burned before the icons. But where we were, on the side corner bench in the total darkness, we felt more detached from the world there than anywhere else. There were no guards and no people praying. It was not hard for me to abandon myself to the excitement and "passion" of this "encounter"; the unexplored mystery of long kisses was urgently alerting me to life—subduing and transforming the imperiously proud independence of a young girl into a slavish, womanly meekness.

The environment and the words were those of our meetings of the year before, but the world that then had lived only in words was now becoming reality. For me as well as for Blok everything seemed transfigured, mysterious, melodious, and full of meaning. The air surrounding us was resounding with those rhythms, those delicate refrains which Blok later captured and brought into his poems. Although I had learned to understand him before, to live with his thoughts, now yet another perception was added, the "tenth perception" through which a woman in love understands her beloved.

Chekhov laughs at Dushenka, but what's so humorous about her? Isn't one of the wonders of nature that perennial capacity of the woman's soul to find, with the accuracy of a tuning fork, a new key to sing in? There is something tragic in this, if you will, because women sometimes lose what is their own too lightly and willingly. They step back and forget their individuality. I am speaking of myself. As though I were being pursued, as though I were aiming for some finish line, I started to run away from everything that was my own and tried to merge into the tenor of Blok's family, which he loved so much. I changed my writing paper, even my handwriting, but this happened later. At that time this was what awaited me: the following day we met again at St. Isaac's, but only fleetingly. Blok said that he had come to tell me not to be upset, that he was not permitted out. He had to stay in bed, he had a fever. He begged me not to worry, but could not say anything else. We agreed to write each other every day. He could write me at school.[57]

In my subconscious I understood that this was something one does not tell girls, but not only did I leave my subconscious thoughts unanswered, I did not even formulate a question. He is ill. It means "oh, poor fellow, he is ill" and that's all. Why am I saying this? Because here I see the explanation of many things. From his gymnasium years physical closeness with a woman meant one thing for Blok: paid sex; and the inescapable result was disease. (Thank God that all this happens in youth; the disease is not fatal.) It was then unquestionably a psychological trauma: it was not a worshipped lover who introduced one to life, but some casual, faceless lover whose body was hired for a few minutes. And the humiliating, agonizing suffering... The two Aphrodites—Aphrodite Urania and the Aphrodite of the streets—separated by a chasm...[58] Even K. M. S.[59] did not play the role in Blok's life that she was supposed to play, and yet she was much more than a "Urania," she was more than a youth needed in his first encounter to expand his adolescent love into love in all its fullness. For Blok this chasm remained for the rest of his life. It was still there in 1914 when, already a mature individual, he had his most meaningful encounters, and it was only the dazzling, sunny, life-loving Carmen[60] who was able to bridge the chasm, and only with her did Blok find his longed-for synthesis of both loves.

To speak about these things is not considered proper; all of it is "taboo," but without these "improper words" there is absolutely no way of understanding Blok's life in the years that followed. These things must be discussed so that we can have some material at least, however incomplete, for a Freudian analysis of events, and such an analysis will protect not only Blok, but also me, from unfair accusations.

And so I have decided at last to discuss the difficulties and complexities which arose because of my basic ignorance in the affairs of life and love. Even years later when I became stronger, sure of myself, and was in the full bloom of beauty and knowledge, it still was not easy for me to overcome these problems. At the beginning, however, I was completely unprepared and unarmed. Hence the foundation of our life together was built on unstable ground; hence the hopelessness of so many conflicts, the broken line of my whole life. But let's talk about this in the proper order.

Naturally, we were not "husband and wife." My God! What kind of husband was he, what kind of a wife was I! In this respect Bely, who was driven to despair by the situation, was right in seeing a "lie" in my relationship with Sasha, but he was mistaken in thinking that both Sasha and I persisted in our marriage out of decency, cowardice, or God knows what. Of course he was right in saying that it was he alone who loved and appreciated me, a flesh and blood woman, he alone who could surround me with that kind of devotion which a woman yearns for and expects. But Sasha was also right in another way—by leaving me alone—and I always took advantage of a person's prerogative to choose his own path, however difficult it might be. I did not strive for the contented life of a woman adored by her lover. Having rejected the first serious "temptation," having remained faithful to my true and difficult love, I paid due homage, later on in life, to all the infatuations that came along. There was no longer a doubt: my course was established, the sail was set, and my "drifting astray" was inconsequential. For this reason there were times later on when I hated Bely; he shook me from my safe, confident position.[61] With a childlike naivete I firmly believed in the uniqueness of my love and in the fact that "some day" things with Sasha would straighten out.

My life with my "husband" (!) by the spring of 1906 was completely shattered. His brief outburst of sensual interest in me in the winter and summer before the wedding soon (in the two months that followed) had spent itself without having succeeded in dispelling my girlish ignorance, since Sasha had taken my instinctive self-protection seriously.

My ignorance in anything pertaining to love was appalling. Furthermore, I could not make my way out of the complex maze of the not-so-simple psychology of such an unusual husband as Sasha. He immediately started theorizing that we did not need physical closeness, that this was "astartism," "darkness," and God knows what else. When I would tell him that I loved this still undiscovered world, that I wanted it, he would theorize further: such relationships cannot be lasting, and no matter what, he would eventually leave me for others. But what about me? "You too would do the same." This drove me to despair. To be rejected even before I was actually a wife—this nipped in the bud that elemental belief which any girl in love for the first time holds—that love is steadfast and unique. I cried my eyes out those evenings with such a passionate despair that I had no tears left. In fact, however, there was no use in crying: everything was following a "predetermined course."

Youth nonetheless draws together those who live side by side. On one of those nights—in the fall of 1904—what should have happened earlier took place. It was all with a mischievous intent on my part and unexpected for Sasha. From that time on infrequent, brief, selfishly male encounters began to take place between us. My ignorance remained the same, the puzzle still unsolved, and I could not fight, since I considered my passivity unavoidable. By the spring of 1906 even this little contact stopped.

The spring of that year was a lengthy "period of inactivity" for a twenty-four-year old woman. I cannot say that I possess the fiery temperament of a southern woman which can drive her to a sick and frenzied state when things do not work out. I am a northerner, and the temperament of a northerner is frozen champagne... Do not trust the quiet coldness of a crystal glass, it conceals a sparkling fire—but not for long! Furthermore, on my mother's side I am a Cossack, for my mother is half-Cossack and half-Swedish. Borya [Bely] correctly sensed in me a "wild recklessness," and I know that he was right. It was the blood of those ancestors who plundered, killed and raped which often surged in me and drove me to free love and shameful actions. There were times when reflection plagued me, the cultural inhibitions that I had also inherited at birth. But sometimes passions burst forth...

That spring, I see it now as I look back, I was thrown at the mercy of anyone who would stubbornly pursue me. If I were now to detach myself mentally from the past and what I could not understand, I would not blame Borya for anything. We all believed him, respected him greatly, valued his judgment, and considered him one of us. I repeat, I was totally ignorant of life and childishly believed that I could do no wrong. Furthermore, I was at that time lionized by Blok's family and his fans from Moscow, exalted without rhyme or reason, and with total disregard for my identity as a human being. My youth had a stange captivating effect on people. I saw it, I felt it; it could have gone to the head of someone even wiser or more experienced than I. I may have shrugged my shoulders in answer to their theorizing on the meaning of "femininity" (of which I was supposedly the embodiment), but how could I not help sensing the power of my eyes and my smiles on those around me, and especially on Borya, the most outstanding one among them? Borya made my head spin as would the most experienced of Don Juans, although he was not a ladies' man. His long monologues, abstract and scholarly, which sometimes lasted four to six hours and which we found very interesting, invariably ended with some disclosure about me; either directly or indirectly it turned out that the meaning of everything revolved around my existence and identity.

Not baskets, but the entire "Bugaev woods" would appear in the parlor. The servants, Nalivaiko or Vladislav, laughing on the sly, would bring in flowers that had been sent to the "young mistress"—to me, accustomed to a life and ambience that was even more than modest! Borya also spoke in the language of the most romantic of songs—he brought me Glinka's "How Sweet It Is to Be with You," "Anxiety of Passion, Abate," and some other songs. He would sometimes sit at the grand piano and improvise. I remember a melody that he used to call his "theme." It used to touch my soul with a familiar note of sadness and pain; it was something I too felt deeply, or at least I thought I did. But I think that he, just like me, did not fully realize the dangers lurking on those paths along which we so thoughtlessly wandered. He had no evil intent; neither did I.

There was something between Sasha and me, a unique feeling which in my childish ignorance of life had seemed irreplaceable, which I regarded as my own "invention," mysterious, unequaled—the "sweet venom" of glances or the penetration of one's soul without a glance or even the touch of a hand, merely by one's presence. I remember the horror I felt when I first asked myself: can all this happen again with someone else? Do such things happen? Am I really looking at Borya that way? And are those eyes, eyes that are not Sasha's, the cause of this fog, this intoxication?

We were returning from one of Count Sheremetev's[62] concerts, from *Parsifal*, which I had attended with the whole family and with Borya. Sasha rode in the sleigh with his mother, and I with Borya. For a long time I had known of his love, for a long time I had been accepting it flirtingly, even encouraging it without understanding my own feelings. Lightheartedly, I was relegating my interest in him to the category of "brotherly" (one of Bely's favorite words) relationships. But then (I even remember where, along the river bank, beyond the house of Peter the Great), as Bely was speaking, I looked at him—and was dumbfounded. The way our glances met—oh yes, it was the same, the same! The "sweet venom" again... My world, the elemental forces to which Sasha no longer wanted to return... How long ago and yet how near was the time when we had abandoned ourselves to them! Feeling all the while the absurdity, incongruity, impossibility of the situation, I could not turn away from it, and from then on confusion reigned. I was shaken no less than Borya. No sooner were we left alone than we felt no barriers between us and, helpless and eager, we could not tear ourselves away from the long and unquenching kisses. Unable to weigh the consequences of this jumble, I once even went to his apartment. Playing with fire, I allowed him to remove my turtle combs and hairpins and my hair fell like a golden cloak. (Are you amused, dear reader, that one's "downfall" began in such a way in my time?) But something awkward and clumsy in his gesture sobered me up (clearly, in these affairs Borya was not much more experienced than I) and with my hair pinned back in place, I ran down the steps, beginning to understand that this was not the way, that another way had to be found out of the confusion that I had created.

(My dear reader, I am now turning to you. I know how difficult it must be for you to believe this story. Let's agree on the following: my version is much closer to the truth than your assumptions about Bely, which are much too flattering.) The fact that I not only did not lose my head, but on the contrary, retreated at the first opportunity for intimacy had a sobering effect on me. The next time I saw Borya I looked at him more dispassionately, and more than anything else in the world I wanted to have a few days alone, or even a week, in order to collect my thoughts, come to my senses, and figure out what to do. I asked Borya to leave Petersburg. I recall the following scene: I was sitting at the piano and he was standing across from me, leaning on it, his face toward the window. I asked him to go away, to give me the freedom to think things over, and promised to write to him as soon as I figured things out. I can still see the look in his wide open eyes. (I used to call them "toppled over"—there was a certain look about them, not quite frenzied and not quite superhuman, everything about them was "toppled over..." "Why toppled over?" Borya would ask, frightened.) He looked at me submissively and believed me. This is where that fraud comes in, about which Borya would complain bitterly afterwards: I gave him no inkling that I was losing interest, that I had already come to my senses. I was depriving him of his only real weapon in such cases—his presence. In reality the course of action that I was proposing would have been an eloquent sign to one more experienced than Borya that I was losing interest. But he still believed in our intoxicating kisses and in the words that I had spoken in moments of inebriation: "Yes, we will run away," "Yes, I love you" and all those other things he wanted to believe in.

No sooner had he left than I started to come to my senses in horror. What's going on? I don't feel anything for him anymore and yet what have I been up to? I felt ashamed of myself and sorry for him, but I no longer had a choice. I wrote to him that I did not love him and asked him not to come to the house. He was furious, sent off streams of letters and complained about me to everybody he happened to meet. This was even more ludicrous than upsetting, and because of it I could not remain friends with him.

We left early for Shakhmatovo, the quiet retreat where more than once we had brought our storms ꞁd where these storms had subsided. There was much that I had to think through; the very make-up of my own soul was undergoing changes. Until now I had been Sasha's humble pupil in everything. If I thought or felt differently than he did, I was wrong. However, the problem now was that a man whom everybody regarded as Sasha's equal had fallen in love with me with the type of love that I longed for, that I waited for, that I considered to be my element. (Later I was told more than once, alas, that I was right.) It means, then, that this kind of relationship is not some "base" realm, clearly it is not "astartism," that darkness unworthy of me, as Sasha was trying to prove to me. It is Andrei Bely who loves me this way, with all the self-oblivion of passion—that very Andrei Bely who was then an authority even for Sasha, and whom our whole family deeply respected, recognizing the sensitivity of his feelings and the acuteness of his judgment. Yes, to run away with him would indeed be a betrayal. L. Lesnaya[63] had a little poem that she often read on the stage during those years when we were both performing at the same theater (Kuokalla, 1914). In it a "Japanese" loved a "Japanese girl," then he started "hugging a black girl," but "he did not speak Japanese to her, did he? Which means that he did not cheat. It means that she was just a passing fancy." I could speak Japanese with Andrei Bely. To run away with him would be saying that I had made a mistake in thinking that I loved Sasha. I would be choosing between equals. I made my choice, but the very possibility of such a choice shook my self-confidence. That summer I experienced a bitter crisis. I repented, I felt despair, I longed for my former stability, but what was done was done. I clearly saw before my eyes the "alternatives," knowing for certain at the same time that I would never "betray"[64] Sasha, however it may appear from the outside. Unfortunately, I was completely indifferent to the opinions and judgments of strangers, and therefore what people said was in no way a curb on my behavior.

My attitude to Borya was inhuman, I must admit. Once I renounced him, I did not feel the least sorry for him. My need and immediate goal were to stabilize my life and make it as comfortable as possible. Borya was trying his best, demanding that I let him spend the winter in Petersburg and that we see each other, if nothing else, simply as friends, but this would have been burdensome, difficult, and trying: at that time Borya's tactlessness was incredible. That winter was threatening to be most unpleasant, but it did not enter my mind that I was guilty, that I had carried my flirtation with Borya and my selfish game too far, that he still continued to love me and that I was responsible for this love... I did not think of any of this and was busy tearing up and throwing into the fire the piles of letters that I received from him. My only concern was how to get rid of this lover whom I no longer needed, and pitilessly and tactlessly I forbade him to come to Petersburg. Now I see that it was I who drove him to extremes, but at that time I considered myself right in acting that way, since I was no longer in love.

The challenge to a duel was, of course, Borya's response to my attitude and to that behavior which he, not believing the things I said, did not understand. Since he felt the same way as before, he could not believe that I could have changed. He still believed in my words and actions of the previous spring and had good reason to be confused. He was sure that I "loved" him as before, but felt that I was cowardly, retreating because of decency and other silly considerations. However, his greatest mistake was his being sure that Sasha was putting pressure on me without having the moral right to do so. This was what he sensed, but need I say that I never told anything about my unhappy marriage to him or anyone else? If I was tight-lipped and secretive about other things, you can imagine how I was about this... Borya did not recognize, however, one of Sasha's basic traits: Sasha always became completely indifferent as soon as he felt that I was moving away from him and toward some new lover. That's how Blok responded now. He would not lift a finger to hold me back. He would not open his mouth, and if he did, it was only to sneer coldly and cruelly as only he could, with humiliating mockery and devastating remarks at my actions and motives and at all the Mendeleev clan into the bargain.

Therefore when Kobylinsky,[65] acting as a second, appeared, right then and there I decided resolutely, as I know how to in critical moments, that I myself must unravel the mess I made. First of all, I reshuffled all the cards and I ruined his plan at the outset.

Bely says that Kobylinsky arrived on the day of Alexandra Andreevna's departure, that is, on August 10 (according to M. A. Beketova's diary). I do not remember any of that, although I remember perfectly what happened afterwards. Sasha and I were alone in Shakhmatovo. It was a rainy autumn day. We used to love to walk on days like those. We were returning from the Malinova mountain and from Prasolova, from the golden splendors of the fall, and were wet up to the knees from walking in the woods in the wet grass. As we walked along the path from the pond to the garden we saw that somebody was walking back and forth in the dining room. We soon recognized who it was and guessed why he was there. Sasha, as usual, was calm and quite ready to meet the worst head on—it was his specialty. However, I decided to take things into my own hands and turn everything my way even before we reached the porch. I greeted Kobylinsky naturally, simply, and joyfully, like a happy housewife. He made an attempt to maintain an official tone and requested an immediate private conference with Sasha. Jokingly, but with sufficient authority to throw him off balance, I asked what secrets there were between them. I said that there were no secrets between Sasha and me and asked him to speak in front of me. So strong was my subtle pressuring that he began to speak in my presence—he, a second! Well, for Kobylinsky everything had gone wrong! I immediately put him to shame for having taken on such a foolish, senseless mission: "But this requires much talking and you must be tired, so let's have dinner first." Quickly Sasha and I changed into dry clothes. Well, at the dinner table it was a simple matter to turn on smiles and the "silent speech of glances." By this time I had learned to master it and knew its effect. By the end of the dinner Lev Lvovich was sitting completely tamed, and the whole matter about the duel was settled...over tea. We parted the best of friends.

*   *   *

The following winter (1906-1907) found me fully ready to enjoy its charms, its "masks," its "bonfires," the casual, entangling love game whirling around us all. We did not pretend, God forbid! Simply and honestly we spent that winter in a state of lightheaded intoxication that did not involve the vital depths of the soul. For a better understanding of that winter, those unfamiliar with it should read Blok's "Snow Mask" or V. P. Ve18gina's recollections of Blok where it is so wonderfully described.[66]

My partner for that winter, my first "fantastic betrayal," in the commonly accepted meaning of that word, probably remembers our carefree love game with no less pleasure than I. Oh, there was everything—tears, my theatrical visit to his wife, and a "scene." But nothing came of it, since his sober wife did not participate in our game and, stunned, waited for us to come to our senses and for her essentially faithful husband to cast aside his reveler mask. But we were irresistibly whirling around and around in the general dance: "the swiftness of the sleigh" (II, 212-213), the "bearskin cover" (III, 20-21), the "burnt out crystals" (II, 236), a little restaurant on the island that everyone loved, with its unthinkably vulgar "private rooms"[67] (that was the attraction) and lightness, lightness, lightness... Georgy Ivanovich,[68] furthermore had a great sense of humor that kept us from "going overboard" in our relationship. Only when he returned my letters a few years ago did he "go overboard." Then his sense of humor failed him, but I was glad to have them back and nostalgically reread the lighthearted, insubstantial delirium: "Oh, yes, I knew that today you would not find the strength to get rid of me, that today I would hear from you. And isn't it strange the way I feel about you? Isn't it absurd that when you leave, something is torn away from me and I feel terribly lonely? Yet I don't need anything from you. Only sometimes I have a great need to meet your glance and to know that you won't leave me. Today I would like to see you. I am home now and will be here all evening. Yours, L.B." And the writing paper is thin, the handwriting light, volatile, almost non-existent.

Don't be surprised, dear reader, at the tender emotion and lyricism that these few winter months evoke in me. Later on there was much that was difficult and bitter in the "betrayals" as well as in the virtuous years (and they were virtuous indeed). Yet that winter offered some kind of respite, some kind of life outside of life. How can I not be grateful for it, not try to conjure up for you, reader, its unforgettable image, so that when reading the "Snow Mask" and other poems of that winter you will associate the snowy witchcraft of our Petersburg with them and see Blok's traveling companions whirling in its blizzard.

*   *   *

Dagobert the courtier[69] was not handsome, but he had a wonderful, supple, strong and lanky body, the movements of a young beast of prey, and he had a wonderful smile that showed a set of teeth as white as snow. His southern accent, the Kharkov pronunciation that he could not overcome, somewhat detracted from his talent, but he was a superb actor, sensitive and intelligent. Later on he rose very high in the theatrical hierarchy, but that particular season he was still a beginner, an actor in our young troupe from which such talents as K. E. Gibshman,[70] V. A. Podgorny,[71] and Ada Korvin[72] emerged. I too was among them, I who held no less promise yet who foolishly wasted everything.

Both he and I felt the surge of youth: we moved along fateful pathways.

One day, after the rehearsal and the dinner, in the few remaining hours before the performance, we were sitting in my hotel room on a small couch. On the table before us there was a French novel that had served as an excuse for Dagobert's visit. He was perfecting his French and I was helping him so that he could work without a dictionary, a task which indeed required a lot of time, and we had so very little of it. For us, however, "the times of Paolo and Francesca had not passed..." (II, 290-91). When the time came for us to shed our clothes, in a surge of belief in the harmony of our mutual passionate feelings, I asked him so persuasively to give me the opportunity to show myself off as I wanted to be seen that he agreed: he went to the window and turned his face away. It was dark. From the ceiling there hung an electric bulb, wretched and banal. In a few movements I took everything off and let the shining cloak of my golden hair fall, wavy, well-groomed as always. In those days such hair was admired, and I was proud of mine. I threw the cover over the headboard. (I would always take a sheet and hang it on the wall covering the headboard by the pillows.) I stretched out against the background of this snowy whiteness and knew that against it the contours of my body were so barely distinguishable that I did not have to fear the coarse, direct light falling from the ceiling, and that my soft, fine, dazzling skin did not have any need for concealing shadows. Perhaps Giorgione, perhaps

Titian... When Dagobert turned around...the celebration began outside time and space. I only remember his exclamation: "Ah, ah...what is this?" I remember how he looked from where he stood, clutching his head in his hands and begging me not to stir... How long did this last? Seconds or slow minutes... Then he came up to me, fell on his knees, kissed my hand, mumbled that he wanted to carry away these minutes and preserve their ecstasy. He saw that I was smiling at him proudly and happily and answering his reverent kisses with a grateful squeeze of my hand.

During our stage performance, of course, my courtier Dagobert moved about darker than a cloud. He had such a strange look that I ran away from him, fearing that the fever burning within me would be noticed by others. Nonetheless, at one point on the stage he managed to whisper to me: "I shall never leave you now..." and the fire started, such a full harmony of sensations, an ecstasy almost to the point of swooning, perhaps even to the loss of consciousness. We did not know or remember anything and returned to the world of reality only with great effort. And yet nothing could equal those first few moments we shared.

This silent adoration, this ecstasy, this magic circle shutting out the world like a physical force—this moment was the very best I experienced in my life. Never had I known a greater "fullness of life," a greater closeness with beauty, with creation. I was the ideal I dreamt about. I was what I had hoped some day to be.

Now, isn't all this "sublimation"? We were young and liked each other. It was desire that drew us together. My attitude to my own body and to the moment that was celebration for me—showing my body off so that he could see it the way I did—estranged him from me. All of this could have turned out disastrously had he been the "wrong one."

Is it possible that there are people who understand each other in everything, who share a common life and the same interests? Is it possible that such happiness exists? I never knew it. I had only one or two things in common and mutually understood with anyone I ever knew. Even later on with my so-called "lovers," with every one, a different interest and only one common chord.

For me Dagobert came the closest to being my holiest of holies. He felt the same reverence for the beauty of the body and his passion was ecstatic and self-oblivious. Let my gratitude for him live on in these sometimes too rough pages. I am grateful to you even now, my courtier Dagobert, in my mature years. I have never lost this gratitude, even though we parted so soon and, for me, so tragically.

Dark, terrible, bewildering months and years followed. When I feel optimistic and believe, I think that there was a reason for them, but now I don't understand. Why was there this sadistic, senseless suffering? Why this terrible stupidity and helplessness on my part? Why didn't I break away right from the beginning, why didn't I defend myself?

From early, very early youth I was absolutely terrified by the thought of having a child. As my wedding day was approaching, I was so worried about the possibility of pregnancy and my whole being so rebelled against it that I decided to have a frank talk with Sasha, who had noticed that I was torturing myself with something incomprehensible. I told him that there was nothing in the world I hated more than motherhood and that I was so afraid of it that there were moments when I was ready to give up marriage rather than face this possibility. Sasha right then and there quieted all my fears: there would be no children.[73]

In that frenzied spring of 1908 I did not give much thought to anything and, as before, I did not know anything about the prose of life. I returned pregnant in May in utter and helpless despair. I firmly decided to terminate my pregnancy but did not do anything about it and hid my head in the sand like an ostrich. Someone had given me the absurd notion that the abortion must be performed in the third month. I decided then to get it in the summer, after the theatrical season in Borzhom.

At that time we were all interested in palmistry. I consistently avoided looking at my left palm; a small red spot had appeared and was becoming brighter—a catastrophe was awaiting me. I was trying with my eyes half-shut to last until August. The feeling that I was at the edge of doom never left me. I did things I never did before or after. I used to go in the evenings to the "floating pub" on the river Kure with an actor, the most obnoxious character of the whole troupe, and who meant nothing to me. We simply sat and drank vodka, facing each other in complete silence. He too had problems and needed to put on a front as I did. When fog enveloped consciousness, he would respectfully take my arm and as silently as before, we would return to the place where our troupe had its summer quarters.

In the "storm of conflicting feelings," I would kiss one of the actors (a sickly, swarthy fellow) one minute and his sister the next. Only her brother's jealous supervision prevented that strange little bird from experimenting with what so attracted her. Dagobert was there too, but we were like strangers. He did not understand at all the agony of my state and the depth of my despair.

Strangely enough, with all that, I played my roles well, some even very well, for example the heroine in the old vaudeville piece *If He Only Knew.* I made her into a colorful and moving "Turgenev woman." The whole troupe commended me greatly for it.

My conduct did not betray my condition. I quietly endured and even delighted in our trip to Abastuman, where our company staged Strindberg's *Miss Julie.* It was supposed to be a pleasant ride of two or maybe three hours —I don't remember exactly. We left early in the morning in order to get there before it got hot. But after half an hour one of the tires blew out. We had no spare, and then the fun started. The driver patched it, but after a few yards it blew out again. Finally he stuffed the tire with grass! And thus, barely crawling, between pushes and jerks we managed to rumble along all day. In addition, the water in the cooling system was boiling and steam was coming out of the radiator as though from a samovar. Every other minute the driver would run off to the river Kure with a bucket, pour fresh water into the radiator, and immediately it would turn to a boil. Every cart passing by enveloped us in a thick cloud of dust. Natalia Butkevich and I were trying not to stir, so as to keep the thick layer of dust that covered us, crunched in our mouths, and blew in our eyes from penetrating further, and all this was under the burning sun. We arrived at nine o'clock in the evening (the show was supposed to have started at eight) and no matter how much they screamed at us, we would not agree to put on our make-up or our costumes until they let us wash from head to toe. I went through all this like a healthy person, that is, with interest, and thoroughly enjoyed the events of that colorful day.

However, August came and I returned to Petersburg. Sasha was there. I started running to doctors, to the best, most respected doctors. They would lecture me and show me the way to the door. I remember my face in the mirror: my skin looked very drawn and I had enormous, half-demented eyes, as never before or since. I would pick up the classified pages of the *New Time* and my hand would fall and I would cry bitterly—I knew I would surely die (the spot on my life line). I had no friends; there was no one who could help me or advise me.

In his own way Sasha also lectured me: banality, abomination, let there be a child, since we don't have one, it will be ours. And I yielded, I resigned myself to it. Le it be. Despite myself, despite what I hold most dear.

Agonizing months of waiting.

I viewed with disgust how the pregnancy was disfiguring my body, enlarging my small breasts, stretching the skin over my stomach. I could not find in my soul even one little corner that could make me accept my beauty's demise. With outward resignation I was preparing myself for the child's arrival and—like other, true mothers—was getting everything ready. Somehow I even reconciled my soul to it.

I felt very much deserted by everyone. Mother and sister were in Paris. Even Alexandra Andreevna was in Revel; she dearly loved children and all kinds of mothering, but she wasn't there. Sasha drank a lot that winter and did not pay any attention to my condition, and none of my girlfriends was in Petersburg. Our old Katya, father's former housekeeper, shook her head mournfully: if only father were alive, I would be looked after; father loved children and grandchildren.

The torture lasted four days: chloroform, forceps, and a temperature of

40° C., almost no hope that the poor baby would survive. He was the exact copy of his father. I saw him a few times through the haze of high fever. I had no milk; they stopped bringing him. I would lie there and before me was the white flatness of the hospital sheet and wall. I was alone in my room and I thought: "If this is death, how simple it is..." But it was my son who died, not I.

After a few weeks I returned home. I suspect that I was deeply traumatized. I experienced everything in a very special way. I remember my first impression at home: a bright spring sun was falling with a slanting ray on the door of the bookcase in Sasha's room. The play of light on the shining surface of the mahogany seemed to me so fantastically wonderful and colorful that it was as if I had never in my life seen either a light or a bright color before. This was after my whiteness, my withdrawal from life.

Yet after this the dominant tone was emptiness and dullness. I even developed peculiarities: I was afraid to cross streets, I was afraid of crowded places, but for some reason no one tried to cure me, and I did not take care of myself. Fortunately, I decided to go to Italy and be healed, as many had been healed, by its art. Naturally, this was the right thing for me to do.

*   *   *

If one listens to critics, even the smartest ones, this is the impression of Blok that one gets: an eighth-grader, knitting his brows and gloomily picking his nose, pondering his "world view" and whether he belongs with the Narodniks or the Marxists... They somehow forget that both in science and in art, when a scientist or a poet first discovers something *new,* it is just as strange to him as it is to other people. He thinks about one thing, applies it to something else that is known and already exists, and the result is something that did not exist before, something new. This "new thing" comes to him in ways that are still very far from being understood and that do not at all fit the image of a clever "eighth-grader" successfully solving difficult problems. It is this image, however, that critics, vying with each other, attempt to foist on every poet, wishing to "praise" him.

Even in the sciences creative processes use the subconscious to the same degree that they use conscious modes of thought. I do not have to reach outside my family recollections in order to remember a striking example. Indeed, ten years of work, conscious research and groping for the truth preceded the invention of the periodic tables...but it was in a subconscious moment that they emerged in concrete form. Father himself used to tell us about it: after a long night at his desk, his day's work completed, he was so tired that he could no longer think. Mechanically, he was looking over the cards with the names of the elements and their qualities, and, without thinking about

anything, was laying them out on the table, and then came a sudden jolt—
a light illuminating everything. On the table before him lay the periodic system. The scientific genius needed a moment of exhaustion, a moment that
opened the locks of the subconsciouss, to make an inroad into the new and
the unknown.

Critics make me laugh. Now, sixteen years after Blok's death (thirty or
so years after the first decade of his artistic activity), pick up his books, read
them, and surely if you are not totally stupid you'll understand more or
less what they are all about, what the sequence of thought from one to another is, what social or literary schools, what moods or ideology these thoughts
fit into.

Having related these observations of his, the critic thinks that he has
said or uncovered something new about Blok's art. And why should he not
think so? Because it's too facile, my dear fellow critic. It sounds a bit too
much like "eighth-grade" work, and it sounds this simple because in hindsight you take something completed and, while speaking of the beginning,
you already know what the ending is going to be. Now, even a schoolboy
knows that "The Twelve" crowns Blok's artistic and personal life, but when
Blok was writing his first poem, he did not know what even the second would
be about, not to mention what would lie ahead....

Try to transport yourself to the end of the nineties, when Blok was already writing the *Poems about the Beautiful Lady*, without suspecting, of
course, that he was writing something of that nature. He caught sounds and
wrote down what sang around him or within him—he himself did not know
which. Try to transport yourself to the times of *World of Art*[75] and its exhibitions, to the times before Merezhkovsky's novels, before the French Symbolists were widely known, even before the founding of the Art Theater.[76]
I remember a wonderful example of the "standards" of that period—a performance in 1900 at the Institute: on the one hand, there was the old, gray,
bearded poet Pozdnyakov[77] emoting "Ahead without Fear or Doubt," reaching out with his arms in imitation of Polonsky,[78] and on the other hand,
Pototskaya,[79] with her high voice affectedly squeezing out something by
Chyumina[80]: "... a little dead bird was lying."

So what if Blok's family was sensitive to literature, if Fet, Verlaine, and
Baudelaire were familiar to him from childhood? Still, in order to write a
poem there has to be a certain burst of inspiration, an unexpected flow of both
rhythm and orchestrated sounds. And it goes without saying that when this
happens there is an absolute *unawareness* of one's pattern of thoughts and
complex of feelings.

I clearly remember how the first poems that Blok showed me in 1901
took me unawares. And yet I had been prepared for the new: the new had
been maturing in me in entirely other layers of my soul than the readily

apparent or superficial ones. Perhaps because I had experienced this process and the birth of the new, it was clear to me just where and how to look for its roots in the "art" of the greats. Judged by outward appearances, I was a member of a cultured family with broad interests in the sciences and arts: the exhibitions of realist art,[81] the *Russian Thought*[82] and the *Northern Herald*,[83] a lot of serious music at home, all the performances of foreign dramatic actresses. But strangely enough, my artistic sensitivity sharpened and my interests began branching out in quite a different direction from my family's, at the root of everything new that was happening there was a special perception of art, a total giving of oneself to it heart and soul. It meant drawing your inner strength from art and not believing in anything else to the same extent that you believed in what a poem might sing to you, what music might say to you, or what might shine through the surface of a painting in the lines of its design.

For me it all began with Vrubel.[84] I was fourteen or fifteen at that time. At home my parents were always buying new books. They bought the *Illustrated Lermontov* in the Knebel edition. Vrubel's illustrations to the "Demon"[85] affected me deeply (why, why?). In a different way they also served as the main attraction when my enlightened mother would show her equally enlightened friends these new illustrations to Lermontov's works. There was no end to the laughter and the stupid jokes that every manifestation of the new caused. I felt bad about it (in a new way!). I could not permit this outrage to continue. I took *Lermontov* away and hid it under a mattress. No matter how much they looked for it, they could not find it. In the same way, Tchaikovsky's Sixth Symphony, performed by Nikish,[86] shook my soul and filled it with new worlds. Everybody was delighted with the "wonderful performance," but all I could do was clench my teeth. I could not utter a word.

I know it is difficult for the contemporary reader to understand me. In other words, it is difficult to imagine that this romantic-sounding "lofty" perception of art, now pretty old-fashioned, was in its time the foremost mover in art and a mover of great power. Not only to recognize with one's mind, but also to feel with one's whole being that art brings the fullest, the most tangible knowledge of the foundations of the universe—here is the key without which it is difficult to understand not only Blok's art, but the art of so many of his contemporaries.

It is one thing to write poems on a premeditated theme, masterfully finding appropriate forms for them. (Critics evidently feel that this was Blok's method.) It is quite anouther thing to listen for melodious echoes (Blok never knew whether they came from within the soul or from the outside), echoes of a world that reveals itself to the poet through its elemental music.

Let's face it, my dear fellow critic, after all, doesn't the poet differ in

some way from you and me, and doesn't he differ from even the most skill-
ful, the most masterly versifier?

*   *   *

How strange it is now to remember that society in which I grew up and
spent my married life. All the people were very impractical and absolutely un-
concerned about money. Whenever they had money they spent it freely;
when they did not have it, nothing was done to acquire it. Money was outside
their interests. Their interests lay outside themselves, outside of that thin layer
of dung that covers the crust of the earth. In order to live, however, we had
to stand with out feet in this dung, we had to eat and somehow organize our
lives, and yet our heads remained high above all that. At my parents' or in my
own house at the dinner table or over tea (which seldom was served without company because either father or Alexander Alexandrovich would always detain someone for dinner) I never heard pedestrian talk, or even worse,
trivial domestic conversation. The latest events in the arts and sciences, but
seldom politics, were the subjects of our conversations. Father would speak
a good deal and with pleasure about what he saw, always synthesizing and
opening broad perspectives on the world. We had frequent discussions at the
dinner table: there were often disputes between Alexander Alexandrovich and
one of his friends or a casual guest. It may seem an inconceivable way of
spending time—a five- or six-hour discussion on an abstract theme, but these
discussions were creative. Blok himself, as well as his guest, found in them a
clarification of his own thoughts, insights, and ideas for new themes. Even the
much disliked "family dinners" never lapsed into vulgarity. Mother loved to
talk and relate things, and often spoke with wit, although paradoxically. She
loved to dispute with interesting people, and such people were not rare
among our relatives. A witty verbal duel engaged everybody's attention. Alexandra Andreevna, somewhat preciously but very sincerely, hated the philis-
tine way of life. During those family dinners, whenever new guests were entertained, she always managed to introduce the element of "scandal" with
intentionally provocative statements. The mode of life around us was deteri-
orating, but the majority of those I saw at my parents' house or in mine—
"What people, *mon cher*!" Among my parents' friends were such people
as the realist painters Yaroshenko, Kuindzhi, Repin[87]—bearded, sincere, big
children, naive and firm believers in established principles and ideas; the brilliant Konovalov[88] (who later became an academician) with his beautiful head
held high. All those who knew father through their work, all the relatives who
visited us—they were all on this truly intellectual plane. You can love your
own self very much, but you should love it only to the extent to which it is
able to perceive what is above it. This motion upwards rather than towards

what surrounds us, or down to what's under our feet, is what is most important.

*   *   *

"My birth was a strange one," said Euzebio in the *Worship of the Cross.*[89] I often asserted this jokingly about my own birth; it was confusing any way you look at it. According to the church records I was born on August 29, 1882; in reality, however, it was on December 29, 1881. Thus, almost until the completion of my gymnasium years I passed for a year younger and later on became so used to it that I did not bother changing the records. This confusion occurred because at the time of my birth the formalities of my father's divorce from his first wife and his religious wedding ceremony with my mother had barely been completed. To christen and register me as his "legitimate" daughter was still impossible, and I remained unchristened until the official time. Thanks to my father's brilliant position in society everything went smoothly; I was christened and registered as "legitimate."[90] Later, as an adult, in the heat of domestic conflicts at the time of my oldest brother's death and of the Lemokhs' demands that our family be declared "illegitimate,"[91] I found out the reason for the "incongruity" in my birthday. The romantic in me was very gratified. I felt that my position was a privileged one: I was a "child of love," and even my name "Lyubov" (Love) set me apart from the commonplace, which at that time suited me just fine. I was happy to knock off one little year.

A "racist" could look with pleasure at Blok—he was indeed the embodiment of the blond, blue-eyed, well-built, heroic Aryan. The severity of his comportment, its militarism, the straight bearing, the conservative manner of dressing, and at the same time his full awareness of his good looks and the lofty way he carried himself—all this complemented his Siegfried-like appearance.[92] Alexander Alexandrovich liked and appreciated his looks; this was by no means the least of his "joys in life." When a year or so before his illness he began to lose hope, when his hair began to thin out at the temples, when he did not stand up straight anymore and his glance was not as clear, he used to look sadly in the mirror and quietly, as though not wanting to admit out loud what had happened, he would say half in jest: "It's not the same any longer; no one looks at me anymore in the trolley...," and this for him was a very bitter reality.

*   *   *

My own transition into old age was not particularly traumatic, mainly because of illness. My heart started to bother me and sometimes nothing mattered as long as I felt no pain. When it did not hurt, I would look in the mirror and think: "It's because of my illness that I look so terrible and not because of old age." Then I did not feel so bad. But fate also helped. When fate is kind, it gives you a break: towards the end it slips you a rogue who is not quite a homosexual and not quite a drug addict, so that you bless the day you finally shed the intoxication of a demeaning infatuation and feel cured for the rest of your life. Then even illness and old age seem incidental. To the depth of my soul I feel that infatuation is loathsome. I don't want any part of it!

*   *   *

And now my home is settled at last. It reflects my soul, as indeed it should. There is much that is amateurish, homemade and unfinished, but it is not lacking in ingenuity. It has nothing in common with the smugly conventional. Here I strive to be modern and European—but how little I succeed! But what is particularly wonderful is that I have a radio. The bathroom is comfortable and well-equipped, as in European homes. The walls are light and do not crowd you in. Here Blok's portrait hangs, bigger than life. The art works are not numerous, but they catch the eye.

From the window, above the flowers, roofs, and pipes there is a view of the sky.

The armchairs and divans for friends are soft and comfortable.

The colorful pillows and the smell of perfume remind one that this is a woman's place.

That is me.

*   *   *

A few additional facts will help the reader understand Alexander Alexandrovich's personality and character. He and I had in common a basic trait that made living together both possible and inevitable, despite our differences in character, in the way we chose to spend our time, and in our outward tastes. We both created our own lives, made things happen, and had the strength not to yield to "ordinary existence" or even to "existence." This, however, is of small significance in comparison with our inner freedom, or rather, with our freedom from externals. Paradoxically, this came about because we—I especially, but Sasha too—always saw ourselves as puppets in the hands of Fate, led down a predetermined path. I knew a little vaudeville song that went:

>You and I are marionettes
>And the days of our lives are not hard...

Sometimes Sasha enjoyed it, but sometimes he got very angry.

In short, here are a few characteristics. I shall speak for myself as well as Sasha whenever I think I am speaking about common characteristics; one can best speak about what goes on inside oneself, for after all, in our case it was a matter of "consciousness shaping our way of life," to turn the Marxist phrase around.

*   *   *

One would have to be utterly stagnant and intellectually shortsighted to live with Blok and not to understand the pathos of the Revolution, not to feel that one's individual concerns were insignificant before it. Fortunately, my way of thinking was not rigid and I had enough freedom from smug egotism when the Revolution came. Having returned from Pskov very "provincial-minded" and with very "provincial" fears of any kind of disorder, even disorders in the kitchen, I quickly came to my senses and found in myself the courage to echo that powerful hymn to the Revolution to which Blok was fully attuned. Into the market place flew the contents of my five trunks of theatrical costumes. It was all for our "daily bread," in the literal sense, for Blok was particularly distressed by the lack of bread—a product especially difficult to obtain at that time. I don't know how to grieve for long and instinctively tend to get rid of everything that oppresses me. If my heart contracted from deathly horror the very first time I had to pick out something salable from my carefully gathered collection of antique kerchiefs and shawls, the succeeding sales merely sent a flutter through my heart like the touch of a little bird's wings. After the shawls went the string of pearls that I adored, and everything, everything else... I am writing this very deliberately. How did we differ from the Roman women who used to bring their jewels to the altar of their fatherland? The Romans used to bring their jewels with hands that were well groomed by their slaves, but we sacrificed our jewels and hands as well, the hands sung by the poet: "Your enchanting hand..." (III, 226), hands that had gotten rough and scaly cutting the frozen potatoes and the smelly herring. Only when I cleaned herring did courage abandon me. I could not bear their smell, their repulsive sliminess, and used to shed bitter tears as I cleaned them on thick layers of paper down on my knees on the floor by the stove, rushing to get rid of the smell and the remains as quickly as possible. And herring was our staple. I remember Olechka Glebova-Sudeikina[93] crying her heart out as she was scrubbing her kitchen. That evening she had to dance at the Comedians' Rest,[94] and she was in tears about her once beautiful hands, now red and swollen.

I gave everything I had to the Revolution, since I had to find the means to keep Blok from starving, and in the process I fulfilled both my obligations and my desire by serving the October Revolution not only with my toil, but with my presence, with my "acceptance." As firmly as Blok, I declared: "No, we will not desert this life for a satisfied life, for a quiet existence." I knew what sort of burden I was taking on, but I did not know that the burden that fell upon Blok would be too strenuous for him—he was still young, strong, and even full of youthful enthusiasm.

* * *

Peals of thunder in the skies. The storm breaks loose. Peals of thunder below in the corridor. "Close the windows! Close the shutters!"

Thus let the image of my father, the thunderer, stand first amid the roar and the whistling of the storm. He reigned in our house like a "divine storm," and his affectionate concern for his children rumbled like peals of thunder and the deafening drumbeat of a spring downpour on the iron roofs of our enclosed terraces.

* * *

...I was always that way. However, I am prodigal. Not only am I prodigal with money, but with my soul, even my spirit. I always gave generously of myself, sacrificing what I considered most valuable and, unfortunately, I did this not only for Blok but for others as well, often for strangers. This was not because I did not have enough esteem for myself, oh no, but because of my ever-present aversion to pettiness. To give of myself in petty ways? No, I must give generously, give what is precious to me.

Now when I look back I see that my potential was essentially very great: I had imagination, resourcefulness, originality in thought and taste. If with all this I did not succeed in my goal—a stage career—it was only because of this one basic flaw of mine: an inability to press on steadily in one direction. I cannot say that it was laziness or lack of love for my work. No indeed, for it was very seldom that I did not work and did not move ahead, but always in different directions. All my life I lacked the capacity to pull myself together and pursue one thing at a time. Yes, even now I would accomplish more if I could only choose: either paper and pen or the living link with the theater through teaching, perhaps also staging. I spread myself too thin.

I possessed a sense of fastidiousness and personal cleanliness greater than was necessary for my life to proceed felicitously. Furthermore, I was totally unable to encourage a man who liked me if I felt that I was motivated by personal gain. Here is an example of how this actually hurt my career: I refused to give a producer (who, by the way, was a cultured and even interesting man) that "consideration" that he regarded simply as his "right," and, as though out of spite, before his very eyes I threw myself at a debauchee named Petka. I did other things of this sort.

*   *   *

Now it seems idiotic to me that I did not take advantage of Blok's position to attain my goals, and it was all because of that same fastidiousness. But it is also true that Blok, as though deliberately, did not do anything to help me along in my career, and, consequently, he even hurt me, because his non-involvement appeared to be a conscious dismissal of my talents stemming from a lack of confidence in me. This could have aroused strong scepticism about me,[95] but if I had only asked him, if I had only explained my feelings to him—surely he would have helped, that I know. Yet his attitude stirred my pride even more and I tried to make it on my own. Everything that I achieved in the theater I achieved not only on my own, without any outside help, but also in spite of the great handicap of two overwhelming names: those of my father and my husband.

Inserts

...It was a life of wealth in comparison to our distinguished, aristocratic, impoverished circumstances. But more about this some other time. The only reason why I am mentioning money is to show how my way of thinking differed from that of the young girls and women of today. I don't know of anyone who would turn down the two or three thousand rubles that Andrei Bely would have immediately realized by selling his estate.

In those days one could have toured the globe with that money and had enough left over to enjoy one more year of comfortable life. Traveling was always my passion, and my burning thirst for life could not be satisfied by the fifty rubles a month that father gave me.[96] Sasha could not spare any of the fifty he received from his father—there was the university, his contribution to his mother's household expenses, and so on. However, it is only now that I am recording these facts. At that time not only did I not weigh the comparative material side of this and that life, but even the very thought of weighing them did not enter my mind. Apropos, I remember Borya, sitting on the small couch in my room, demonstrating for the hundredth time that our "brotherly" relations (he always used this word to define that closeness which had grown little by little, first from our friendship and later from his love for me) were more meaningful than my love for Sasha, that they compelled me to take decisive steps, to alter my life. As proof of the possibility of extreme decisions, he told me of his intention to sell the estate so that we could run away together and travel to the ends of the world. I listened to all sorts of propositions, but the seemingly impressive amount of money did not even capture my attention, and I let it slip in one ear and out the other. In all those talks I always asked Bely to wait and not to rush me into making a decision.

*　　*　　*

Without any doubt, Blok and his entire family were not quite normal—I understood this much too late, only after their deaths. The diaries of Maria Andreevna,[97] which fell into my hands after her death, and the letters of Alexandra Andreevna made things especially clear to me. They are full of signs of mental illness. My first impulse, out of respect for Sasha, was to burn his mother's letters, as he undoubtedly would have done, since this had been his intention. Right then and there, however, I realized that I must not destroy them. It is only at the present time that literary research is so empirical, elementary, and satisfied with triviality, but in five, ten, or twenty years it will arrive at exact methods, at the scientific examination of handwriting, of psychological states, of the influence of genes and heredity. On Blok's side (Lev Alexandrovich), on the Beketovs' (Natalia Alexandrovna), on the Karelins' (Alexandra Mikhailovna Markonet and Maria Andreevna Beketova)—everywhere one finds unmistakable symptoms of clinical insanity. And Blok's cousin is a deaf mute: these are only the extreme, medically proven manifestations of their aristocratic degeneration and inbreeding. An imbalance, an extreme "borderline condition" (as psychologists call it)—this is what they all had in common. If one takes this into consideration and puts it in perspective, one will look upon their words and actions in a different way, and one will view differently Blok's tragic position in this family which he loved, but which so often made him suffer and from which, so helplessly and hopelessly, he sometimes wanted to escape. It is no wonder than my elemental health was for him such a longed for, peaceful haven. There is not even a hint of the pathological in me. If sometimes I was hysterical and hypersensitive, the reason was no different from what causes hysteria in so many women: a sex life which is abnormal right from the very start. Here is the proof of the normalcy of my nature: when old age came upon me, I accepted my new status painlessly and without regrets, without a humiliating clutching at youth. The egotism of my youth, which I also consider normal (it is ugly only in old age, but youth without egotism is probably also close to pathology), turned into a complete shifting of interests outside myself, just as joyous and passionate as my youth had been. I am not lonely: my scholarly interests and my work with my priceless pupil, her theatrical successes and all that concerns them are just as enjoyable to me now as novels were in my youth. Since I did not have an abnormal psyche, I could not, in my youth or middle years, understand the Beketovs. I did not take into account that two-faced nature of theirs which is typical of the abnormal personality. Their actions were at odds with their words, and I, unable to understand the root of the problem, was indignant at their falseness. It was more than falseness, though; it was a much deeper spiritual flaw. For example, in my presence they would vie with one another in praising me: they "loved" me very much, yet...they were never willing to let go of Sasha completely and fought against that elemental health of mine which I wanted so much to give to him—to bind him. And what does one find in Maria Andreevna's early diaries and in Alexandra Andreevna's letters? They spared no words in abusing me. "She is homely, she is immature, mean, petty, dishonest, 'just like her mother and just like her father.' " (This is from Alexandra Andreevna.) A clearly transparent envy drove one sister, and a wild jealousy drove the other to this! Is this normal? To call Mendeleev dishonest—this can only be foaming at the mouth in a fit of insanity. Of course I did not know anything about this underhanded talk and it was carefully kept from Sasha as well. ("Lyuba is amazing, Lyuba is unique"—this was meant for his ears.)

In all our interactions, their secret hatred seethed. I am subconsciously very sensitive and susceptible. How else could I have felt it? It drew me into a whirlpool of shouting, protests, and arguments. I can say, by the way, with absolute conviction that I never "asked for trouble." Alexandra Andreevna's constant interference in my life provoked immoderate reactions from me. Her tactlessness had no limits and from the very first moments of our life together she made me burn with indignation. For example, I have already told the reader about the first year of my marriage. Once that year Alexandra Andreevna suddenly bursts into my room: "Lyuba, you are pregnant!" "No, I am not pregnant." "What are you hiding it for? I gave your underwear to the laundry. You are pregnant!" (Straight into a girl's soul with her boot—the soul of a young girl who was not even a woman yet!) Lyuba, of course, answers impudently: "So what? This only means that the women in my time are cleaner and not as untidy as they were in yours. But it seeems to me that my dirty underwear is not an interesting topic for discussion." So there it is— I insulted her, I was rude and so on and so forth.

Or let's take the time of our ill-starred life together in the difficult year 1920. I am in the kitchen rushing to get the dinner ready. Having run home from the People's Union after a rehearsal, and having grabbed on the way our food ration of about one-and-a-half to two poods (54-72 lbs.), I had carried it home on my way back from Khalturin Street. I was cleaning the herring, an occupation from which I was almost in tears, I so despised their smell and nauseating sliminess. "Lyuba, I want to clean my little boy's room. Where is the broom?" "In the corner, in its place." "Oh, yes, here it is. Oh, what a dirty, dusty rag; don't you have a cleaner one?" Lyuba is already burning up. Who needs that kind of "help"? "No, Matryosha will bring it tonight." "How horrible! Listen, Lyuba, don't you smell the stench from the bucket?" "Yes, I do." "It should be taken out!" "I haven't had time to do it yet." "Well, of course, with your rehearsals, your theater and all, there is never any time for your home!" Well, la-di-da! Lyuba lost her patience, she rudely showed her mother-in-law the door, and consequently, Mama complained to Sasha: "She has offended me, Lyuba hates me. . ." and so on.

If I had only known, if I had only understood that I was dealing with a woman who was practically insane, or anyway almost irresponsible, I could have let matters ride, I would have looked at her as at an empty place. But Sasha took his mother seriously, and I followed his example. His letters will show a careful future researcher what a mistake that was, a mistake that brought Sasha and me much grief. It is a great relief for me to shed the responsibility of judging this eighteen-year-old quarrel among the three of us. I prefer to pass it on to Freud's pupils.

Fragments from a Diary

September 24, 1921

[. . .]

On May 17, on Tuesday, when I came home I found Blok lying on the couch in Alexandra Andreevna's room. He called me and told me that he probably had a fever. We took his temperature: it was 37.6. We put him to bed, and in the evening the doctor came. Blok's whole body ached, especially his hands and legs, as, in fact, they had all winter. At night he had a bad dream, he was in a sweat, and in the morning he did not feel rested; it was his nightmares that particularly tormented him. All in all, the condition of his psyche immediately struck me as abnormal. I pointed it out to Dr. Pekelis, and he agreed, although it was impossible to single out obvious abnormalities. When we discussed it, we came to this conclusion: Sasha's usual everyday condition already presented a considerable deviation from the norm. In an average individual changes of mood from a childish, wholehearted gaiety to a gloomy, despondent pessimism would be regarded as "illness," as would the inclination Sasha had not to resist anything evil and to lash out in irritation, banging on furniture and breaking dishes. (When this occurred, even before his illness, he would begin to cry, almost in terror, and would clutch his head in his hands and say: "What is the matter with me? Look what I'm doing!" At such moments, no matter how much he may have offended me before, he at once became like a child to me, and I was horrified that I had spoken to him as if to an adult and that I had expected something from him. My heart would break and I would take him into my arms and he, as swiftly and childishly as before, would give himself over to my soothing, protecting embrace, to my caresses and words, and soon we would be "friends" again.) And now when this behavior pattern became even more painfully accentuated, it was still only an extension of his "normal" state of health. In Sasha those symptoms were not an indication of abnormality, but had they manifested themselves in an ordinary person they would surely have presented a picture of real mental illness.

Gloom, pessimism, a deep unwillingness to get better, also a terrible irritability, an aversion to everything—walls, pictures, things, me. One morning he got up and did not want to lie down again; he was sitting in the armchair by the round table next to the stove. I was trying to persuade him to lie down again and telling him that his legs would swell; he was getting terribly irritated and had tears in his eyes: "What do you bring up such nonsense for! What do I care for my legs when I have terrible dreams and terrible visions as soon as I begin to fall asleep..." And with this he grabbed everything from the table and threw it on the floor—whatever was there, including a big, blue, handcrafted vase that I had given him and that he had been fond of. He also smashed the little pocket mirror that he always used when shaving, or when he rubbed his lips at night with pomade or his face with boric vaseline. The mirror broke into little pieces. This happened in May; I still could not drive from my heart the horror I felt at his deliberately breaking this mirror, and so this horror has remained lurking down deep. I never told anything about it to anyone, but I painstakingly swept the room and threw away the bits and pieces.

From the beginning of his illness he had a terrible need to beat and break: a few chairs, dishes and such. Once, again in the morning, he was walking back and forth in the apartment, irritated. Then from the corridor he walked into his room and closed the door behind him. Immediately I heard blows and the noise of something crumbling. I walked in, feeling that he might hurt himself, but he had just finished taking a poker to the Apollo that was standing on the bookcase. This destruction appeased him, and he calmly answered my exclamation of surprise, which was far from approving, with: "I wanted to see into how many pieces his dirty snout would break." It was a great relief when, later, at the end of June, we took down all the pictures and frames, and Vasilevsky[98] bought and carried everything away. Also, part of the furniture was taken away and part was chopped up for the stove.

*   *   *

1929

The concerned tenderness of our relationship in no way fitted into the framework of usual human relationships—brother-sister, father-daughter... No!.. It was more tender, painful, impossible... Immediately after our first year of marriage a kind of game began: we found "masks" for our feelings and surrounded ourselves with imaginary beings which for us were quite real, and our language became symbolic. Thus speaking "concretely" was quite impossible, yet everything we said could be fully comprehended by a third party. In Blok's poems the forest sprites, all the childish things, the crabs, the donkey in the "Nightingale Garden"—all of them reflect that special world. And that is why, no matter what happened to us, no matter how life separated us, we always could escape into a world where we were firmly inseparable, loyal and pure. In it there was always light and hope, even if we cried at times about our earthly misfortunes.

When Sasha became ill he could no longer journey there. Yet even in the middle of May he drew a caricature of himself from that world—it was to be his last. His illness deprived him of even that last solace. Only a week before his death, having come out of oblivion, he suddenly asked *in our language* why I was all in tears. It was his last tender gesture.

* * *

KORNEI CHUKOVSKY

Excerpts from *A. A. BLOK: THE MAN*

> Такой любви
> И ненависти люди не выносят,
> Какие я в себе ношу . . .
> *Александр Блок*

> The love
> And hate that I have within me—
> No one could endure . . .
> *Alexander Blok*

I

Blok liked to think of himself as a homeless vagabond, and yet it seems that one would have to go far back into the past to find anyone in Russia whom life had surrounded with so much comfort and affection. From early childhood:

> Он был заботой женщин нежной
> От грубой жизни огражден.

> He was shielded from life's coarseness
> By women's tender care.

His great-grandmother, grandmother, mother, nurse and Aunt Katya formed a wall of warmth and protection around him. Were there not, perhaps, too many doting women? When he recalled his childhood, Blok always stressed the fact that it had been the childhood of a nobleman, "a golden childhood, a veritable Christmas tree of aristocratic overindulgence." In the poem "Retribution" he sometimes called himself "the Fates' favorite" and at other times his "family's idol and favorite." For his family he had but one epithet—aristocratic. He stressed it repeatedly in "Retribution":

> В те дни под петербургским небом
> Живет дворянская семья.

> In those days beneath the Petersburg sky
> Lives a family of noble rank.

In this poem he called his mother "a delicate girl of noble birth," noted that his father bore the stamp of the ancient nobility, and characterized the hospitality of his grandparents as the old-fashioned aristocratic sort. "A Wonderful family," he wrote, "their hospitality was that of the old nobility, their thoughts were luminous, their feelings simple and austere."

He believed that his family belonged to the ancient nobility rather than the new gentry. "It was steeped in the old ways, it was closed to the new." He even described it in archaic language: "This ancient vessel" *(Siya starinnaya ladya)*.

Compared with him all the rest of us were foundlings without ancestors or a real home. We did not own an estate outside Moscow, where jam was kept perpetually simmering beneath century-old linden trees. We did not have locks of hair as splendid as his, nor so many grandfathers and great-grandfathers, nor did we have so many toys or a horse so white and stately. Ancestors were not our strong suit, only descendants. But both as a man and a poet, Blok was totally preoccupied with his ancestry. He was the last poet-nobleman, the last Russian poet who could adorn his house with portraits of his grandfathers and great-grandfathers.

The aristocratic manner of his patrician family was enhanced by the high culture of all its members, who, from generation to generation, devoted themselves to scholarship. This cultural tradition was the prerogative of noble families such as the Aksakovs, the Beketovs, the Maykovs. Blok too received the kind of classical education that is no longer available. It was only in the Russia of Pushkin's time that poets were so well educated. It seemed as though fate had deliberately arranged that Blok's grandfather, father, and father-in-law be professors, and his mother and all his aunts be writers for whom books were a source of life and a sort of religion.

To the very end of his life Blok never broke away from his family's cultural tradition. A young *raznochinets*[1] might leave his family without a backward glance, but Blok maintained close ties with his remarkable mother, Alexandra Andreevna, to his dying day. He shared with her practically all of his most intimate thoughts and feelings, as though the umbilical cord joining mother and son had never been cut. It was moving to hear him—a forty-year-old man—consistently refer to his mother as "mama" and his aunt as "auntie," even among people he hardly knew.[2] When, at Professor S. A. Vengerov's request, he wrote a short autobiographical sketch, he considered it essential to speak not so much about himself as about the literary work of his ancestors. When I told him in jest that instead of an autobiography he had submitted a biography of his relatives, he replied unsmilingly: "They played a very important role in my life."

His demeanor was also aristocratic: dignified, correct, somewhat haughty. Even in his last years, collarless and wearing a beret, he resembled a patrician in disguise. And his enunciation too was aristocratic, overly refined and bookish. Moreover, he would give recently assimilated words a foreign pronunciation, i.e., *"meuble"* instead of the Russian *"mebel"*; *"trottoir,"* pronouncing the last two vowels as one, instead of the Russian *"trotuar."* He also pronounced *krokodil* as a foreign word, clearly enunciating the two "o's." No one speaks that way any longer. Once, when I told him that in his famous poem "It is time to give in, sir," he had incorrectly rhymed *"ser"* [sir] with *"kover"* [carpet], he replied after a long silence: "You are right, but for me this word has a sound reminiscent of Turgenev. That is how my grandfather would have pronounced it, with a tinge of French—like a noble-man of the old school."

Blok's grandfather was such an old-world aristocrat that whenever he met a peasant he would say: *"Eh bien, mon petit."* Describing his grandfa-ther in the poem "Retribution," Blok said that "the French language and Paris were perhaps closer to him than his own language and country."

From early childhood Blok was called a *"prince."* His future father-in-law would say to the little boy's nurse: "And what's your prince doing? Our princess has already gone for her walk." According to Bely, Blok and his wife were indeed like a prince and princess.

Blok's wedding ceremony was in the grand style: it was held not in the parish church, but in an ancient chapel near their estate in Shakhmatovo. When the young couple left the church they were greeted by the peasants, who, in accordance with ancient custom, presented them with white geese and bread with salt. Peasant women and girls dressed in their finery gathered in the courtyard during the wedding celebration to sing the praises of the bride and groom, for which, as was the custom at every such landowner's wedding, they received presents and money.

Blok's marriage put an end to the "Poems about the Beautiful Lady." He married in August 1903, and the last poem of the cycle was dated Decem-ber of that year. Such poems could only have been created in the sort of idyllic family environment characteristic of the old aristocracy. It is diffi-cult to imagine a *raznochinets* enmeshed in the trivia of his bourgeois exist-ence experiencing love as such an exalted, prolonged, and unearthly emo-tion . . .

II

On the face of it, his seemed a most idyllic, peaceful, and radiant life. But strangely enough, one has only to read any of Blok's poems, rather than his biography, and the whole idyll explodes as if someone had hurled a bomb right into the middle of it. Where does it all fit in—all this aristocratic com-fort, with its *fleur d'orange,* its trout[3] and French phrases? Blok's well-mean-ing biographer, Maria Beketova, writes, for example, that the poet spent the autumn of 1913 on his estate and there, like a child, diverted himself by playing charades, "shaking with laughter and beaming with pleasure."[4] From his poems, however, we know that if he was "shaking" that autumn, it was certainly not with laughter. This is what he was writing then:

Милый друг, и в этом тихом доме
Лихорадка бьет меня.
Не найти мне места в тихом доме
Возле мирного огня!
Голоса поют, взывает вьюга,
Страшен мне уют.
Даже за плечом твоим, подруга,
Чьи-то очи стерегут!

> Dear friend, even in this quiet house
> I burn with fever.
> There is no place for me in this quiet house
> By the peaceful hearth!
> Voices sing, the blizzard calls;
> All this comfort terrifies me.
> Even over your shoulder, my friend,
> Someone's eyes are watching.

His life was serene and untroubled, but a frenzied terror runs through his poems. Even in tranquility he sensed catastrophe. From early youth he was haunted by premonitions of doom. While still an adolescent he had written:

Увижу я, как будет погибать
Вселенная, моя отчизна

> I will see how the universe,
> My native land, will perish.

When he spoke of his muse, he first pointed out that all her songs were songs of doom:

Есть в напевах твоих сокровенных
Роковая о гибели весть.

> There are in your secret melodies
> Fateful omens of doom.

Throughout his life he considered himself doomed, exiled from his comfortable family refuge. In one of his early articles he had mused: "But what is one to do? The home fires are no longer burning . . . the doors are open onto a square where a blizzard is raging." It was at this point, or perhaps even earlier, that Blok, the idol of *a loving home,* who had been pampered by "gentle women," came to think of himself as a kinless vagabond and began writing most of his poems as though he were a desperate, homeless man, lashed by a merciless wind.

In reading his poems one would never suspect that they had been composed under the shade of century-old linden trees, in the bosom of an old aristocratic family. There is not a single idyllic line in them—only indignation, longing, despair, or the "trampling of cherished, sacred things." In his art, if not in his personal life, he rejected all that spelled contentment, and was from his youth the poet of discomfort, adversity, and doom.

Look closely at this photograph of him. He is in the garden, sitting with his family by the samovar, surrounded by roses and tender smiles—a perfect aristocratic idyll. But his expression is frightening and forlorn, à la Lermontov, completely at odds with these smiles and roses. He faces away from the others as though even in his own home he had neither a family nor a place to call his own. And it was the same in his art: he lived a dreary and self-destructive life. His art was saturated with an apocalyptic sense of the End—an end that was inevitable and imminent. He reacted with apprehension to the catastrophe in Messina. This earthquake, which had destroyed so many peaceful homes, echoed with that same sense of doom which possessed Blok throughout his life. Halley's comet (1910) and some other "poison-tailed" comet also shook him profoundly because they too carried omens of death. There was no place in his soul for any feeling of ease and contentment: it responded only to the tragic. It is no wonder that his "Constant Companions"[5] were such unfortunate, homeless, and doomed wanderers as Apollon Grigoryev, Gogol, Vrubel, and Catiline. Blok loved these men because they were "damned," because they were "on the verge of shipwreck," and because they all might have said: "Ours is a hopeless cause...."

. . . From 1905 to 1917 Blok constantly reiterated his warnings of catastrophe. And it is striking that not only was he not afraid of it, but he summoned it more and more fervently as time went on. Only in revolution could he see a reprieve from his "prison-like tedium." And he called for revolution loudly and insistently:

> Эй, встань и загорись, и жги!
> Эй, подними свой верный молот,
> Чтоб молнией живой расколот
> Был мрак, где не видать ни зги!

>> Hey, arise, catch fire, and burn!
>> Hey, lift your faithful hammer,

So that the pitch-dark gloom
Is split by living lightning. (1907)

No one believed in the power of the Revolution as strongly as Blok did; to him the Revolution was omnipotent, and he made enormous demands of it, without doubting for a moment that they would be satisfied. Let the Revolution come, and when it does, it will fulfill all expectations. The articles in Volume 7 of Blok's works are all imbued with this boundlessly optimistic faith in the Revolution's liberating role. In one of them he wrote: "Sooner or later everything will be different, because life is beautiful." These words could serve as an epigraph to the entire volume. Life is essentially beautiful, but we do not see its beauty because it is spoiled by all kinds of rubbish. The Revolution will burn away all this rubbish, and life will appear before us in all its beauty. Blok would accept nothing less, no half-measures—it was all or nothing. "Life is worthwhile," he said, "only when one makes boundless demands of it: all or nothing; expect the unexpected; so what if it is not here now and will not be here for a long time. Life will justify our expectations because life is beautiful." In another, earlier article he wrote that he was rightfully and hopefully awaiting the "new light" that would appear in the "new age."

What, then, did Blok expect from the Revolution?

III

First and foremost, he wanted the Revolution to transform people, to make the nobodies into somebodies. This was his primary demand. No one, it seems, has realized until now how much Blok was tormented all his life because he felt that people were not truly "human." Once, as we were riding in a trolley car, he said to me: "I close my eyes so as not to see these apes." "Are they really apes?" I asked. And he replied, "You mean to say you can't tell?"

"Heaps of human trash," he would say, "human roastbeef," "gray specters of wet boredom."

When still an adolescent of eighteen, he had written disdainfully:

Смеюсь над жалкою толпою,
Но вздохов ей не отдаю.

> I laugh at the pitiful crowds,
> But do not give them the tribute of a sigh.

. . . Only those whose spiritual life is not obscured by petty cares and activities deserve, in Blok's estimation, to be called "people." But such people are rare, and all the rest are merely two-legged animals... These were the people people who were to be transformed by the catastrophe. Blok was firmly convinced that the humanoid creatures who survived the catastrophe would attain true humanity. For Blok the sign presaging this tragic catharsis, this regeneration through catastrophe, was the earthquake in Calabria. His article devoted to this disaster was not sad, but joyful. This calamity showed the poet that people who are purified by a mighty storm become immortally beautiful.

"So this is how man is," wrote Blok, "more helpless than a rat, but loftier and more beautiful than the most illusory and incorporeal vision. Such is the *ordinary man*. He is neither a Peredonov[6] nor a tyrant, neither a libertine nor a villain. His actions are terribly simple, and in this simplicity is revealed the precious pearl of his spirit. And the true value of life and death can be determined only when things come down to just that—to life and death."

This faith accounted for Blok's extreme optimism in calling for revolution. He was convinced that the Revolution would succeed in bringing to light "the precious pearl of the spirit" hidden within this human refuse. In the fires of revolution the rabble would be transformed into "real people"...

At times, however, Blok was seized by despair, and then it seemed to him that even the Revolution would be powerless to transform our squalid existence into a beautiful one. It was at one such moment that he wrote his mother: "I see now more clearly than ever before that as long as I live I shall neither accept nor submit to anything in contemporary life: its shameful structure fills me with disgust. It is too late to remake anything—no revolution can or will."[7]

But these moments of despair made his faith stand out even more vividly. In them one could perceive with special clarity the extent of his hatred for the "old world" and all its dreadnoughts, its Kaiser Wilhelms, its hotels, health resorts, newspapers, and kept women. He would never accept this "old world." In another letter from abroad (1911) he wrote: "One can clearly see the monstrous absurdity that our civilization has become. It is reflected in the tense faces of rich and poor alike, in the bustling traffic devoid of any inner significance, in the press: mercenary, talented, free and vociferous"...

In general, his articles and letters are full of maledictions against a despicable European system that produces disgraceful rubbish instead of people... There was not a single phenomenon of life that did not conjure up for him the "fateful omens of doom." He saw in doom the only possible justification for his home, for his personal life, for all of civilization; in his eyes our lawless epoch, which was sowing the seeds of disaster for itself, was worthy of respect only because it was doomed. Blok was one of the first to feel that the self-destructive blood

> Сулит нам, раздувая вены,
> Все разрушая рубежи,
> Неслыханные перемены,
> Невиданные мятежи . . .

>> Swelling our veins,
>> Destroying all boundaries,
>> Heralds unheard-of changes
>> Unprecedented rebellions.

From his youth on, from the very moment when he first came face to face with the dismal way men live, he was on the path of rebellion. Neither within himself nor in his art was there even a hint of his earlier idyllic life, his close family ties, his old aristocratic home. His art was at odds with his way of life. What he lived by in his life he burned to ashes in his art.

IV

In stating that Blok's cataclysmic art was at odds with his way of life, I do not mean to imply that his old-fashioned aristocratic lifestyle did not leave its stamp on his art. On the contrary, I agree beforehand with those who will study his works and eventually prove that:

1) basically, even his revolutionary feelings were the outgrowth of old aristocratic attitudes;

2) his division of mankind into two unequal parts, the rabble and the non-rabble (even if the criterion for judgment is their spiritual enlightenment) is a peculiarity of feudal thought;

3) Blok's characteristic hatred of civilization and of all the theories of progress could have arisen only in an old, aristocratic, Tolstoi-like milieu of landed gentry;

4) even in the enormous, exorbitant demands that Blok made on the Revolution, in his contempt for its compromises and prosaic aspects, as well as in visions that it would lead to the fiery transformation of all mankind—even in this maximalism one could recognize the patrician who was extraordinarily remote from that "pile of human rubbish" which, despite all its apparent unattractiveness, is the true material of revolution;

5) even his pathos-laden *poetry of doom* has its roots in the old aristocratic culture, since this doomed culture could not help but inculcate in its geniuses the inherent tragic sense of its own end . . . .[8]

V

Like all of Blok's works, "Retribution" is a poem about doom. In it the poet depicts the gradual destruction of his ancestral home. The hero of the poem is this home—not a particular individual in it, but the entire house...

From the middle of the nineteenth century destructive forces from every direction—each one a harbinger of revolution—press against the walls of this "kind house." But the house remains standing, unaware that it is doomed. It is comfortable and bright, and its inhabitants are happy and content. But Blok sees that the house is threatened by impending calamities, and he knows that the blood-stained dawns that cast their crimson reflection on the peaceful windows of this comfortable house are the ominous glow of an approaching revolution.

Depicting with masterful strokes the dull and stagnant era of Alexander III, he irradiates it with this same image of the bloody dawn.

Раскинулась необозримо
Уже кровавая заря,
Грозя Артуром и Цусимой,
Грозя девятым января.

> Already the bloody dawn
> Has spread across the boundless horizon,
> Warning of Port Arthur and Tsuchiyama,
> Warning of January ninth.

The destruction of the house was gradual. In the 1860s a *raznochinets*, a "nihilist in a *kosovorotka*"[9] broke into the house. The house shook, but it did not collapse. It withstood the blow. This was the first omen of revolution.

In the 1870s the whole house was shaken by the terrorists' threat... The house tottered, but again it withstood the shock. And perhaps it would have remained standing until now if, at the beginning of the eighties, that most dreadful of agents of destruction, a "plunderer," a "hawk," a "demon," and "vampire"—Alexander Blok's father—had not burst into it. He was the herald of the *inner* revolution, who came to shatter the spiritual complacency of the nobility. He reduced to ashes once and for all the idyll that the inhabitants of that kindly home had erected over the abyss. He stripped the house of its soul, of its comfortable way of life, and thereby ensured its destruction.

"Retribution" is a prophetic poem with a broad grasp of world history, similar in many respects to Pushkin's "The Bronze Horseman." It remained unfinished, but from some of Blok's other verses we know what "Retribution" does not state outright: in this kind house a child was born. Youth is retribution: the son of that dreadful demon who only knew how to destroy was himself born to be destroyed, and all his life he was to consider himself a homeless wanderer, cast out into the blizzard. From the very beginning he had no home. True, the walls were still standing, but already they were, in Blok's words, "impregnated with poison." In his house the hearth had vanished, leaving only the wind:

Как не бросить все на свете,
Не отчаяться во всем,
Если в гости ходит ветер,
Только дикий, черный ветер,
Сотрясающий мой дом.

Что-ж ты, ветер,
Стекла гнешь?
Ставни с петель
Дико рвешь?

> How can one not reject everything on this earth,
> How can one not despair of everything,
> When the only guest is the wind
> The wild black wind
> That shakes my house?
>
> Why, oh wind,
> Do you beat against the window panes?
> Savagely tear
> The shutters from their hinges?

From 1905 on, the images of homelessness and wind predominate in Blok's lyrics. He knew how to depict homelessness masterfully—a frantic, destructive homelessness...

Blok was acutely aware that his comfortable haven was without comfort. And in the end, when during the Revolution his house was actually destroyed and his estate at Shakhmatovo was looted and demolished, he did not even notice this loss. I remember his telling me about this destruction; he waved his hand and said with a smile, "It serves it right." Within his soul his house had already long since crumbled into a heap of ruins.

VI

When the Revolution came, Blok greeted it with a kind of religious exultation—as the festival of the *spiritual* transfiguration of Russia.

It required a great deal of courage for Blok, an aristocrat, an "esthete," to declare himself a "bolshevik" to the circle of people among whom he lived.

He knew that it meant losing friends, resigning himself to loneliness and being scorned and abused by those he loved. He knew that he would be torn to pieces by a rabid pack of journalistic hounds who only the day before had been submissively wagging their tails before him. But he accepted this cross without flinching, for he was accustomed, in life as well as in literature, to obey only the dictates of his own truth, unaffected by either the love or the ill-will of others.

This kind of courage was always characteristic of Blok. When in 1903 he embarked on a literary career, journalists mocked him as a decadent who had lost his wits. None of those who were close to him (except his wife and his ever-understanding mother) could comprehend his poetry. But he refused to make any compromises and followed his own path to the end.

Later, in 1908, he again stood alone against all others when he welcomed the newly-emerging people's intelligentsia. He boldly contrasted this intelligentsia with that of our so-called "cultured" society and predicted that a bloody collision between the two intelligentsias was inevitable—a collision from which we, the cultured, would not emerge victors. At the time this prediction angered many people, and some of his best friends broke with him. But Blok remained faithful to his own truth.

It was the same when the Revolution came. Blok remained steadfast under a deluge of insults and slander; he was still as cheerful, happy, and optimistic as ever. The long-awaited event which those bloody dawns had foreshadowed had at last occurred. Joyfully he went his way alone and against everybody, for he felt completely in harmony with chaos. One day early in January 1918, at the house of some friends, he defended the October Revolution in a noisy argument. His friends had never before seen him so excited. He usually argued calmly and with decorum, but now he gesticulated and even shouted. At one point in the course of the argument he said, "I see angels' wings behind the shoulders of every Red Guardsman." His statement evoked many sarcastic comments. Blok left—and wrote "The Twelve." It seemed then that this was just the beginning of another long and heroic struggle for him. But a month passed, and Blok fell silent. It was not that he had ceased to love the Revolution or had lost faith in it. No, but in the Revolution he had loved only its ecstasy, and now it seemed to him that the ecstatic period of the Russian Revolution was over. True, the storm and fire of revolution continued, but at a time when many people all around him were eager to see them subside, Blok, on the contrary, demanded that they grow even more fiery and violent. He remained faithful to the Revolution to the very end and disliked only those aspects of it which he considered unrevolutionary—everything in it that was commonplace, miserly, cautious, slavish and compliant. He remained a maximalist to the end, but his maximalism was not of this world. It demanded of people the impossible: that they live exclusively in the spirit of tragedy and desire only destruction; that they be "people." This was the maximalism of one who contemplated the Revolution from afar. He did not wish to allow the human race, after it had experienced catastrophe, to turn once more into a "pile of rubbish." It seemed to him that everything ought to be different after the great storm, that people whose lives had been purified by it would no longer dare to be petty and dissolute. It was not the Revolution that disappointed him, but the people: no revolution could change them. What had he been waiting for all these years? Had the red dawns blazed for him in vain? Was this what those dawns had portended?

Even after the coming of the Revolution the poet remained homeless— a bird without a nest. Until the end of his days he could not forgive the Revolution for being unlike the one he had dreamed of for so many years. But he had never been promised that it would resemble his dream revolution. This was a real revolution—with real fire and smoke in it—it was mad and at the same time cunning, but Blok wanted it only to be mad. And this accounts for his terrible depression in the final years of his life. He found himself outside the Revolution, outside its festivals, victories, defeats, and hopes. And he felt that only one thing was left to him—to die.

Once, in Moscow, in May 1921, I was sitting backstage with him at the Press Club. On the stage some "orator" or other (of whom there are so many in Moscow) was cheerfully demonstrating to the crowd that as a poet Blok was already dead: "I ask you, comrades, where is the dynamism here? These verses are just dead rubbish written by a corpse." Blok leaned over to me and said, "That's true." And although I could not see him, I felt instinctively that he was smiling. "He's telling the truth, I have died."[10] I disagreed with him then, but I see now that in the last years, when he and I met especially often and I had the opportunity to observe him from day to day, he was gradually dying. He fell ill in March 1921, but the process of dying started much earlier, in 1918, immediately after he wrote "The Twelve" and "The Scythians." Day by day the great poet was dying while still in the full bloom of his talent, and whatever he did and wherever he went, he felt that he was a corpse. He was not ill. On the contrary, he had enough strength left to carry cabbages on his back from distant cooperatives, to take his turn guarding the entrance to his house at night and to chop frozen firewood. But even his way of walking became funereal, as though he were following his own coffin. One could not watch his eerie, slow walk—so proud and yet so mournful—without feeling depressed.

He "died" right after he wrote "The Twelve" and "The Scythians," for it was just at that time that something happened to him which was essentially equivalent to dying. He became deaf and dumb. That is, he could hear and speak like everyone else, but that wonderful ear and seraphic voice that only he possessed abandoned him forever. Suddenly a grave-like silence fell upon everything. He said that while he was writing "The Twelve" there was an incessant rumbling or roaring in his ears for several days in succession, but that it all suddenly stopped, and he came to perceive this seemingly loudest and shrillest of epochs as total silence.

One day in March 1921, as he and I were walking across the Palace Square and listening to the rumbling of the guns, Blok said: "To me even this is silence. All this din simply puts me to sleep... In fact, I have been in a state of drowsiness for the past few years now."

But the most dreadful thing of all was that in the midst of this silence he ceased to create. As soon as he started thinking of himself as someone already lying in the grave he buried the very thought of art. That is, he continued writing, even wrote quite a lot, but he no longer wrote poetry. He wrote reports, official documents, and commissioned articles.

They would tell him: "Make a list of the one-hundred best writers." And obediently he would draw up not one, but several lists. And walking in his funereal way, he would go off God knows where, to some conference or other at which these lists would be discussed, only to be discarded immediately afterwards. They said to him: "Write a play about ancient Egyptian life." And he obediently got hold of Maspero[11] and sat down to carry out this task. They said to him: "Edit Heine's works." And for whole months he plunged into the tedious work of collating texts. He read many untalented translations, selected the least untalented ones, corrected them, and then reworked them. He wrote long letters to the translators,explaining why this or that line needed revision or that, in another line, a syllable was missing. They said to him: "Review these manuscripts and let us know as soon as possible which of them should be published." And with that conscientiousness peculiar to his genius, he would write several reviews in succession about whatever books came his way...

Already in November 1918, when he was employed by the theater division, he told me that now he had nothing left, not even dreams: "All my life I have had wonderful dreams, but now they are gone. Either I don't dream at all, or I dream of work: telephones, reports, meetings."

His creative writing stopped, not because he lacked time or because the conditions of his life had become too difficult, but for another, more ominous reason. No doubt his life was hard: he did not have a separate study, he had no servant in his apartment; often he did not put pen to paper for weeks because he had no lights. And it can hardly have been good for his health to walk, as he did, enormous distances, almost everyday—from the end of Ofitserskaya Street to the offices of "World Literature." Yet it was not this that weighed on him so heavily. If he had not suddenly become aware of the "silence," he might never have noticed these inconveniences.

Whenever I asked him why he was not writing poetry, his answer was always the same: "All sounds have stopped. Haven't you noticed that there are no sounds at all?"

Once he wrote me a letter about this absence of sound. "I have not heard any new sounds in a long time; they have all vanished for me and probably for all of us... It would be blasphemous and deceitful to try deliberately to call them back into our soundless space."

For Blok, space had formerly been filled with all kinds of sounds and he had been accustomed to refer to objects as "musical" or "unmusical." Once, writing to me about an anniverary celebration, he described that day as "not empty, but musical."

He had always been aware of the music of the world around him—a music that he absorbed not only with his ears, but through his skin and his whole being. In the preface to "Retribution" he had written that all phenomena in a given epoch had for him a unified musical import; together they formed a single musical impulse. He could tune into this music of the epochs like no one else. Indeed, he had a seismographic ear; he heard the music of war and revolution long before those events took place. It was this music that had now ended... "And the poet dies because he cannot breathe."[12]

VII

. . . This was all the more terrible because before this silence engulfed him he had been overflowing with music. He was one of the favored children of music who experienced no effort or strain in creating, and for whom creating only meant listening attentively to the sounds. Doesn't it stagger one's imagination to realize that he wrote the whole of "The Twelve" in two days? He began writing from the middle with the words "With my little knife/ I'll slash, I'll slash!"("Uzh ya nozhichkom/Polosnu, polosnu") because, as he pointed out, the two "zh's" in the first line seemed to him particularly expressive. Then he turned to the beginning and completed practically the whole poem in one day—eight sections, up to the lines that read "Lord, may the soul of Thy servant rest in peace. What tedium."

Almost the whole poem in one day! Extraordinary creative energy!.. There was no sign of strain, and no unnecessary squandering of inspiration: for Blok creating was as easy as breathinng. It was nothing unusual for him to write two, three, four, or even five poems in succession in a single day . . . . As I have already mentioned, Blok's poems were not separate entities, but essentially one continuous, indivisible poem spanning his entire life. His own life was a poem that flowed on uninterruptedly from day to day for twenty years, from 1898 to 1918. That is why the sudden cessation of this poem was such an enormously significant fact. Until now it had never been interrupted, and now it stopped. The man who could write 800 poems in succession on just one theme—the "Beautiful Lady," 800 romantic hymns to one woman—that incredible litany—had suddenly fallen into a total silence and over a period of several years was unable to write a single line. And this is why I say that the end of his creative work, which occurred more than three years ago, was in reality his death.

After he had written "The Twelve," he tried all throughout the last three-and-a-half years of his life to understand what it was that he had written. Many people can remember how keenly he would listen when anybody spoke of "The Twelve" in his presence. It was as if he were waiting to find someone who would at last explain to him the meaning of this poem, a meaning that was not quite clear even to him, as if he were not responsible for what he had created, as if not he but someone else had written the poem, as if he had simply taken it down at someone else's dictation.

On one occasion Gorky said to him that he considered "The Twelve" a satire, "the most malicious satire on all the events that took place during those days." "A satire?" Blok asked, and thought for a moment. "Is it really a satire? Hardly. I don't think it is. But I don't know..." And indeed, he did not know. His lyrics were wiser than he. Simple, straightforward people often asked him to give them an explanation of what he had meant to say in "The Twelve," but despite the best of intentions, he could not answer them. He always spoke of his poems as though they were the products of some other person's will, a will he could not help obeying, as though they were not just poems, but a revelation from above.[13]

I remember the occasion in June 1919 when Gumilyov delivered a lecture on Blok's poetry at the Institute of the History of Arts. Blok was in the audience. Gumilyov mentioned in passing that the end of "The Twelve" (where Christ appears) seemed to him to have been tacked on artificially and that the sudden appearance of Christ was a purely literary effect. As usual, Blok listened unperturbed, but after the lecture was over he said in a thoughtful and guarded way, as though he were listening to something else: "I, too, dislike the ending of 'The Twelve.' I would have preferred a different one. When I finished the poem, I too was surprised: why Christ? But the more I looked into it, the more clearly I saw Christ. And right then and there I wrote in my notebook: '*unfortunately, Christ.*' "

Gumilyov looked at him in his usual haughty way. Always the master, even the captain, one might say, of his own creative impulses, Gumilyov did not approve of poets thinking of themselves as spineless victims of their own lyrics. But to me Blok's admission seemed invaluable: the poet's helplessness in the face of his own talent was such that while he himself was amazed at, regretted, and struggled against what had poured from his pen, he still felt that what he had written was a higher truth independent of his own wishes.

He had greater respect for this truth than he had for his own personal tastes and beliefs.[14] He believed this truth to be outside the realm of literature, and he disliked "literature" precisely because he saw in it a diminution of this truth. He disliked the "literary man" in himself and considered that expression a derogatory term. He would refer to himself by that term only in those moments when he felt most dissatisfied with himself.

> Был он только литератор модный,
> Только слов кощунственных творец—
>
> > He was only a literary man of fashion,
> > Only a creator of blasphemous words—

He had once said this reproachfully about someone. I asked him who this person might be. He answered: "myself." There had been a stage in his life when he almost became a man of letters. He always regarded that period as a low point.

He knew, not from books, but from his entire creative experience, that poetry was not simply a matter of linguistic technicalities; that it was regarded as such in our time by our younger generation seemed to him a sinister sign of our epoch. He viewed the currently popular approach to poetry, with its concentration on purely formalistic analysis of poetic techniques, as the death of poetry. He hated all the poetry workshops that appeared in the last few years, for he found in them that same spirit of death that he felt all around him...

VIII

. . . He suffered torments when he was with people he disliked, for he felt their presence with his whole being, and this gave him physical pain. A person who was distasteful to him had only to enter the room and deathly shadows would instantly descend upon his face. It was as though imaginary hands were reaching out from every person and object and wanted to scratch him.

Last spring [1921], at a poetry recital in Moscow, as he was about to read his last poems, Blok caught sight of an unpleasant individual in a large hat who was standing near the rostrum. After forcing himself to read two or three poems, Blok left the hall, telling me that he was not going to read anything else. I begged him to return to the platform. I told him that the man in the hat was only one individual, that it was unfair to punish everyone else because of him; but I looked at Blok's face and stopped. His whole face was shaken by minute tremors. His eyes had dimmed, his wrinkles deepened.

"But he is not the only one," he said, "over there each and every one of them is wearing a hat like that!" Nevertheless he was persuaded and returned to the stage. He stepped forth, frowning gloomily, but instead of reading his own poems, recited some Latin verses by Poliziano, and the audience was greatly amazed:

> Conditus hic ego sum picture fama Philippus
> Nulli ignota meae gratia mira manus
> Artificis potui digitis animare colores
> Sperataque animos fallere voce Diu . . .[15]

Many were angry, but I saw that he could not have behaved otherwise, that this was not some whim of his but an illness. It was precisely this hypersensitivity that made him a great poet, but it was also what destroyed him...

IX

. . . In May, 1921, I received a distressing letter from him: "Now I have neither soul nor body left. I am sick as I have never been before: my fever refuses to go away and my body aches all over... And so I can no longer say '*We are thriving even now*.'[16] Our vile, sniffling mother Russia has gobbled me up like a sow its own suckling pig."

He did not want to leave Russia, no matter how hard life may have been for him. It was only later, shortly before his death and on the urgent advice of his doctors, that he began to hope for a cure abroad. But prior to this time it seemed to him that leaving Russia was a form of betrayal. He had learned by heart a recently published poem by Anna Akhmatova, which he recited to Aliansky and me during our train ride to Moscow:

> Мне голос был. Он звал утешно,
> Он говорил: иди сюда,
> Оставь свой край глухой и грешный,
> Оставь Россию навсегда . . .
>
> Но равнодушно и спокойно
> Руками я замкнула слух,
> Чтоб этой речью недостойной
> Не осквернился скорбный дух.

> I heard a voice. It called soothingly,
> It said: "Come here,

> Leave your wild and sinful land,
> Leave Russia forever..."
>
> But calmly and dispassionately
> I covered my ears with my hands,
> So that my grieving spirit
> Would not be profaned by these contemptible words.

"Akhmatova is right," he said, "this kind of talk is contemptible. To run away from the Russian Revolution is disgraceful."

He did not fear the Revolution; on the contrary, he loved it very much. Only one thing disturbed him: what if the Revolution was counterfeit? What if there were no such thing as a real revolution? What if the "real" one had only been a figment of his imagination?..

X

Blok's attitude toward those writers who had fled Russia and were now vilifying those who had remained behind was one of unusual irritation. He spoke of them vehemently, as I do not believe he ever spoke of anyone else...

. . . But political differences did not interfere with Blok's love for his old friends. In 1918, even after he had been boycotted by Merezhkovsky and Gippius because of his poem "The Twelve," he continued to speak of them just as affectionately as always. Here is an excerpt from his letter to me dated December 18, 1919: "If the subject should come up, tell Z. N. (Gippius) that I do not think that she drew the right conclusions from these poems of mine, that I love her as before, sometimes—even more than before..."

An "Evening of Blok" was held at the end of April, at the Bolshoi Dramatic Theater (formerly the Suvorin Theater). My lecture on Blok was a fiasco. Even as I spoke I felt that every word I uttered was wrong, out of place, irrelevant. Blok was standing backstage and listening, and this upset me even more. For some reason he had believed in this lecture and expected a great deal from it. Having somehow or other stumbled through a haphazard performance, I immediately ran into one of the dressing rooms so as to avoid facing him. But he found me there and comforted me as though I had been taken seriously ill. He brought over the actors and actresses of the theater, who warmly applauded my performance. Blok himself had enjoyed an enormous success on the stage, but he sympathized wholeheartedly with me in my failure. He gave me one of the flowers that had been presented to him, and then suggested that we be photographed together. And this is how the picture turned out: I looked thoroughly dejected, while he looked kind and very sympathetic—like a doctor at his patient's bedside. This was the last picture ever taken of Blok...

On our way home Blok said a great deal more to console me, but it was also clear that he had no intention of concealing from me the fact that he disliked my lecture. He put it this way: "There were many things in your lecture that were incorrect. My wife did not like it at all." This was one of Blok's distinctive traits—he never lied concerning matters of art and even when he wanted to comfort someone he would not deviate from the truth; he might articulate it with difficulty, as if he were being forced, but he always spoke candidly and unambiguously. Once a certain spoiled and very successful author asked Blok how he liked his latest play. Blok did not answer. He thought for a long time in silence, and at last he said remorsefully: "No, I did not like it." And after a while, even more contritely: "I didn't like it at all." It was as though he felt guilty that the play had turned out to be a bad one.

About many of my own writings he used to say in reproachful tones: "Clever, very clever." But coming from him it was always a sign of disapproval.

XI

Blok was no stranger to the Bolshoi Dramatic Theater, where the last "Evening of Blok" was held. He had been one of its directors and an administrative chairman for the last two years (since 1919). Perhaps I am mistaken, but I believe that this theater was a kind of haven for Blok during those terrible days. He dedicated himself to the theater wholeheartedly and worked for it enthusiastically. He commented on the plays that were being prepared for staging, then explained roles to the actors and delivered introductory statements to the audience before the curtain went up. He would urge the actors not to squander their energies on neurotic "quests" and meaningless "innovations," but to learn from Shakespeare and Schiller. His influence invariably had an inspiring and ennobling effect on their work.

"Dear friends," he told the performers in one of his speeches (May 5, 1920), "one cannot help being wearied by the sensuousness of 'the quest'; on the other hand, fresh mountain air preserves our strength. Breathe that air, breathe it while you can, it is our protection... Through your humble service to the *Great* in art you will succeed in preserving *It;* strange as it may seem, your selfless labor will preserve that modicum of human culture that must and will be saved."

The actors idolized the poet who inspired them. A. N. Lavrentev told me, "Blok was our conscience," and N. K. Monakhov remarked to me recently: "We revered him in accordance with the Third Commandment..."

In an affectionate letter to Monakhov, Blok made a startling comment:

"I have never had to tell a lie." How many other people can say this at the age of forty-one?

I felt that Blok's straightforwardness and truthfulness were related to another characteristic trait of his, one which for some reason even frightened me: his exceptional neatness and cleanliness. There was such an oppressive order about his room and his desk that one felt tempted to mess things up just a little. Even the old books in his library seemed brand new, as though just from the bookstore. His belongings were never piled up in disorderly heaps, but seemed to arrange themselves of their own accord in geometrically straight lines. More than once I told him that he had only to hold some worn-out volume in his hands and it would automatically become clean and new again. He disliked briefcases and never carried them. Instead he gathered up all the manuscripts he needed for a meeting, wrapped them up in paper in his extraordinarily elegant way, and tied them with a ribbon...

All the letters Blok had ever received, from anyone at all, were kept in individual folders under a special number, and in some sort of super-human order; and, I repeat, there was something frightening in this order. In this inordinate neatness I always sensed chaos.

XII

What can I say about the last trip he made to Moscow before his death? One day in conversation he told me with a sad, ironic smile that the walls of his house were impregnated with venom. The thought occurred to me that perhaps a trip to Moscow would distract him from his problems at home. He did not want to go at all, but I insisted, hoping than an enthusiastic, successful reception in Moscow would have a beneficial effect on him. During the train ride he was gay and talkative. Once in a while, however, he would rise from his seat, stretch out his aching leg and say with a smile: "It hurts!" (He thought he had gout.)

His illness grew worse in Moscow. He wanted to return home but felt obliged to appear on stage every evening, and this weighed heavily on him. "Why the devil did I come?" sounded like a repeated refrain in all his conversations...

. . . At the Italian Society, Blok was accorded an unusually warm welcome. He read his poems slowly, in his deep, melodious, suffering voice. Never before had Moscow heard him give such a strikingly moving performance. But on the following day a sad and disturbing incident took place that proved to me that his illness was both serious and dangerous. He read his poems at the Union of Writers, then we went to the small, cramped apartment of Professor P. S. Kogan, where he was staying. We sat down to tea, but

Blok went into his room instead. A moment later he returned, saying: "How strange! I can't make heads nor tails of anything. I completely forgot that we were at the Union of Writers and was just now about to sit down and write them a letter of apology for having been unable to attend."

This alarmed me. He had been at the Union of Writers not one or two days before, but that very day, only ten minutes earlier, so how could he have forgotten about it, he who was so punctual and who had such a good memory? And the next day something happened which alarmed me even more. It was evening and we were sitting together drinking tea and talking. I had said something without looking at him, when suddenly I looked up and I almost cried out in shock: before me sat not Blok but some other man completely different from Blok, without even a vague resemblance to him, a stiff, wasted figure with vacant eyes that seemed to be covered with cobwebs. Even his hair and ears looked different. And above all, he was clearly detached from everything, blind and deaf to everything human.

"Is it you, Alexander Alexandrovich?" I cried out, but he did not even look up.

And now, no matter how hard I try, I cannot believe that this was the same man whom I had known for twelve years.

I picked up my hat and left quietly. This was my last meeting with him.

XIII

Now, when I try to recall our recent meetings, all that I seem to remember are the conferences. It is as if there had been one continuous conference that dragged on with no beginning or end for three long years....

Towards the end these meetings became a great burden to him, since his fellow committee members (two of them especially) aroused in him a feeling of hostility. It all began in the spring of 1920 when he was editing the works of Lermontov. He approached this task in his own way and wrote the kind of introduction that only he could write, about Lermontov's prophetic dreams and about Lermontov's visions of God. I remember that he was very pleased with his new assignment, for Lermontov was his favorite poet. But suddenly at one of the meetings they told him that his introduction wouldn't do at all, that what was important about Lermontov was not that he had had this or that vision, but that he had been a "progressive figure," a "great cultural force." Blok was urged to rewrite the introduction in a more popular, "culturally enlightening tone." He said nothing, but I could see that he was offended. If a "culturally enlightening tone" was what they wanted, why did they turn to him? Weren't there enough literary hacks in Russia?

The more they tried to prove to Blok that he must write differently ("the point is not that Lermontov had visions, but that he wrote 'On the Death of Pushkin' "), the more melancholy, reserved and haughty the expression of his face became. This marked the beginning of his estrangement from other committee members with whom he had been obliged to associate, and with each passing week his alienation grew.

When Blok realized that, as Blok, nobody needed him, he abstained from all participation in our work and simply sat in at all the conferences in silence. And if he ever did say anything, he talked only of his own work, and then, not at the meetings, but during the breaks . . . . He talked more often with Gumilyov than with anyone else. The two poets carried on an endless argument with each other about poetry. With his usual boldness, Gumilyov would attack Blok's symbolism: "Symbolists are mere swindlers. They take a weight, write 'ten pounds' on it, but then they hollow out the middle and proceed to fling it this way and that; but—it is empty all the same." Blok would answer in a monotone: "But this is done by followers and imitators of every school. It has nothing to do with Symbolism. Anyway, what you are saying does not sound Russian to me. It's the sort of thing that could be said very well in French. You are too much of a litterateur, and what's more, a French one to boot."

These outspoken arguments culminated in Blok's article on Acmeism, in which he said many caustic things about Gumilyov's theories. The public was not destined to see this article, however, since the *Literary Gazette* was never published.

The debaters did not finish their argument. And Russia was unable to decide which one of them was the Acmeist and which the Symbolist...

XIV

When Blok spoke of his own poetry it was in either solemn or mocking tones. He had the habit, which was reflected in many of his plays and poems, of referring ironically to himself and everything pertaining to himself. In this connection we have only to recall his article, "On Love, Poetry, and Government Service." While he may have defended the Symbolists staunchly in this article, he included only a few of them in his list of the "One Hundred Best Writers." When I asked him the reason for this, he replied, "I do not like those young men." And after a while he added, "I don't understand anything about those young men." He called these fifty- and sixty-year-old poets "young men."

About the programs prepared by Gumilyov he said: "Nikolai Stepanovich wants to publish only the 'good' and the 'absolute.' In that case one must offer only Pushkin, Lermontov, Tolstoi, Dostoevsky and no one else. All other writers are of questionable value." I reminded him of his favorite Tyutchev, and to my astonishment he answered: "Well, what about Tyutchev? It's all just little bits and pieces of writing. Furthermore, his poetry is German."

He often spoke in the same tone of the things that were dearest to him—of the Beautiful Lady, for instance. If this tone had not come instinctively to him, he could never have written *The Puppet Show*. Sergei Gorodetsky, in his "Reminiscences of Blok," writes that Blok once as a joke called his book *Nechayannaya radost (Unexpected Joy)— Otchayannaya gadost (Awful Trash)* and referred to himself as Alexander Klok.[17] He felt a need to laugh at experiences which he had once held sacred. He actually enjoyed V. P. Burenin's parody which mocked his high-sounding poem "The Footsteps of the Commander." Showing me the issue of the *New Times* in which this parody had appeared he said, "Look at it. Really, isn't it very funny?":

В спальне свет. Готова ванна.
Ночь, как тетерев, глуха.
Спит, раскинув руки, Донна Анна,
И под нею прыгает блоха.

> There is a light in the bedroom. The bath is ready.
> The night is deaf as a black cock.
> Donna Anna sleeps with outstretched arms,
> And underneath her a flea is darting about.

I had the impression that he preferred this sort of open mockery to the praise and compliments of the "refined esthetes," whom he despised. . . .

In 1919 Blok was still able to laugh, but later his laughter ceased, and his last poem, dedicated to the memory of Pushkin, was unlike anything he had ever written. Many will remember the magnificent speech which Blok delivered at the House of Literature in February 1921 at the ceremony commemorating Pushkin. When I visited him a few days later, I learned that he had also written some verses dedicated to the poet: "But I'm afraid they are very bad," he said. "Someone telephoned me to say that the Pushkin House wanted me to write a few lines on Pushkin for their album. I wrote them, but they seem to have turned out poorly. I've lost the habit of writing poetry—I haven't written any for the last few years."

And then he read me these lines:

Имя Пушкинского Дома
В Академии Наук!

Звук понятный и знакомый,
　　　Не пустой для сердца звук!

Это — звоны ледохода
　　　На торжественной реке,
Перекличка парохода
　　　С пароходом вдалеке.

Это — древний Сфинкс, глядящий
　　　Вслед медлительной волне,
Всадник бронзовый, летящий
　　　На недвижном скакуне.

Наши страстные печали
　　　Над таинственной Невой,
Как мы черный день встречали
　　　Белой ночью огневой.

Что за пламенные дали
　　　Открывала нам река!
Но не эти дни мы ждали,
　　　А грядущие века.

Пропускали дней гнетущих
　　　Кратковременный обман,
Прозревали дней грядущих
　　　Сине-розовый туман.

Пушкин! *Тайную свободу*
　　　Пели мы вослед тебе!
Дай нам руку в непогоду,
　　　Помоги в немой борьбе!

Не твоих ли звуков сладость
　　　Вдохновляла в те года?
Не твоя ли, Пушкин, радость
　　　Окрыляла нас тогда?

Вот зачем такой знакомый
　　　И родной для сердца звук —
Имя Пушкинского Дома
　　　В Академии Наук.

Вот зачем, в часы заката
Уходя в ночную тьму,
С белой площади Сената
Тихо кланяюсь ему.

The name Pushkin House
In the Academy of Sciences—
Has a clear and familiar sound,
A sound full of meaning to our hearts!

It is the sound of the drifting ice
On a majestic river,
It is one steamship hailing
Another in the distance.

It is the ancient Sphinx—its eyes
Following a lagging wave,
It is the bronze horseman, flying
On his motionless steed.

Our passionate sorrows
Above the mysterious Neva,
As we met the black day
With a fiery white night.

What flaming distant vistas
The river threw open before us!
But it was not these days we awaited,
But centuries to come.

We let the short-lived illusions
Of our oppressive days slip by,
We discerned the blue-pink haze
Of coming days.

Pushkin! Following in your traces
We sang of secret freedom!
Give us your hand in troubled times,
Help us in our silent struggle!

Was it not the sweetness of your sounds
Which inspired us in those years?
Was it not your joy, Pushkin,
Which lent us wings in those days?

That is why the name Pushkin House
In the Academy of Sciences
Is a sound so familiar
And dear to our hearts.

That is why in the hour of sunset
As I depart into night's darkness,
I bow silently to him
From the white Senate Square.

With the exception of some rough drafts for the poem "Retribution," these were the last verses that Blok wrote. Even at that time I was struck by the line, "As I depart into night's darkness." Truly, he did "depart into night's darkness," but before departing he made a final farewell bow—to Pushkin.

His death was an agonizing one. Soon after the end, a young girl who was a close friend of Blok and his family sent me (I was in the country at the time) an account of his last days, and I will now quote a few passages from her letter:

"His illness progressed by fits and starts, so to speak; there were periods of improvement, and at the beginning of June it began to look as if he might recover. He could not grasp or hold on to any thought, and his heart was causing him terrible pain all the time; he was constantly gasping for breath. After the twenty-fifth of July his condition grew considerably worse. We thought of taking him to the country, but the doctor said that he was too weak to be moved. By the beginning of August he was unconscious almost all the time. At night he was delirious and he shrieked in the most terrible way. For as long as I live I shall never forget his screaming. He was given morphine injections, but they did not relieve his pain. Nevertheless we thought that we must make one last attempt to take him away to Finland. The exit visa was signed, but on August 5th it turned out that some Moscow agency had lost its questionnaire forms, and therefore a passport could not be issued... On August 7th I was supposed to travel to Moscow with power of attorney... I was to travel in N. N.'s railway coach, but both N. N. and his secretary turned out to be drunk when we met to make arrangements. The next morning at seven o'clock I ran to the Nikolaevsky station; from there to Konyushennaya, where I announced that I was leaving anyway, even if I had to ride in the buffer car... But before leaving I learned by telephone that Blok had died, and I hurried off to Ofitserskaya Street... Alexandra Andreevna (Blok's mother) was sitting by the bed, stroking his hands... Whenever visitors called her out of the room, she would say to me, 'Go to Sashenka,' and these words (which she had spoken so often during his lifetime) took away one's belief in the reality of death... I chose the burial place myself, at the Smolensk cemetery, beside his grandfather's grave, under an old maple tree... We carried the open coffin ourselves. There were a great many flowers. The funeral rites were held in the Church of the Resurrection, in the Smolensk cemetery...."

MAXIM GORKY

A. A. BLOK

... I wonder at times whether the Russian mind is not frightened to death of itself. It tries to circumvent thinking; it dislikes reason and even fears it.

That wily serpent, V. V. Rozanov, laments bitterly in *Solitaria*: "O my sad experiments! Why did I want to know everything? Now I can no longer die in peace as I had hoped."

Lev Tolstoi in his *Diary of My Youth* (May 4, 1851) states austerely: "Consciousness is the greatest moral evil that can befall man."

Dostoevsky spoke in a similar vein: "An acute consciousness is a sickness indeed, a real disease ... a heightened consciousness or even any consciousness at all is a disease. That's my opinion."

The realist A. F. Pisemsky cried out in his letter to Melnikov-Pechersky: "Damn this habit of thinking, this itch of the soul!"

Leonid Andreev said: "In reason itself there is something of the spy, of the saboteur." He surmised: "It is very likely that reason is that old witch, conscience, in disguise."

In Russian writers one can find dozens of such aphorisms, all of them bearing clear witness to their distrust of the power of reason. This is very much in keeping with the mentality of a people who live in a country where life is hardly ever ruled by reason.

It is significant that even P. F. Nikolaev, the author of the book *Active Progress*, to all appearances a man of a different persuasion, wrote to me in 1906: "Knowledge raises one's demands, demands create dissatisfaction, a dissatisfied man is unhappy, and that is why he is sociologically valuable and personally likeable." A totally incomprehensible, somewhat Buddhist thought! By the way, Montaigne too sighed wistfully: "Why arm ourselves with futile knowledge? So sweet and soft is the lot of the chosen—ignorance and simplicity of heart!" He attributed the longevity of the barbarians to their ignorance of science and religion, unaware that both science and religion were already present in them in embryonic form. The Epicurean Montaigne lived in times of religious wars. He was endowed with a lively wisdom and regarded the cannibalism of barbaric tribes less repugnant than the tortures of the Inquisition. Three hundred years later, Tolstoi said of him, "Montaigne is trivial."

Tolstoi's thought was religious in both form and content. I do not think that dogmatism pleased him, and I doubt that the process of thinking delighted him to the extent it delighted philosophers such as Schopenhauer, who was fascinated by the development of his own thought. As I see it, thinking was for Lev Nikolaevich a necessary curse, and it seems to me that he always bore in mind Tertullian's words reflecting the despair of a fanatic afflicted by doubt: "Thought is evil."

Is it not in the Bible that the dogmatist finds the roots of man's fear and his hatred of thought? "Azazel taught men how to make swords and knives . . . . He taught them various crafts and explained to them the course of the moon and stars . . . . And a mighty godlessness came upon the earth and the paths of men became crooked . . . ."

All this came back to me after yesterday's unexpected conversation with Blok. As we were leaving the offices of Universal Literature he asked me what I thought of his "Collapse of Humanism."[1] He had given a talk a few days earlier in which he had read a brief paper on this theme. It had seemed to me unclear, yet full of dark forebodings. Blok, as he was reading it, reminded me of a child lost in the woods in a fairy tale: sensing that monsters are approaching from out of the darkness, he mutters some incantations in their direction, hoping to frighten them away. As Blok turned the pages of his manuscript, his hands shook. I could not figure it out: did the notion of the decline of humanism please him or upset him? He is not as supple and talented in prose as he is in poetry, but he is a man whose feel for life is very deep and pessimistic—in other words, a "decadent." Blok himself, I think, was not too sure about what he believed; his words did not penetrate the depths of the thoughts that were destroying him and that were leading him to believe that humanism was collapsing. Certain ideas in his lectures seemed to me insufficiently worked out, for instance, his notion that "to educate the masses is impossible and unnecessary," and that "discoveries are giving way to inventions."

The nineteenth and twentieth centuries are so fantastically rich in inventions because they witnessed the most numerous and significant discoveries in science. Furthermore, to speak of the impossibility and futility of educating the Russian people is clearly "Scythianism"[2]—in my opinion a concession to the instinctively seditious sentiments of the Russian masses. And besides, what does Blok need "Scythianism" for?

I told him all this as tactfully as I could. It is difficult to talk to him. It seems to me that he despises anyone who regards his world strange or incomprehensible, and his world is incomprehensible to me. Lately I have been sitting next to him twice a week at editorial meetings for Universal Literature, and we often argue over whether certain translations conform to the spirit of the Russian language or not. Arguments of this sort do not bring people together. His attitude to work, like that of almost everyone on the editorial staff, is one of indifference and formality. He said that he was pleased to see me liberating myself "from the habit of solving social problems, a habit peculiar to the intelligentsia." He said: "I have always felt that this was not the real you. In the *Little Town of Okurov* one can already see that you are deeply concerned with the 'child question'[3]—the most profound and frightening of all." He was mistaken, but I did not argue; let him think what he likes or needs to feel! "Why don't you write about these questions?" he kept on pressing me. I told him that such subjects as the meaning of life, death, or love are strictly personal and intimate, concerning the individual alone. I do not care to discuss my feelings with anyone, and if I do so involuntarily, I always sound incompetent and awkward. To speak of oneself is a subtle art—I do not possess it.

We entered the Summer Gardens and sat down on a bench. There was an almost frenzied expression in Blok's eyes. By the gleam in them, by the tremor in his cold, tormented face, I saw that he was eager to talk, to ask questions. As though trying to erase with his foot the lacy design of sunlight on the ground, he said reproachfully, "You are holding back. You are concealing your thoughts about the spirit, about truth. Why?"

And before I could answer, he began criticizing the Russian intelligentsia in an irritating manner, in words which were especially out of place then, after the Revolution. I told him that in my opinion a negative attitude toward the intelligentsia is in itself a typically "intellectual" one. It is not the attitude of a *muzhik* who knows the intellectual only in the person of a selfless country doctor or a devoted country teacher, or of the workman who owes his political education to the intellectual. A negative attitude is wrong and harmful, not to mention the fact that it undermines the respect of the intelligentsia for itself and for its own historical and cultural work. Our intelligentsia has played, plays, and will continue to play the role of the workhorse of history. Thanks to its tireless work, it has elevated the proletariat to the heights of a revolution unprecedented for the depth and breadth of the tasks that it raised and that demanded immediate solution. He did not seem to be listening to me and was staring gloomily at the ground, but when I stopped, he again started speaking of the intelligentsia's doubts about Bolshevism and, by the way, he was quite right in saying: "Having invoked from the darkness the spirit of destruction, it is not fair to say: 'We didn't do it, they did.' Bolshevism is the inevitable result of all the efforts of the intelligentsia in universities, in publishing houses, in the underground..."

A nice-looking woman greeted him warmly, but his response was cool, almost contemptuous. She walked away with an embarrassed smile. Glancing after her at her short, hesitant steps, Blok asked me: "What do you think of immortality, of the possibility of immortality?" His voice, the persistent look in his eyes demanded an answer. I said that perhaps Lamennais was right: since the quantity of matter in the universe is limited, it must be presumed that its combinations will be repeated in infinity, an infinite number of times. Hence it is possible that in a few million years, on a gloomy spring night in

Petersburg, Blok and Gorky will again be speaking of eternity, as they sit on a bench in the Summer Gardens. Blok asked me: "Are you serious?" I was surprised and somewhat annoyed by his persistence, although I felt that he was asking not out of sheer curiosity but from an apparent desire to banish or suppress some disturbing and oppressive thought.

"I have no reason to consider Lamennais' opinion any less serious than others' on this subject."

"But you, you personally, what do you think?" He even tapped his foot. Until that evening he had seemed to me reticent, untalkative.

"Personally I prefer to picture man as a mechanism that converts the so-called 'dead matter' into psychic energy and which will in some unfathomably distant future transform the whole world into pure psychics."

"I don't understand. What's this—pan-psychism?"

"No. Someday nothing will exist except thought. Everything will disappear after having been transmuted into pure thought; thought alone will survive, incorporating in itself all human thinking from its dawn to the moment of its final explosion."

"I don't understand," Blok repeated, shaking his head.

I suggested that he picture the world as an unceasing process of dissociation from matter. As it disintegrates, matter constantly releases such forms of energy as light, electro-magnetic waves, Hertzian waves and so on. Radioactive phenomena are, of course, part of this process. Thought is the result of dissociation of atoms in the brain; the brain is composed of elements of "dead" inorganic matter. Within the human brain, this matter is constantly undergoing conversion into psychic energy. I like to think that at some future time all the "matter" absorbed by man will be converted into a single form of energy—the psychic. It will then find internal harmony and ultimately turn to self-contemplation, to reflection over the infinitely varied creative possibilities concealed within itself.

"What a gloomy fantasy," said Blok with an ironic smile, "It is comforting to remember that the law of the conservation of matter disproves it."

"And I, on the other hand, find it comforting to think that the laws discovered in laboratories may not coincide with universal laws still unknown to us. I am convinced that if from time to time we could weigh our planet we would see that its weight is gradually diminishing."

"All this is boring," said Blok, shaking his head. "It's all a lot simpler. It's all because we have become much too clever to believe in God, but not strong enough to believe in ourselves alone. Life and faith can be built only on a belief in 'God' and oneself. Mankind? How can one believe in the wisdom of mankind after this war, and on the eve of inevitable and still crueler ones? No . . . this fantasy of yours is terrible! But I don't think you are serious."

He sighed: "If we could only stop all thought, if only for ten years! If only we could extinguish that deceptive little swamp-light which draws us closer and closer to the world's night, and listen with our hearts to the harmony of the universe. The brain, the brain ... It is an unreliable organ, monstrously huge, hideously developed, a swelling like a goiter..." He remained silent awhile, his lips tightly pressed, and then said in a low voice: "If we could only stop motion, let time stand still!"

"It would stand still if all motion were reduced to the same speed."

Blok glanced at me out of the corner of his eye, raised his eyebrows, and began speaking rapidly and incoherently, and I could no longer understand him. I had a strange feeling: it seemed to me that he was ripping off his worn, tattered clothes.

Suddenly he got up, offered me his hand, and walked off to the trolley-car. His gait at first glance seems steady, but a closer look reveals it to be shaky and faltering. And, however well he may dress, one would prefer to see him dress differently, not like anyone else. Gumilyov even in the fur outfit of a Laplander or a Samoyed would not stand out, but Blok, since he *is* different, requires something out of the ordinary.

No sooner had I finished jotting down my conversation with Blok, than B., a sailor from the Baltic fleet, came in to borrow some "real interesting books." He is extremely fond of science and expects it to resolve all "the riddles of life," and speaks of it with joy and faith. Today he brought some amazing news: "Do you know, they say that an American scholar has invented a wonderfully simple machine: a binocular, a wheel, and a handle. Turn the handle and you can see everything: analysis, trigonometry, criticism and, in fact, the whole meaning of the history of one's life is there. This machine will show it all and, furthermore, it whistles."

What appealed to me most of all was the fact that it whistled.

A young woman from the Nevsky and I were talking in the Pekar restaurant: "That little book of yours," she said, "is it by that famous Blok? I met him too—only once, to be sure. It was a fall day, very late in the evening, slush and fog, you know; the Duma's clock was pointing to midnight, I was dead tired and about to go home when suddenly, at the corner of Italyanskaya, a nicely dressed, good-looking guy with a proud face invites me to go with him. I even said to myself, I bet he's a foreigner. We start walking along Karavannaya Street—it's not far from here—No. 10 has rooms to let. We're walking and I'm talking, but he's quiet and I feel kind of uncomfortable and strange. I don't like impolite people. We get there, I ask for tea. He rings, but the servant doesn't come, so he goes into the hall to call him, and I'm so tired, you know, so cold, that I fall asleep sitting on the couch. Then suddenly I wake up and what do I see: he's sitting at the table across from me, with his elbows on the table, holding his head and he's looking at me sternly—what terrible eyes! But I'm so ashamed that I'm not even frightened. All I can do is think, O, God, he must be a musician! He has curly hair. 'Excuse me,' I say, 'I'll get undressed right away.'

"But he smiles politely and answers: 'You don't have to, don't worry.' He sits next to me on the sofa, puts me on his lap and, strokes my hair, saying: 'Go on, sleep a little longer.' And imagine, I fall asleep again—it's terrible! Of course I understand that this isn't the right thing to do, but I can't help it. He rocks me so gently and makes me feel so comfortable! I open my eyes, I smile, he smiles too. And I think I must have even been asleep when he shook me gently and said: 'Good-bye, I must leave now.' He puts twenty-five rubles on the table. 'Excuse me,' I say, 'but what for?' Naturally I'm terribly embarrassed. I excuse myself, everything seems so funny, so strange. But he laughs quietly, shaking my hand, and even kisses it. Then he leaves. As I was walking out the servant says: 'Do you know who it was you were with? That was Blok, the poet. Look!' And he shows me his picture in the paper. And I see it's true. It's him. 'God,' I think, 'how stupid the whole thing turned out to be.' "

She stopped, and indeed across her face, with its turned-up nose and saucy expression, mischievous like that of a homeless puppy, there passed a shadow of real sorrow and—disappointment. I gave her all the money I had with me, and from that time on I understood Blok and felt him to be close to me.

I like his serious face and his head—the head of a Florentine of the Renaissance.

1923

ANNA AKHMATOVA

REMINISCENCES OF A. BLOK

In the fall of 1913, on the day we were to celebrate Verhaeren's arrival in Russia at some restaurant or other, a large private reception (for students only) had also been planned for him at the Bestuzhev Institute for Women. It occurred to one of their organizers to invite me. My assignment was to pay homage to Verhaeren (a poet I dearly loved), not for his celebrated urban poetry, but for his small poem, "On a Little Wooden Bridge at the End of the World."

I visualized the elaborate celebration at the Petersburg restaurant. For some reason such celebrations resemble a funeral banquet: the tuxedos, the good champagne, the bad French, the toasts, and so I decided in favor of the students.

The sponsors, who had dedicated all their lives to the struggle for women's equality, also came to this reception. One of them, the writer Ariadna Vladimirovna Turkova-Vergezhskaya, who had known me from childhood, said after my reading: "Congratulations, Anichka has won equality for herself!"

I met Blok in the dressing room before the reading. I asked him why he was not at the restaurant reception for Verhaeren. The poet answered with a winning straightforwardness: "Because I would be asked to speak and I don't speak French."

A student came over to us with a program and said that I was scheduled to read after Blok. I implored: "Alexander Alexandrovich, I cannot read after you!" He answered chidingly: "Anna Andreevna, we are not both tenors!" At that time Blok was one of Russia's best known poets. For the last two years I had been reading my poems at the Poet's Guild, in the Society of Lovers of Literature and at Vyacheslav Ivanov's Tower, but this was an entirely different matter. While an ensemble performance may conceal the individual, a solo performance in a variety show exposes him mercilessly. A variety show is something like the executioner's block. I think I knew it then for the first time. The audience begins to seem to the performer like the many-headed Hydra. Controlling such an audience is very difficult. The master of this art was Zoshchenko. Pasternak was pretty good at it too.

Nobody knew who I was and when I came in, I could hear them murmuring: "Who is she?" Blok had advised me to read "We Are All Revelers Here." I objected and said: "When I read 'I put on a narrow skirt' they all laugh," and he countered by saying: "When I read 'And the drunks with their rabbit eyes'—they also laugh."

It seems to me that it was at another literary evening, not at that one, that Blok, after hearing Igor Severyanin, returned to the dressing room and said: "He has a slick lawyer's voice."

*   *   *

On one of the last Sundays of 1913, I brought Blok his books to inscribe for me. In each he simply wrote: "To Akhmatova—Blok." Here are the *Poems about the Beautiful Lady.*[1] But in the third volume, the poet wrote a madrigal dedicated to me, " Beauty is a frightening thing, they will tell you..."[2] I never had a Spanish shawl like the one I am depicted wearing in that poem, but at that time Blok was wild about Carmen and made me Spanish too. It goes without saying I never wore a red rose in my hair either. It was not accidental that the poem uses the stanza of the Spanish *romancero.*[3] And at our last meeting backstage at the Bolshoi Dramatic Theater, Blok came up to me and asked: "And where is your Spanish shawl?" These were the last words he ever spoke to me.

*   *   *

The one time I was at his house, I reminded Blok in passing that the poet Benedikt Livshits had complained that his writing of poetry was hindered by Blok's very existence. Blok did not laugh, but answered quite seriously: "I understand it. Leo Tolstoi hinders my writing."[4]

*   *   *

In the summer of 1914, I visited my mother in Darnitsa, in the suburbs of Kiev. At the beginning of July, I went home to my village Slepnyovo by way of Moscow. In Moscow I took the first train that came along. I was smoking on the open platform. As we approached a deserted station, the engine slowed down and a bag of mail was thrown in. Suddenly Blok's figure loomed before my amazed eyes. I yelled out: "Alexander Alexandrovich!" He turned around and since he was not only a great poet, but a master at asking questions tactfully, he asked: "With whom are you traveling?" I had just enough time to answer, "Alone," before the train pulled away.

Today, after fifty-one years, I open Blok's *Notebook* and read in the July 9th entry: "Mother and I went to take a look at a sanatorium near Podsolnechnaya. The devil is tempting me. Anna Akhmatova is on the mail train."

*   *   *

Somewhere else Blok writes that one day Delmas, E. Yu. Kuzmina-Kara-vaeva, and I wore him out with our phone calls. I think that I can explain what happened. I called up Blok. Alexander Alexandrovich, with his typical direct-ness and habit of thinking out loud, asked: "You are probably calling because Ariadna Vladimirovna Turkova told you what I said about you." Dying of curiosity, I went to see Ariadna Vladimirovna on the day she received visitors and asked her what Blok had said. But she was unrelenting: "Anichka, I never tell my guests what others say about them."

*   *   *

Blok's *Notebook* rewards the reader by recovering from the well of oblivion half-forgotten dates: and once again the burning wooden St. Isaac's Bridge floats toward the estuary of the Neva, and my companion and I stare with horror at the unprecedented sight, and this day has a date: July 11, 1916, as recorded by Blok.

*   *   *

And once again, after the Revolution (January 21, 1919), I met Blok in the theater restaurant. Grown thin, with a crazed look in his eyes, he tells me: "Here people meet as if they were already in the hereafter."

And here we are, the three of us—Blok, Gumilyov, and I—dining (August 5, 1914) at the Tsarskoselskaya Station in the first days of the war. (Gumilyov was already wearing a soldier's uniform.) Blok at this time was visiting the families of recruits and was offering them his help. When Kolya and I were left alone, Kolya asked: "Is it possible that he too will be sent to the front? That's like frying nightingales."

And over a quarter of a century later, in that same Dramatic Theater, at a reception commemorating Blok (1946), I read the verses I had just written:

Он прав—опять фонарь, аптека,
Нева, безмолвие, гранит . . .
Как памятник началу века,
Там этот человек стоит—
Когда он Пушкинскому дому,
Прощаясь, помахал рукой
И принял смертную истому
Как незаслуженный покой.

He was right—again a street lamp, a pharmacy,
The Neva, silence, granite . . .

Like a monument to the beginning of the century
Stands this man—
When he, upon parting, waved his hand
To the Pushkin House
And accepted the embrace of death
As an undeserved rest.

*   *   *

Akhmatova's reminiscences end here. What follows is a poem that she wrote in answer to one that Blok had dedicated to her, "Beauty is a Frightening Thing, They Will Tell You." It was published for the first time together with Blok's poem in the journal Lyubov k tryom apelsinam *(I, 1914), for which Blok was the poetry editor.*

Я пришла к поэту в гости.
Ровно полдень. Воскресенье.
Тихо в комнате просторной,
А за окнами мороз.

Там малиновое солнце
Над лохматым сизым дымом...
Как хозяин молчаливый
Ясно смотрит на меня!

У него глаза такие,
Что запомнить каждый должен;
Мне же лучше, осторожной,
В них и вовсе не глядеть.

Но запомнится беседа.
Дымный полдень, воскресенье
В доме сером и высоком
У морских ворот Невы.

I came to visit the poet
On Sunday, promptly at noon.
There is silence in the spacious room
And frost outside the window pane.

Up there—a raspberry-colored sun
Above gray and grizzled smoke...
And here—the glance of my silent host
Brightly shines on me.

He has the kind of eyes
That one can't help but remember;
Being cautious, I'd best
Not look into them at all.

But our meeting will live in my memory,
That smoky noon, that hazy Sunday,
In the tall, gray house
By the sea gates of the Neva.

BLOK THE ARTIST

N. S. GUMILYOV

A REVIEW OF ALEXANDER BLOK'S COLLECTED POEMS IN THREE VOLUMES. *Vol. I.* POEMS ABOUT THE BEAUTIFUL LADY. *Vol. II.* UNEXPECTED JOY. *Vol. III.* SNOW NIGHT. *(MOSCOW: 1912)*

A poet usually gives his works to the public; Blok gives his very self. What I mean is that Blok not only does not concern himself with large, general questions—literary ones, as did Pushkin, philosophical ones, as did Tyutchev, sociological ones, as did Hugo—but does not even raise such questions. He simply describes his own life, which to his good fortune is so wonderfully rich in inner struggles, catastrophes, and illuminations.

"I don't listen to fairy tales, I am a simple man," says Pierrot in *The Puppet Show,* and one would like to see these words as an epigraph to the three volumes of Blok's poems. Nonetheless, he possesses the purely Pushkinian gift of making one feel the eternal in the ephemeral, of disclosing with each casual image the shadow of genius that guards his destiny. I said that this was a Pushkinian characteristic and shall not take back these words. Is it not true that even the "Gavriliada"[1] is imbued with a greater religious feeling, however strange it may be, than the many thick tomes of various "Words and Meditations" on the same theme? And are not Pushkin's Album Poems a sacred hymn to the mysteries of a new Eros?

There were many conjectures about the Beautiful Lady. Some wanted to see in her the Wife enveloped by the Sun, others the Eternal Feminine, others the symbol of Russia. But if we were to picture her simply as a girl with whom the poet had fallen in love, it seems to me that not a single poem would refute this notion, and that this image, having become more familiar, would become even more enchanting and be infinitely enhanced from an artistic point of view. We would understand then that what the book reveals is a new face of love: as Dante revealed it in *La Vita Nuova,* Ronsard in his *Sonnets,* Goethe in *Werther* and Baudelaire in *Flowers of Evil.* This is a love that yearns for blinding rapture, that feeds on presentiments, that believes in omens and sees unity in everything because it sees only itself; a love that proves once more than man is more than a civilized ape. And we will be on the poet's side when he, in the words of that same Pierrot, cries out to the mystics gathered around him: "You will not deceive me; this is Columbine, this is my bride!"

In his second book, as though for the first time, Blok took notice of the material world surrounding him, and having done so, was elated beyond words. Hence its title, *Unexpected Joy.* But here is where the tragedy begins. The poet was sincerely delighted by this world and forgot the difference between it and himself, the possessor of a living soul; with a rather strange ease he immediately accepted and loved everything: the little swamp priest, doing God knows what in the swamp but surely not just healing frogs' legs; the dwarf, clutching a pendulum in his hand and mortally striking a child with it; little demons begging not to be taken to Holy Places; and deep below in this unlikely kingdom, like an empress in the silks and rings of the Unknown Lady *(Neznakomka)*, Hysteria and her servant Alcohol reign.

The Unknown Lady is the leitmotif of the book. It is the deceptive promise of matter to bring absolute happiness and at the same time the impossibility of it; an Unknown Lady not pure and silent like the stars, whose meaning and truth are in their unextinguishable light, but one who teases, calls and excites, like the moon. She is the water nymph of the city, demanding that those in love with her renounce their very souls.

But Blok, the poet with a child's heart, did not choose the lure of adventure. He chose death instead, and half of the *Snow Night,* which had at first been part of *Earth in Snow,* is permeated with the constant and persistent thought of death—not the concern with the world beyond, but with the moment of transition into it. The "Snow Mask" is that very same Unknown Lady, but one who in her frustration wishes the death of the lover who is slipping away from her. In the poems of this period we not only hear a hysterical elation or a hysterical anguish, but we already sense the festive approach of the Spirit of Music, victorious over demons. Music is what unites the material and spiritual worlds. It is the the soul of things and the body of thought. In the violins and bells of *Night Hours* (the second half of *Snow Night)* there is no more hysteria; these are happy times for the poet. All the lines are pure and firm, and at the same time there is not one esoteric image, all are alive in the fullest sense of the word, all quiver, surge, and float into "the land of distant violins." The words are like notes, the phrases like chords. And the world, ennobled by music, becomes humanly wonderful and pure—the whole world, from Dante's tomb to the faded curtain above the sick geraniums. I don't think that anyone can tell what other forms Blok's poetry will flow into from now on—Blok least of all.

VALERY BRYUSOV

ALEXANDER BLOK

I

The stations along the road traveled by Alexander Blok "in the twelve years of his conscious life," as he himself put it, as well as those in succeeding years, are very clearly delineated in his poetry; they could indeed be said to be etched in black. This was a road that led from solitary contemplation to fusion with life, from attempts to fathom the mystery of the world through the power of dreams to a quiet and somber observation of reality, from mysticism to realism. At the same time it was a journey from adolescent dreams of the poet's crown, of ideal love and ideal life, to a realization that his sole vocation was poetry. It was on this journey that he came face to face with the complexities and rude realities of contemporary life, realities which slowly but inexorably filled his soul and found in it unexpected echoes. To the poet himself this second part of his journey, in the course of which he had to renounce the unattained and unattainable ideals of his youth, seemed a kind of "fall." Yet Blok's poetry has broadened and deepened with each passing year, flowering in new colors. At the same time, however, somber moods, verging at times on hopelessness, have gradually overtaken the early radiant hymns: optimistic faith has given way to skeptical pessimism.

Blok's first collection of poems, with the characteristic title *Poems about the Beautiful Lady,* appeared in 1905, but consisted of poems written much earlier (1898-1904). While still in his teens and living in Petersburg, Blok joined a small circle of young Moscow poets that included, among others, Andrei Bely and Sergei Solovyov, and which was strongly influenced by the ideas of Vladimir Solovyov and the then new religious preaching of D. S. Merezhkovsky. Together with Vladimir Solovyov, these young dreamers were sure that "the end of the world" was close at hand and that a great worldwide cataclysm which would fundamentally alter the life of mankind was destined to occur soon—almost any day. Their excited imagination discerned everywhere clear portents of things to come. These young men interpreted all events, indeed everything going on around them, as secret symbols of some loftier reality, and in every mundane phenomenon they tried to uncover a mystical meaning.

Such are the moods that inform Blok's first volume. In the "Beautiful Lady," regardless of with whom he associated her in real life, Blok perceived the divine, eternally feminine principle that must, once it permeated the world deeply enough, transform and redeem it. In this respect Blok was a faithful disciple of Vladimir Solovyov, who not long before his death had prophesied:

> Вечная женственность ныне
> В теле нетленном на землю идет.

>> The eternal feminine now
>> In incorruptible flesh is descending to earth.

The poet depicts himself as this "Lady's" humble and obedient servant, as "the Queen's slave," *servus Reginae,* and defines his own task:

> Светить в предьверьи Идеала
> Туманным факелом своим.

>> To light with my humble torch
>> The threshold of the Ideal.

In his poems he portrays himself in many guises: as the "custodian of the temple" who "keeps the icon-lamps burning," as one of the faithful slaves who guards the entrance to the Empress' chambers, as one "who performs his simple ritual in the dark temple" in anticipation of the "Beautiful Lady," as a page who follows behind Her, holding Her mantle... The entire book is filled with the pathos of expectation; the words "I wait," "we wait," "he waits" are repeated over and over, and one of his earlier poems expresses this feeling with special force:

> Предчувствую Тебя. Года проходят мимо,—
> Все в облике одном предчувствую Тебя.

> Весь горизонт в огне и ясен нестерпимо,
> Я молча жду,—тоскуя и любя.

>> I sense your approach. Years pass, but still
>> My vision of You remains unchanged.
>> The whole horizon is aflame and unbearably bright,
>> Silently I wait in longing and in love.1

Perpetually absorbed in his dreams, the author of the poems about the "Beautiful Lady" shuns life. Over and over he reiterates that life "torments" him and that for him the earth is a "wasteland." He imagines himself in some unearthly "ancient cell," in a "monastery," or on some mysterious "royal road," following a "pillar of fire." The poet defines his hopes as "dreams of the unrealizable," as a "sacred dream," and all his secret prayers resolve into one: may the idea of the body vanish, "may the spirit be resurrected and the flesh slumber." The greater part of these poems is filled with a disdain for the "body" and for this earth and the craving for the celestial and "incorporeal."

Consequently, nothing in the poems about the "Beautiful Lady" seems real—all the feelings and all the inner experiences are transposed into some ideal world. Every event of the poet's life assumes in his early poetry an allegorical meaning: a river is not simply a river, but a symbol of the boundary that separates him from the Ideal; the faraway white church, which in the morning seems closer, is not just a church; "chamber," "door," "steps," "road," "dawn," "skies"—these words are almost always used in a special, symbolic sense. One must learn this allegorical language if one is to understand the meaning of the poems about the "Beautiful Lady," and only then will the charm of a poem such as this clearly emerge:

Я, отрок, зажигаю свечи,
Огонь кадильный берегу.
Она без мысли и без речи
На том смеется берегу.
Люблю вечернее моленье
У белой церкви над рекой,
Перезакатное селенье
И сумрак мутно голубой.
Покорный ласковому взгляду,
Любуюсь тайной красоты,
И за церковную ограду
Бросаю белые цветы.
Падет туманная завеса,
Жених сойдет из алтаря,
И от вершин зубчатых леса
Забрезжит брачная заря.

> A young lad, I light the candles,
> And watch the censer's fire.
> Without thinking or speaking
> She laughs on the other shore.
> I love the evening prayer
> At the white church above the river,
> The village before sunset
> And the hazy blue twilight.
> Yielding to her caressing glance,
> I delight in beauty's mystery,
> And toss white flowers
> Over the church fence.
> The misty curtain will fall,
> The bridegroom will descend from the altar,
> And the nuptial dawn will gleam
> From the forest's jagged tops.

Only in the final poems of this book do the images become more concrete and alive: outlines of living people emerge from behind the masks of angels, and walls of simple, ordinary houses, and even a factory, rise from behind the cupolas of mysterious temples.

II

Between Blok's first and second books lies the difficult period of the years 1905-1906. These were years which could not fail to be instructive in many ways to anyone at all capable of learning. At that time, Blok, like others who had shared his views and trusted too naively in their own mystic intuitions, could not help but realize that the fulfillment of his expectations was not as imminent as he had originally assumed. Those same feelings which the whole of Europe had experienced around the year 1000 A.D., when it expected the end of the world and the Last Judgment, were relived on a smaller scale at the turn of the twentieth century in the circle of young Moscow mystics. But the fateful time came and went and their prophesies had not come true. A period of disillusion and disbelief followed, which led them at times to mock what they had once held sacred.

In Blok's second book, which was given the unfortunate title *Unexpected Joy* (1907), the demonic breaks into his poetry. It appears at first in the guise of "creatures of spring," "imps," "priestlings of the swamps," and wizards personifying the pagan principle, powers which are forever leading the human soul astray from the Almighty, tempting it with the age-old fascination of the transient. Lovingly and in great detail, Blok depicts this world of elemental creatures who live in unison with nature, who are foreign to sin just as rocks, plants and clouds are, but who also feel no attraction whatever for things supernatural. We are face to face with

> ...мохнатые, малые каются,
> Униженно в траве кувыркаются,
> Подымают копытцами пыль...

> ...the shaggy little creatures contritely
> And meekly turn somersaults in the grass,
> Raising the dust with their little hooves.

The poet assures one of his little imps: "Like you, I am a child of the woods," and then, as if echoing the prayer of his "priestling of the swamps," he says:

Душа моя рада
Всякому гаду,
И всякому зверю,
И о всякой вере.

> My soul rejoices
> In every snake,
> In every beast,
> And every creed.

Later the same demonic principle which is embodied in the image of the "Dark-Visaged One" enters Blok's poetry. It invariably comes to the poet at the hour of twilight to torment him with the terror of dark forebodings....

It is here that we encounter entirely new themes, unexpected ones from the "faithful slave of the Queen, the humble servitor of the 'Beautiful Lady.' " As though forgetting his temples, his monastic cells, his church porches and lilies—all the customary props of his early poems—Blok tells us how

По вечерам, над ресторанами,
Горячий воздух дик и глух...

> In the evenings, above the restaurants
> The sultry air hangs wild and stale.

He now confesses that

В кабаках, в переулках, в изливах,
В электрическом сне наяву
Я искал бесконечно красивых
И бессмертно влюбленных в молву.

> In taverns, in alleyways, on street corners,
> In an electric waking-dream
> I searched for the endlessly beautiful
> And eternal lovers of small talk.

The poet who once had "silently awaited" the "Beautiful Lady" now asks himself as he wanders aimlessly along the gas-lit street,

Не увижу ли *красной* подруги моей?

> Shall I not see my *scarlet* girl?

And sure enough, coming toward him is

Вольная дева в огненном плаще.

A loose girl in a flame-colored cape.

This transition from the "Beautiful Lady" to the "scarlet girl" was expressed even more sharply in Blok's "Lyrical Dramas," which appeared in 1908 shortly after *Unexpected Joy*. In these plays, Blok openly mocks his own youthful dream of the Eternal Feminine, by embodying it in the figure of Columbine, who in the end turns out to be only a "cardboard bride,"[2] and by bringing his "Unknown Lady" into a circle of vacuous and seemingly blind people. What had previously impelled Blok to compose prayers and sing hymns has now become for him a subject of farce.

True, in *Unexpected Joy*, Blok sometimes tries to return to his earlier inspirations and even assures us that,

Я не забыл *на пире хмельном*
Мою заветную свирель...

I did not forget *at the drunken feast*
My cherished reed pipe.

But at the same time comes his despairing statement:

Ты в поля отошла *без возврата*...
. . . .
О, исторгни *ржавую* душу,
Со святыми меня упокой!

You have gone off to the field *never to return*...
. . . .
O, wrest from me my *rusted* soul!
Grant me repose among the saints!

In these last words he seems to be saying that his self—his former self, that is—is dead.

III

The struggle between two principles, the divine and the demonic, continues in Blok's third collection of poems, *The Earth in Snow* (1908), which the author himself has called "a goblet of bitter wine."

In this book the images of the "Snow Mask" and of the "Unknown Lady" are the personification of the demonic: they draw the poet's soul into a world of sensual passion previously alien to his poetry.

Вот явилась. Заслонила
Всех нарядных, всех подруг,
И душа моя вступила
В предназначенный ей круг,—

> And there she was! She outshone
> Her friends in their fine attire,
> And my soul stepped into
> Its predestined circle—

and thus the poet's words introduce us to the drama of passion which he portrays. Then, having set forth as his new precept the conviction:

Что путь открыт, наверно, к раю
Всем, кто идет путями *зла*,—

> That the road to paradise, no doubt, lies open
> To all those who tread the paths of *evil*,—

he describes, step by step, this "path of evil" leading to paradise, a path on which sorrowful complaints escape his lips:

Возврати мне, Маска, душу!

> Give me back, oh Mask, my soul!

or:

Убей меня, как я убил
Когда-то близких мне!

> Slay me, as I slew
> Those once near and dear to me!

The poems from *The Earth in Snow* (especially those in the second part of the book) are among Blok's most powerful. They have all the immediacy of life and in places they impress us as the frank confessions of a human soul rather than the creations of a poet. This is a poetic diary, set down in nervous, fragmentary and deeply stirring verse. The mood that dominates these poems is anticipation of doom, an ultimate doom which seems to draw and tempt the poet. More than once he cries out:

Тайно сердце *просит* гибели...

Secretly the heart *begs for* doom...

И погибнуть мне *весело*...

And for me dying is *joyful*...

The book concludes with the image of a bonfire in which the poet sees himself crucified—in the flames, on the cross of passion.

This acceptance of passion, an earthly feeling, also brought Blok into contact with all the concrete realities of the earth. On almost every page of *The Earth in Snow* images from everyday life flash past. First a "weary brown nag" shuffles along, then we see "the street, the street...the shadows of people who are silently scurrying to sell their bodies," next comes a description of a young girl on whom a molester is "forcing his will," then we are told how the alleyways "smell of the sea" and how "the factory sirens sing." At one point we find the coarse exclamation, "Hey, Fyokla, Fyokla," breaking into the verse, and at another the poet summons us to the most ordinary of street dances:

Гармоника, гармоника!
Эй, пой, визжи и жги!

Accordian, accordian!
Hey, sing, shriek and burn!

The Earth in Snow is already infinitely remote from the poems about the "Beautiful Lady," and the poet at one moment says: "Forget my luminous words," and the next moment, recalling his poems from *Unexpected Joy* about how She had "gone off to the fields, never to return," bitterly calls himself "an unresurrected Christ."

IV

Thus, in his poetry, Blok little by little renounces his youthful ideals. Passionate verses about the "scarlet girl" and the "Snow Mask" replace his mystical devotional hymns to the "Beautiful Lady"; songs about the joys and sorrows of the "grieving earth" and simple descriptions of daily life now supplant the poetry of obscure allegories, mysterious temples, white steps, expectation and worship. The youth who had dreamt of being a prophet has become a poet.

Perhaps the very nature of Alexander Blok's talent made such a path inevitable. Art is always an embodiment; it must express and define in images even the vague and the ineffable. The domain of inspiration that produced the poems about the "Beautiful Lady" was limited; to infuse new vigor into his poetry, Blok had to turn to the everyday, to real life. Thus the ancient fable of Antaeus, who drew fresh strength from touching the earth, was re-enacted.

In his fourth book of poems, *Night Hours* (1911), Blok makes an attempt to renounce once and for all the general conceptions underlying his youthful poetry. He no longer seeks a reconciliation between the two eternally warring principles of existence, but is content with the more modest role of poet-observer and poet-depictor. In Blok's new poems we read of the "low smoke hovering over the barn," of "three old harness straps" fluttering, of a gendarme standing on a railroad platform in front of a woman who has been crushed by a train; we see a fashionable man of letters, the "creator of blasphemous words," a "tavern bar," a "private room in a restaurant," the "Elagin Bridge," the "swiftly flying sleigh," and in it someone who "lightly tucks in the bearskin cover as the sleigh dashes along" and "deftly slides [his] arms around [her] slender figure." Then we see scenes of Italian cities: Ravenna, Venice, Florence... There is much more first-hand observation in these poems, much fresh imagery, and a genuine insight into human psychology. Here we find solemn stanzas "on the death of an infant," verses on the "fierceness of a final passion," and the poet's bitter admission:

> И стало все равно, какие
> Лобзать уста, ласкать плеча,
> В какие улицы глухие
> Гнать удалого лихача—

> And I no longer care
> Whose lips I kiss, whose shoulders I caress,
> Or into which lonely streets
> I press the dashing cabdriver—

Then there are his stern observations about one who wrings his hands in anguish, and whom

> Вся жизнь, ненужно изжитая,
> Пытала, унижала, жгла...

> A wasted useless life
> Has tormented, debased and burned...

And here, too, we find reflections on the poet's homeland, on the destiny of Russia, meditations to which Blok has been returning more and more frequently... In some of the poems in *Night Hours* one senses the poet's sorrow for his irretrievable past, as in those lines where, after describing the "familiar hell" which gazes into his "hollow eyes," he exclaims:

> Где спутник мой? — О где ты, Беатриче? —
> Иду один, *утратив правый путь.*

> Where is my companion? O where are you, Beatrice?
> I walk alone, *having lost the right way.*

V

But Blok was not destined to remain for long in such a conciliatory frame of mind. His most recent poems (1912-1915), which have been appearing in journals, almanacs and newspapers since the publication of *Night Hours,* testify anew to his tragic awareness of the contradiction between his present and his past. Blok could for a time resign himself to the humble destiny of being merely a poet, and still can, temporarily, create such beautiful stanzas of pure poetry as his latest Italian poems (with scenes of Venice, Florence, Sienna, etc.), but he lacks the strength to stifle permanently recollections of his youthful, loftier dreams. Themes from *The Earth in Snow* reappear in Blok's new poems, but without that "fascination with doom" which, like a fiery glow, had previously eclipsed all his other moods. Now a sense of the irreparable and fatal loss of something higher and finer emerges stark and unconcealed, a feeling that sometimes imbues Blok's poems with exceptional power and depth.

"Yes, I *was* a prophet... A tsar I shall not be... A slave I shall not become... I am a man..." thus the poet defines the road he has traveled. Blok calls himself a "fallen angel"; he confesses that "having abandoned his vigil," he "crossed over to the enemy camp by nightfall," and that his "dreams had not been enough to last even half a lifetime." Finally, he admits:

> Как тяжело ходить среди людей
> И *притворяться непогибшим...*

> How hard it is to walk among men
> And *to pretend to be still alive...*

In the poem "To the Muse," Blok recalls that

...была роковая отрада
В попираньи заветных святынь...

> ...there was a fatal joy
> In trampling on what was most holy...

And for his "barren, wasted soul," he can point to only one remedy: drunken oblivion:

Ах, не все ль мне равно!
Вновь сдружусь с кабацкой скрипкой,
Монотонной и певучей!
Вновь я буду пить вино!

> Oh, isn't it all the same to me.
> Again I'll make friends with a tavern violin,
> Monotonous and melodious!
> Again I will be drinking wine!

This pathos of "tragic despair" perhaps attains its greatest power in those poems where the emphasis shifts from the poet himself to a depiction of life as he perceives it. In the two poems entitled "Totentanz" ("Dance of Death") Blok portrays a pharmacy; in the first, a certain visitor, having procured a vial labeled "venena" (poision, Lat.) from the Jewish chemist, afterwards "takes it from under his cloak and thrusts it upon two noseless women"; in the other the poet is ready to admit that nothing can exist in this world except "absurdities" and "dreariness":

Ночь, улица, фонарь, аптека,
Бессмысленный и тусклый свет,
Живи еще хоть четверть века,
Все будет так. *Исхода нет.*
Умрешь – начнешь опять сначала...

> Night, a street, a lamp, a pharmacy,
> A meaningless, dull light.
> Even if you live another quarter-century
> Nothing will change. *There is no way out.*
>
> *You'll die—you'll start again from the beginning...*

This thought is carried to its conclusion in another poem that says that *everything* in the world must,

Как этот мир, лететь *бесцельно*
В сияющую ночь...

> Like this world, fly *aimlessly*
> Into the shining night...

"The aimlessness of existence"—here we have the polar opposite of those sentiments that once had impelled the adolescent Blok "to light candles" and "to guard the incense fire." Now what frightens the poet most is not that he has "trampled" with "fateful joy" on "what was most holy," nor that, to use his own vivid expression, he was "scorched by the tongues of *infernal fire*" (significantly followed by: "I conceal nothing from you"), but rather that the future has nothing to offer save more of the same. In his remarkable eight-line poem "The Ring of Existence Grips Tight," Blok tells us that as he peers ahead into the "mist of the future" he sees "always one and the same fate":

> Опять — любить Ее на небе
> И изменять Ей на земле,

> Again—to love Her in heaven
> And betray Her on earth.

Blok's most recent romantic drama, *The Rose and the Cross,* seems to us an attempt "to love Her in heaven." This drama is permeated with the mystical sentiments of the romantic Middle Ages. The heroine of the play, Izora,[3] loves an unknown singer whom she has never met but whose image she has created in her dreams. Like a leitmotif, the singer's refrain is repeated several times:

> Сердцу закон непреложный —
> Радость-Страданье одно!

> The heart has an immutable law:
> Joy and Suffering are one!

Yet even in the play this yearning "to love in heaven" ends in "betrayal on earth." When Izora meets her singer and he turns out to be old and ugly, she betrays him for the handsome page Aliskan.

VI

Despite all these tragic inner experiences, Blok has remained a true poet and a genuine artist in each phase of his creative career. His moods may have fluctuated; at times his soul may have been full of "childlike faith," at others it may have felt "desolate," but his artistic sense has always prevailed. Just as Blok earlier had been able to find appropriate rhythms and words for his mystical expectations, for his depictions of the "Beautiful Lady," and later of the "Unknown Woman" and the "Snow Mask," he can now just as successfully find rhythms and words for his poems of passion and death, for his realistic pictures of Petersburg night life, and for his poems on the beauty of Italian cities. By the same token, for all the diversity of moods expressed in his poems, Blok has always succeeded in preserving that unique style that distinguishes him from other poets and makes him *maitre* and founder of that distinct Blokian school that already numbers many adherents.

In verse technique and creative devices Blok is a disciple of Fet and Vladimir Solovyov, and if the later Blok fell under the influence of other poets, including Pushkin, this does not alter the already distinctive character of his verse. Although Fet's technique provided him with a point of departure, Blok in his early poems was already transforming that technique into something original and independent, and he has continued ever since to develop and perfect his verse. His art has always remained purely lyrical; he always chose expressions and epithets not in order to describe realistically objects and phenomena, but according to his own subjective attitude toward them. In his verses, the poet never vanishes behind his images: his personality is always before the reader. Because of this, Blok's youthful poems as well as his later works require much effort and close attention on our part. One must fill in for oneself what is not stated explicitly and reconstruct the link between the various images—a link that is obvious to the poet but not always clearly expressed—and above all, one must interpret each individual poem as a chapter in a long series of other chapters that supplement and explain it. Thus, for example, only one who has an intimate knowledge of Blok's poetry as a whole can fully comprehend a poem such as the following:

Ты оденешь меня в серебро.
И, когда я умру,
Выйдет месяц, небесный Пьеро,
Встанет красный паяц на юру.
Мертвый месяц беспомощно нем...
Никому ничего не открыл.
Только спросит подругу — зачем
Я когда-то ее полюбил.
В этот яростный сон наяву
Опрокинусь я мертвым лицом.
И паяц испугает сову,
Загремев под горой бубенцом...
Знаю — сморщенный лик его стар
И бесстыден в земной наготе.

Но зловещий исходит угар —
К небесам — к высоте — к чистоте.

> You will clothe me in silver
> And, when I die,
> The moon will appear, that celestial Pierrot,
> The red clown will rise in the open sky.
> The dead moon is helpless dumb...
> It has never revealed anything to anyone.
> It will only ask my lady friend
> Why I once came to love her.
> It this frenzied daydream
> I topple blan-faced.
> And the clown will frighten the owl,
> Rumbling under the hill with his bells...
> I know his wrinkled face is old
> And shameless in its earthly nakedness.
> But the malefic fumes spiral
> To the skies—to the heights—to purity.

Another related factor is Blok's disinclination to name the *dramatis personae* in his poems; he merely uses impersonal verb forms: "[they] rose out of the darkness of cellars," "[they] went out," "[they] laughed," leaving it up to the reader to guess *who* rose and *who* went out or laughed.

Blok's verse is almost always musical. He is able to achieve a melodious quality through combinations of sounds (for example, "Po veche*ram* nad resto*ran*ami") and even tends to avoid a strict adherence to meter, so that it is not unusual to find occasionally an extra foot in one of Blok's lines. No Russian poet has written such successful combinations of bi- and tri-syllabic feet (a verse form also common in Heine's *Book of Songs*). More often than other modern poets, Blok rejects the monotony of regular quatrains and gives us his own free, non-stanzaic verse with alternating long and short lines, for he possesses an unerring ability to find the meter appropriate to each feeling. At the same time Blok's poetry has a distinct originality which assures it its own independent place in Russian literature.

Blok's treatment of rhyme is equally free. He often consciously chooses to replace it with alliteration *(gibeli-vyveli; prorubyu-postupyu)* or off-rhymes...[4] His great sensitivity to verbal music and his refined artistic taste enable him to emerge the victor from these risky experiments. Moreover, in the liberties that Blok takes there is nothing ostentatious or designed solely for effect. He likes his own audacity, but knows how to conceal it so that only the attentive reader is aware of it.

Blok holds a distinctive position among contemporary poets. He does not repeat the themes of other writers but with extreme candor draws the content of his poems out of the depths of his own soul. This gives his poetry a unique freshness, imbues it with vitality, and enables him to discover fresh sources of inspiration continually. Blok created his own individual style, but he has not let himself become confined to it, and in each new work he has sought new paths for his art. A great master of verse, although not one who strives for new forms at any and all costs, Blok is always attractive and engaging. His verses seem made for music, and in fact many of them have been set to music. No one reading Blok's intimate poetry for the first time would be likely to reject it, but thoughtful attention and immersion are required for a true understanding. One must enter the sphere of the poet's experience if one is to respond fully to it; Blok's poems must be read very carefully to be appreciated in all their originality and beauty.

1916

YURY TYNYANOV

BLOK

Blok's "literary judgments," in the strictest sense of the term, do not even enter into consideration when his image comes to mind. Hardly anyone remembering him now would even think of his articles.

What we have here is an organic trait. Whereas Andrei Bely's prose is close to his poetry and even the outcries in his "Diary" are literary and melodious, in Blok there is a sharp distinction between prose and poetry; on the one hand, there is Blok the poet, and on the other, Blok, the writer: the journalist, the historian and the philologist.

It would seem then that what we are mourning is the loss of the poet. But this grief is so genuine, so real and personal, that it touches even those who are not concerned with literature. Clearly there is another, a truer explanation for this grief, one that we all know deep within: it is the man that we are mourning.

And yet—did anyone really know this man? In Petrograd, where the poet lived, brief reminiscences appeared in an art journal immediately after his death. It is significant that these articles were not obituaries but *reminiscences*—to so great a degree was Blok a unique phenomenon, one ready to assume its place in the history of Russian poetry. And the reminiscences themselves were typical: Petrograd writers and artists recalled their incidental, fleeting encounters with the poet, the spare words uttered by him, and their conversations on such diverse matters as apples and book illustrations. This is the way the leading figures of long ago, such as Dostoevsky or Nekrasov, are remembered.

Very few people really *knew* Blok. As a person, he remained an enigma even to literary Petrograd, to say nothing of Russia as a whole. Yet throughout Russia they *know* Blok the man; they firmly believe in the authenticity of his image, and should a person by any chance come upon his picture, he would feel at once that he knows him thoroughly.

But where does this knowledge come from?

II

Herein, perhaps, lies the key to Blok's poetry, and if we cannot now answer the above question, we can at least pose it as comprehensively as possible.

The main theme of Blok's lyrical poetry is Blok. (This theme appears as an intriguing one for a new form of the novel, one not yet brought to birth or perhaps not even conceived.) It is about this *lyrical hero* that people are talking now. He was essential to them and a legend already has formed around him. Nor is this legend something new: it surrounded him from the very beginning. It seems to have even preceded Blok's poetry, so that his poetry merely filled in and completed an already existing image. His readers "personify" all of Blok's art into this image. When people talk about his poetry, they almost always subconsciously substitute a *human face* for it, and it is this *face* and not the *art* that everyone has come to love.

This "lyrical image" found the confines of the Symbolist canon constricting. The symbol embodied by the word drove Blok to the complex verbal structures of the "Snow Mask," while, on the other hand, the word could not endure the emotional strain and abandoned itself to the free spirit of the song. (By the way, his musical model was the traditional romance-ballad (*romans*) "Of valiant deeds, heroic feats and glory [III, 67],[1] the gypsy *romans*, and the factory workers' song—"Accordion, accordion" [II, 280]). However, this "lyrical image" had to strive to constrict itself into the rigid confines of the traditional verse novella. Among Blok's "verse novellas" (no matter whether they are in cycles or scattered throughout his works), those in which this happens stand apart: Ophelia and Hamlet, the Tsar's daughter and the Knight, the Knight and the Lady, Carmen, the Prince and the Maiden, the Mother and the Son.

Blok's image, familiar to all, originated here even in its physical features:

Розовая девушка встала на пороге,
И сказала мне, что я красив и высок.   1, 279

————

Влюбленность расцвела в кудрях
И в ранней грусти глаз.   11, 130

    A pink-cheeked maiden stood on the threshold,
    And told me that I was handsome and tall.

————

    Love flowered in his curly hair
    And in the early sadness of his eyes.

A vacillating light falls upon this image. Blok complicates it with the theme of the *other*, the *double*. At first this "other" appears separately and independently (the Clown), merely as a contrast to the first image, but in later poems it appears as a double:

> И жалкие крылья мои,
> Крылья вороньего пугала...   11, 9

> And my pitiful wings—
> The wings of a scarecrow...

In "Night Violet" ("Nochnaya fialka") the theme of the double is reduced to that vague "recollection of a previous existence" so dear to the Romantics:

> Был я *нищий бродяга,*
> Посетитель ночных ресторанов,
> А в избе собрались короли;
> Но запомнилось ясно,
> Что когда-то я был в их кругу
> И устами касался их чаши
> Где-то в скалах, на фьордах,
> Где уж нет ни морей, ни земли,
> Только в сумерках снежных
> Чуть блестят золотые венцы
> *Скандинавских владык.*   11, 29-30

> I was a *penniless wanderer,*
> A habitué of late-night cafes,
> And in a hut kings had gathered;
> But I clearly remembered
> That once I had been in their circle
> And my lips had touched their cup.
> Somewhere among the rocks, in fjords
> Where there is no longer either sea or land,
> But only, in a snowy twilight,
> The faint glimmering of the golden crowns
> Of *Scandinavian lords.*

In *Gray Morning (Sedoe utro)* Blok reintroduces the motif found in Musset and Polonsky[2] of the "aging youth" who "smiled impudently" (III, 16). The emotional power of this image lies precisely in this vacillating dual light: the knight who carries *spring* on the *point* of his spear and the *dishonorable and venal creature with dark blue circles under his eyes* (II, 115) merge into an image indefinable in concrete terms, yet emotionally complete *(the darkness of city streets).* Blok created several other lyrical images on this same pattern (in the "Unknown Lady" ["Neznakomka"], for instance), but his readers abstracted the double from them and identified it with Blok's lyrical hero.

And yet there is (or there seems to be) still one more image:

...Как тяжело ходить среди людей
И притворяться непогибшим,
И об игре трагической страстей
Повествовать еще нежившим...   111, 27

> How hard it is to walk among men
> *And to pretend to be still alive,*
> And to tell those who have yet to live
> Of passions' tragic game.

...Забавно жить, забавно знать,
Что все пройдет, что все не ново,
Что мертвому дано рождать
Бушующее жизнью слово.   11, 287

> It's amusing to live! Amusing to know
> That there is nothing new under the sun,
> *That dead men can give birth*
> *To words teeming with life.*

But readers do not think about this cold persona; for them it is eclipsed by the knight, the sailor, and the vagabond. Perhaps Blok first glimpsed it in Gogol, about whom he wrote: "A meeting with Gogol can hardly have been a pleasant, friendly encounter. It was easy to sense in him an old enemy; his soul gazed into the souls of others with the dim, lackluster eyes of the old world. One might easily have flinched from such a gaze."

Perhaps it was not by chance that the poem from which I have just quoted appeared in print next to the following poem:

Ведь я — сочинитель,
Человек, называющий все по имени,
Отнимающий аромат у живого цветка.   11, 288

> But I am a poet,
> A man who calls things by their name,
> Who removes the scent from the fresh flower.

This principle of personification, this *informing of words with a human face*—what does it consist of? How does it work?

Even a cursory glance at those lyrical subjects we have enumerated will convince us that what we have here are familiar, traditional figures. Some of them, such as Hamlet or Carmen, are so shopworn as to have become cliches.

Harlequin, Columbine, Pierrot and the Commander—favorite characters of Blok's lyric novellas—are also stereotypes. Sometimes it would seem that Blok deliberately chooses such epigraphs as the one from Kean[3]: "Be silent, you accursed strings!"

His images of "Russia" are equally traditional;some stem from Pushkin:

Когда звенит тоской острожной
Глухая песня ямщика!   111, 255

>When the coachman's muffled song
>Is heard in all its jail-like loneliness!

Others from Nekrasov:

Ты стоишь под метелицей дикой,
Роковая, родная страна.   111, 268

>You lie beneath a raging snow storm,
>My fateful native land.

Sometimes he borrows a lyrical theme from A. K. Tolstoi: "Uzh vecher svetloi *polosoyu.*" He does not even mind quoting directly:

В час равнодушного свиданья
Мы вспомним грустное прости.

>At the time of our indifferent encounter
>We shall remember our sad farewell.

>(K. M. S. "Luna prosnulas." Quoted from Polonsky.)

И молча жду, *тоскуя и любя...*

>Silently I wait, *in longing and in love.*

>("Predchuvstvuyu tebya." From Vladimir Solovyov.)

Затем, что *Солнцу нет возврата...*

>Because the *Sun will not return.*

>("Sny bezotchetny." Kupava in Ostrovsky's *Snow Maiden.*)

И вспоминая, сохранили
Те баснословные года...

And by remembering them we have preserved
Those legendary years.

("Proshli goda." From Tyutchev.)

Теперь проходит предо мною
Твоя *развенчанная тень...*

Now thy *uncrowned shadow*
Passes before me.

("Svoimi gorkimi slezami." From Pushkin.)

...И словно облаком суровым
Грядущий день заволокла.

And like a threatening cloud
It enveloped the approaching day.

("Opyat nad polem Kulikovom." From Vladimir Solovyov.)

What is significant here is the fact that Blok not only borrows images from other poets, but also underlines them and quotes their authors.

For Blok, theme and image are not important in themselves: their importance lies in their emotional power, as in dramatic art:

Тащитесь, траурные клячи,
Актеры, правьте ремесло,
Чтобы от *истины ходячей*
Всем стало *больно и светло.*　　　　11, 823

Drag along, you mournful nags,
You actors, ply your trade,
So that *pain and light* might
Come to all for *commonplace truth.*

He prefers traditional, even shopworn images (commonplace truths), because in them is preserved some long-standing emotionality. Slightly rejuvenated, the power of this emotionality is greater in strength and depth than the feeling conveyed by a new image, for novelty usually distracts one's attention from the emotion and directs it toward the object itself. For the same reason, where symbols are concerned, Blok does not shun strictly allegorical images, symbols long since ossified, or colloquial and commonplace metaphors:

Прохладной влагой синей ночи
Костер волненья залила...　　　　111, 67

With the cool moistness of the dark blue night
[Eternity] quenched the *fire of excitement*...

...По бледным *заревам искусства*
Узнали *жизни* гибельной *пожар!*..   111, 27

So they may recognize in the *pale glow of art*
The devouring *fires of life!*..

...Мой сирый дух — *твой верный пес*
У ног твоих грохочет цепью...

...My orphaned spirit—*thy faithful hound*
Rattles his chain at thy feet...

Над *кадилом мечтаний*...   111, 186

Above the *censer of dreams*...

Nor does Blok avoid the old-fashioned allegorical ode (as in the poem "Night"):

В длинном черном одеяньи,
В сонме черных колесниц,
В бледно-фосфорном сияньи
Ночь плывет путем цариц.   11, 48

Clad in long black garments,
With a swarm of black chariots,
In pale phosphorescence
Night flows in regal splendor.

He is not afraid to use such a banal, commonplace image as:

Тень Данта *с профилем орлинным*
О Новой Жизни мне поет.   111, 99

Dante's shade with its *eagle profile*
Sings to me of a New Life.

because these images are designed to play a specific role in the general composition of his art without calling attention to themselves. And by the same token, new images (of which he has many) must carry correspondingly new emotions:

И вздохнули духи, задремали ресницы,
Зашуршали тревожно шелка...   111, 25

And her perfumes sighed, eyelids grew heavy,
And her silks whispered anxiously...

Подурнела, пошла, обернулась,
Воротилась, чего-то ждала,
Проклинала, спиной обернулась,
И, должно быть, навеки ушла.   111, 219

Her face darkened, she walked away, turned around,
Came back, waited for something,
Cursed, turned her back
And left, probably forever.

Here we have completely new composite images that are incompatible from the standpoint of objective reality (that is, actions occurring on different temporal planes are presented side by side as though they were occurring simultaneously, and verbs of different aspects are grouped together: "vzdokhnuli dukhi" [her perfumes sighed], "zadremali resnitsy" [eyelids grew heavy], "podurnela" [her face darkened], "poshla" [she walked away], "proklinala" [cursed]).[4]

This is the reason why the *romans*, the most primitive and emotional of forms,[5] was the musical composition that served as a prototype for Blok's lyrics. By using epigraphs from gypsy *romansy*, Blok underscores his affinity with them: "Ne ukhodi, pobud so mnoyu" ("Don't go away, stay with me a while), "Utro tumannoe, utro sedoe" ("A foggy morning, a gray morning"); at the same time, however, he uses these epigraphs to establish a set melodic pattern; when reading the poem "Dym iz kostra struyoyu sizoi"("Smoke from the bonfire in a bluish-gray stream") one cannot help but yield to its melodic command. "Byla ty vsekh yarche, vernei i prelestnei" ("Brighter you were than the others, truer and lovelier")-a stylization of Apukhtin's poem—should also be read in the same purely lyrical, *romans* spirit.

It is no accident that in Blok's poems one so often encounters the familiar form "ty" [thou] with its direct ties to the reader and listener—a standard device in the *romans*.

But it is not only in these extreme forms of emotive art that we encounter the emphatic intonation of ordinary speech in a lofty lyrical theme:

Я, *наконец,* смертельно болен,
Дышу иным, иным томлюсь,
Закатом солнечным доволен
И вечной ночи не боюсь.   111, 67

At last, I am deathly ill,
I breathe a different air, I pine for other things.

> I am gladdened by the sunset
> And do not fear the everlasting night.

Here the parenthetical "at last," taken from everyday speech, influences the whole tonal coloring of this stanza, making it sound like a fragment of animated conversation.

And just as in the melodrama, that most emotional genre of dramatic art, the finale or denouement takes on a very special significance, so too, in Blok, the *end* of a poem plays a very special role.

In his early works the end repeats the beginning and joins with it to form a closed circle within which the emotion fluctuates; once the emotional key has been given, the emotion starts building up and at its highest point of tension falls back toward the beginning—in this way the end interlocks with the beginning to form a complete unit that continues, as it were, beyond the ending of the poem.

In Blok's later poems, however, the highest point—the climax toward which the entire poem seems to be directed—characteristically comes at the very end. Thus, the poem entitled "Already the brightness of the glance has dimmed" ("Uzhe pomerkla yasnost vzora") ends as follows:

> Когда в гаданьи, еле зримый,
> Встал предо мной, как редкий дым,
> Тот призрак, тот непобедимый...
> *И арфы спели: улетим.*   111, 185

> When I was in a mystic trance, that spirit
> Barely visible, like thin smoke,
> That invincible one rose before me
> *And the harps rang out: "We will soar."*

Here the highest point of tension is not just in the last stanza; it is reached only in the last *line* and even in the last *word*.

This trait is even more conspicuous in the poet's longer poems. In the "Unknown Lady," the theme of the restaurant in syncopated paeans, "Зала-мывая котелки" (Cocking their bowler hats), "Испытанные остряки" (The tried and tested wits) is replaced by the theme of the "unknown lady" expressed in iambs,

> И каждый вечер, в час назначенный
> (Иль это только снится мне?)...   11, 185

> And every evening, at the appointed hour,
> (Or am I only dreaming?)...

and tension builds up toward the end as the result of a monotonous sequence of sentences. In "The Twelve" as well, the last stanza with its highly lyrical structure caps a series of light verses in *chastushka* style,[7] in which Blok deliberately employs street vernacular. Not only is this stanza the high point of the poem, it also contains the poem's entire emotional theme, and consequently the work itself seems to be made up of variations on, fluctuations of, and deviations from this concluding theme.

That emotional quality that emerges from Blok's poetry strives toward intensification and embodiment and leads to the *human face behind that poetry.*

1921

B. M. EIKHENBAUM

BLOK'S FATE

He has praised God long enough.
He is no longer a voice, just a moan.

A. Blok

Blok's death has shaken us all, and not merely because he will no longer be writing poems—let us not be hypocritical before his fresh grave. Let those pretend who make it a custom to greet the emergence of a new poet with cruel laughter and follow his remains with sentimental tears. We did not laugh then and we do not weep now, because we live and die in an iron age where tears have no place. Death has become our true friend; let us behave with dignity in its silent presence, because our so-called "friends" can be crueler than our supposed enemy and it is them that we must learn to fight.

No, the reason why Blok's death has made a deep impression on us is not because he will not be writing any more poems. It would be exaggeration to think that art is so necessary to life, at least to what we normally call life. School teachers speak of our need for it out of naivete, bureaucrats because it is required of them. Blok himself answered them: "Putting hearts to the test of harmony is not a soothing process which will guarantee the mob that external events will follow a smooth and successful course." Art has much stronger ties with death than with life: because Life is lighthearted, talkative, and frivolous, while Death is serious and knows how to pick the most deserving people as its friends.

Furthermore, Blok had not been writing verses since 1918, and among those few who consider art truly valuable and necessary, Blok's name has already become an echo of the past. These is no need to hide the fact that as the fashion for Blok grew, a hostility toward him, not of a petty or incidental nature but organic and inevitable, also mounted and intensified. It was the hostility of a whole generation toward the "dictator of feelings," feelings which had lost their hypnotic power, their poetic impact, hostility toward the poetic canon which he had created and which had already become rigid in its immobility. This is not meant to be derogatory: only hostility and hate can save art when it becomes mere fashion.

There was something ghost-like in Blok's last collections of poems, *Beyond the Edge of Days Gone By* and *Gray Morning*. They were greeted with bewilderment. What many had perhaps been expecting after "The Twelve" was not there. No new paths at all, only old poems written between

1898 and 1916, which had been cast aside and not included in previous editions. Their titles seemed anachronistic, as though Blok were already dead.

Rumors began to spread about the "decline" of Blok. Almost simultaneously with his death, a review of *Gray Morning* appeared in the Moscow press. It is a good thing that Blok did not get to read it and that the author of the review did not know how eerie his words would sound. "Admirers of Blok, 'you girls,' you future lady dentists and deputies' girlfriends, secretaries and assistant secretaries, etc., etc., whatever you are called today or may be called tomorrow—*Blok is dead*. What do we find in this book? Pages filled with deadly anguish, inexpressible horror and inarticulate prayers into a void. Decay without bounds... Why did Blok publish this book? It must be that he could not help himself and with this book he pronounced his own sentence: *'from now on he is dead.'* "[1]

The harsh words of this critic turned out to be strangely prophetic. Now Blok in reality *"is dead."* And we are shaken because his death appears to us not just as a simple coincidence, but a preordained tragic denouement, the fifth act of the tragedy that we were all watching. Above all we are shaken because we are confronted with two coinciding deaths: the death of a poet and the death of a man.

Not long ago Blok himself had warned us of this denouement:

Как тяжело ходить среди людей
И притворяться непогибшим,
И об игре трагической страстей
Повествовать еще нежившим.

И, взглядываясь в свой ночной кошмар,
Строй находить в нестройном вихре чувства,
Чтобы по бледным заревам искусства
Узнали жизни гибельной пожар.

> How hard it is to walk among men
> And to pretend to be still alive,
> And to tell those who have yet to live
> Of passions' tragic game.
>
> And gazing into one's own nightmare,
> To find order in the chaotic whirlwind of feeling,
> So that they may recognize in the pale glow of art
> The devouring fires of life.

All we saw in these words was the "tragic play" of familiar emotions. Summoning us from the "pale glow of art" to the "fires of life," Blok led us away from real art, but did not bring us to real life. He became for us a tragic actor playing himself. Instead of a real (and of course impossible) fusion of life and art, we got an eerie stage illusion that destroyed both life and art. We no longer saw the poet and the man. What we saw was the mask of the tragic actor, and we fell under the hypnotic spell of his performance. We watched the mimicry of emotions almost without listening to the words. The knight of the Beautiful Lady, a Hamlet reflecting on non-existence, an habitue of taverns who abandons himself to the charms of gypsy girls, the gloomy prophet of chaos and death—all this was for us the consistent logical development of a single tragedy whose protagonist was Blok himself. Blok's poetry became for us the emotional monologue of a tragic actor, and Blok himself was this actor, made up to look like himself.

And then came the abrupt end of this tragedy: the stage death to which the whole course of the play has been directed turns out to be a real death... and we are shaken as spectators are when, in the fifth act of the tragedy and before their very eyes, the actor bleeds real blood. The footlights are turned off; Hamlet-Blok is truly dead:

И гибну, принц, в родном краю
Клинком отравленным заколот.

    And I am dying, prince, in my native land
    Pierced by a poisoned blade.

We always *contemplated* Blok, but did not look at him; we contemplated him as one does an exciting artistic phenomenon. Our attitude to his poetry was too emotional, our attitude to him too esthetic. Although he was the poet closest to us, bound to us by ties of profound spiritual affinity, he remained at the same time the most alien, the least understood. He "walked among men" in the aura of those emotions which he himself aroused. He died a mature man, but in our imagination he will always remain young. To imagine Blok as an old man is just as difficult as to imagine Tolstoi young. This is not surprising. The heroes of tragedies live before our eyes for a day or a few days and then perish without reaching old age. Such is the law of tragic genre. The tragedy of old age always runs the risk of turning into a comedy. King Lear needs a clown in order to maintain his own tragic stature.

Blok himself called his double an "aging youth":

Вдруг вижу, — из ночи туманной,
Шатаясь, подходит ко мне
Стареющий юноша (странно,
Не снился ли мне он во сне?).
Знаком этот образ печальный,
И где-то я видел его...

Быть может, себя самого
Я встретил на глади зеркальной?

> Suddenly I see, out of the misty night,
> An aging youth who, staggering, approaches me. (Strange,
> Was it in a dream that he appeared to me?)
> His mournful image is familiar,
> And I saw him somewhere...
> Or was it, perhaps, myself I met
> On the mirrored surface?

Blok's youthful appearance harmonized with his poetry, as the make-up of a tragic actor harmonizes with his monologue. When Blok appeared, it was almost frightening: he was so much like himself— a cabin boy from a northern vessel, agile and yet at the same time a bit clumsy, a bit angular in his movements, impetuous but strangely calm, with a smile almost childish yet at the same time enigmatic, with a voice that was dull and monotonous, with overly limpid eyes, reflecting, as it were, the pale waves of northern seas, with the gentle face of a youth which seemed burned by the rays of the polar glow....

We looked at him from afar, and could not bring ourselves to talk to him about life—although he acted simply with everyone and looked as though he were expecting questions... but the spectators were silent, observing with trepidation the "passions' game"....

The second generation of Symbolists is living through its moral crisis, its tragic catastrophe, and catastrophe demands victims, and the victims are always former leaders. Blok was destined to become the first victim because he had been the most powerful leader. Tired of being the dictator, he became the victim. He was in the grip of a deadly melancholy—and when he gave his speech on Pushkin (a writer's confession in which he clearly foretold his own death), he spoke gloomily and without hope, no longer as the captain of his destiny but as its victim: "What killed Pushkin was not D'Anthes' bullet, what killed him was lack of air... *Peace and freedom*: they are essential to the poet for the feeling of harmony. But peace and freedom too are being taken away. Not an external peace, but a creative one; not a puerile freedom, the freedom to play the liberal, but the creative freedom, the hidden freedom. The poet dies because he can no longer breathe; life has lost its meaning."

A victim—that is what Andrei Bely, another leader, also considers himself as he runs back and forth shouting and demanding "peace and concentration." In his *Diary of a Writer*, also a writer's confession, he shouts frantically for all Russia to hear, imagining that, worn out and hungry, she will listen to the histrionic complaints of a man of letters: "I am ill... don't summon me, a sick man—let my illness run its course; let Bely's mortal, suffering self sink into eternal sleep and write a will before death . . . I do not want to die without having said what is most essential . . . Thus I stand before my destiny with bitter pride; and realizing my inner strength, I address Russia straightforwardly and say with confident words 'You need me! And I know precisely why!' " But Russia remains silent, she could not care less about either literature or Andrei Bely's fate, or about the fate of Symbolism. Not only can she not save, but she has even forgotten how to bury, she has grown weary....

In Blok's death and in Andrei Bely's hysterical cries, the destiny of an entire generation is expressed, the destiny of the entire Symbolist movement, living itself out amid the horrors of our iron century. And this destiny is tragic because it did not happen by chance, it did not come crushing from without, but was unfolding for a long time, progressing from within.

We get lost in the mass of facts and of events which surround us on all sides; we don't know what to make of them, but we feel that there is an indissoluble organic bond among them. We do not know the fundamental causes which explain all things, but we see that our historical destinies are inwardly related to Symbolism, the principle of our spiritual culture. The ideologues of Symbolism who regarded themselves as missionaries, bearers of the new truth, and their art as a mystic service to truth, also sensed this bond and did not reject it. The "Scythianism"[2] of the Symbolists is not a chance phenomenon, nor is their passionate "maximalism," which prompted some to become censors and led others to the idyllic philosophy of permanent rebellion, some to anthroposophy and others, like Blok, to despondency and death: "life has lost its meaning." The prophets of the Revolution are now its gloomy observers. Bely, amid loud wails about his literary destiny, suddenly declares triumphantly: "We, the *humanists,* the freethinking *philosophers* who decry and lament violence, are the most refined oppressors, executioners and tyrants. The state monolopy of thought is the reflection of ourselves: we are the 'gate keepers,' and, oh yes, we are the Bolsheviks."[3]

Painfully and intensely Blok perceived all these hidden connections and felt himself a part of them. He felt the imminent tragedy of his generation and his own tragedy as its leader; not by chance did he speak so often of Destiny, Fate and Retribution. His favorite prose device was the "juxtaposition of phenomena, phenomena taken from various spheres of life that seemed to have no relation to one another." *(Catiline)* He sought analogies from the past in order to understand his own century and to justify his own destiny. Juxtaposing the Roman revolution and Catullus' verse, he speaks like a scientist: "I am convinced that only by means of these and similar comparisons can the key to an epoch by found, its pulse be felt, its meaning clarified." Yet this is not simply a "research method,"it is an inner necessity, applied Symbolism. Milyukov's[4] lecture, Andrei Yushchinsky's[5] murder in

Kiev, the stifling summer ("when grass was burning at the roots"), the strikes of railroad workers in London, the popularity of French wrestling in Petersburg's circuses, aviation, Stolypin's[6] murder—that is what 1911 was all about for Blok. "All these facts which seem so dissimilar have for me a single musical meaning. I am accustomed"—and here he repeats one of his recurring thoughts—"to juxtapose facts from all the spheres of life accessible to my vision at a given time, and I am convinced that they all create a unified single musical dynamic." (Preface to the last chapter of "Retribution.") Here Blok's thought coincides fully with that of a writer akin to him in spirit, Apollon Grigoryev, who wrote in his *Wanderings:* "Yes, in terms of history we do not live on as individuals; what lives on is ideas *(veyaniya)* of which we, the individuals, are more or less important representatives.... The parallels between world events in various spheres thus become absolutely plain—the strange, mysterious coincidences of the creation of Don Quixote and Hamlet, of revolutionary aspirations and Beethoven's music, etc."

Blok watched the events of everyday life keenly and anxiously, as though sensing that this life would demand retribution and compel us to listen. It is no accident that the poem "Retribution" is built on the juxtaposition of historical and family events: the life of one family and the "retribution of history, of the milieu, of the era." Blok also explains the transition from the melodic anapest to the Pushkinian iamb in terms of his era: "I think that the iamb was the simplest expression of the rhythm of that time when the world, anticipating prodigious events, was so vigorously and systematically developing its physical, political and military muscles. This is probably why I, who had so long been driven around the world by the lashes of the iamb, let myself be carried away by its resilient wave for long periods of time." This is a dangerous motivation for art, but to Blok, exhausted under the weight of a Symbolism replete with "juxtapositions of facts," it seemed essential, its salvation. He turned to it as a justification for his last step, a step which surprised many, but which was logically predetermined, an omen of the denouement: his transition from intimate lyrics to the poem "The Twelve," intentionally vulgar, convulsively harsh. Speaking of Catullus, Blok refers allegorically to himself: "Catullus' personal passion, like the passion of every poet, was permeated with the spirit of his epoch; its destiny, its rhythm and its beat, like the rhythm and the beat of the poet's verses, were inspired by the time he lived in, for in the poetic perception of the world there is no break between the personal and the general: the more sensitive the poet, the deeper he feels that what is 'his' and what is 'not his' are indissoluble. Thus in times of storm and turmoil even the most gentle and intimate aspirations of the poet's soul become filled with storm and turmoil."

The first generation of Symbolists was permeated with the pathos of a *mystic fusion* of contradictions into a single current of symbols, a current in which people, objects, and art itself were submerged. It did not feel the need to "juxtapose facts"; it did not have, nor could it have had a sense of the times, of actual historical reality, just as it did not and could not have had an awareness of what man was like. The magic of symbols was a cultural principle. Life had to be reduced to a shadow in order to fit into this system of symbols. A thing was recognized as valuable only if its spiritual essence "transpired," in other words, if it was not a thing. Finally, a word was recognized as worthwhile only if it possessed the magic power to evoke dim, amorphous images.

Fateful questions confronted the second generation. Stifled by this abstract culture, life demanded attention. Art demanded freedom from symbolism. "Things" rose up in mutiny, wanting tangible form and substance. The crisis of Symbolism began as both a cultural and an artistic awareness and Blok was destined to be saddled with the weight of the whole tormenting course of this crisis. He himself (in the preface to "Retribution") defines exactly when it all began: "The year 1910 was the crisis of Symbolism, a crisis about which much was then being said and written, both in the Symbolist camp and by the opposition. That year certain trends appeared which took an openly hostile stand toward Symbolism as well as to each other: Acmeism, Ego-Futurism, and early Futurism." Blok remained in the Symbolist camp, but instead of that blissful mystic radiance which had filled the first generation, there came into his soul *"the tragic awareness of both the incompatibility and essential unity of all things*, an awareness of irreconcilable contradictions demanding reconciliation." Instead of the inspired soaring to symbolic abstractions or the aspiration to capture the symbolic essence of reality, the "juxtaposition of facts" begins. In place of or next to the works of Swedenborg[7] there is an ordinary newspaper. Blok remembers the all-night discussions when he "first became *aware of both the essential unity and the incompatibility of art, life and politics.* Consciousness which probably had been raised by pressures from the outside was knocking simultaneously on all these doors and was *dissatisfied with the mystic fusion of all things* into one, a fusion that had been simple and possible in the true mystical haze preceding the first revolution and in the false mystical hangover that followed."

Here, in these nocturnal discussions of the year 1911, is the beginning of Blok's tragic destiny, the beginning of "retribution." From the depths of Symbolism itself, from Blok's own lips, came its condemnation as a principle of spiritual culture, as a principle of consciousness. The mystical "hangover" of the post-revolutionary period caused Blok to sober up. A realization of contradiction had arisen; a split in consciousness had appeared, leaving its imprint of tragic unrest upon the entire second generation. A split had occurred between mysticism and estheticism, between the question of proselytizing and the problem of craftsmanship. Blok began to feel "pressure from the outside," and it gradually grew stronger and more persistent. Revolution was followed by war. From this time on, Blok's voice sounds constrained and somber:

Рожденные в года глухие
Пути не помнят своего.
Мы—дети страшных лет России—
Забыть не в силах ничего.

Испепеляющие годы!
Безумья ль в вас, надежды ль в весть?
От дней войны, от дней свободы—
Кровавый отсвет в лицах есть.

     Those born in years of stagnation,
     Do not remember the path they trod.
     But we—the children of Russia's terrible years—
     Cannot forget anything.

     Years which burn everything to ashes!
     Do you herald madness or hope?
     The days of war and the days of freedom
     Cast a bloody glow on people's faces.

Russia replaces the Beautiful Lady; the period of the "patriotic" poems begins, the period of "Scythianism." The tragic realization of the "incompatibility and the essential unity" enters a new phase and becomes an esthetic theme:

Буду слушать голос Руси пьяной,
Отдыхать под крышей кабака.
. . . .
Да, и такой, моя Россия,
Ты всех краев дороже мне.

     I'll be listening to the voice of drunken Russia,
     I'll be resting under the tavern roof.
     . . . .
     Yes, and even this way, my Russia,
     You are dearer to me than all other lands.

Gypsy motifs combine in an original manner with civic ones—Fet and Polonsky with Nekrasov and Nikitin. Blok's lyric poetry turns to those traditions which in the beginning had been alien to his art:

И опять мы к тебе, Россия,
Добрели из чужой земли.

And back to you again, o Russia,
We trudged back from a foreign land.

But the roar of life, raging wildly over the conquered fields, grows deafening, and Blok begins anew his restless search for a fusion of art, life and politics. 1918 is the year of his maximalism: his article "Russia and the Intelligentsia," the poem "The Twelve," and the book on Catiline, a Roman "Bolshevik," as Blok sees him. This is an attempt to listen attentively to the "music" of the Revolution, an attempt to drown out his "personal" tragedy and anxiety in the roar of the world orchestra. Instead of his tragic mask, he now wears the mask of a stern prosecutor and preacher: "Woe to those who expect to find in the Revolution merely the realization of their dreams, however high and noble they may be. The Revolution, like a threatening whirlwind, like a snow storm, always brings the new and the unexpected. It deceives many cruelly; its maelstrom is quick to maim those who should be spared; it often leads to shore, safe and sound, those who least deserve it—but all these are isolated instances. They do not alter either the general flow of the current or its frightening and deafening roar. Nonetheless, this roar always means something *great*... Life is beautiful. Why should anyone—nation or person—live, who deep within no longer believes in anything? Life is worth living only if one makes unlimited demands upon it."

This is Blok's last attempt to reconcile contradictions, a problem which Symbolism had bequeathed him. He becomes the rhetorician and the sophist of the Revolution. This does not suit him at all, yet he must tear away the poet's mask of intimacy and tenderness—and expose a new mask beneath it. Here a contrast is called for and Blok changes his voice and his diction. Instead of a "juxtaposition of facts" there is a new attempt to fuse them, to drown out contradictions in the symbolic current of the Revolution. "Do not be afraid if fortresses, palaces, paintings, and books are destroyed. They should be preserved for the people, but even if they are lost, the people do not lose everything. A palace which has been destroyed is no longer a palace. The Kremlin erased from the face of the earth is no longer the Kremlin... What did you expect? That the Revolution would be an idyll? That creation would destroy nothing along its path? That people are angels?... Are you not perhaps the ones who should be awakened from your centuries-old sleep?... This is because from you who love little, much is expected, more than from anybody else."

Cicero's Latin is filtered through the tradition of a religious-philosophical society, the knight of the Beautiful Lady poses as a tribune, and Revolution, a "Snow Maiden," is surrounded by music and wind: "It is the business, the obligation of the artist... to listen to the music that fills the wind-torn air." "The Twelve" is born—an attempt to fulfill this obligation: to overcome, once and for all, the tragic awareness of the impossibility of fusing art, life, and politics, of finding among them any mystic bond. Christ, who appears unexpectedly at the end of the poem, is meant to fuse all contradictions into a single symbol. This is Blok's last attempt to save himself from his tragic fate, the last outcry of dying Symbolism. As usual the denouement occurs at the very moment when the hero of the tragedy thinks that he has been saved. Thus Wallenstein,[8] before falling asleep for the last time, asks not to be awakened early.

When the artist speaks of "obligation," he betrays art, and art does not forgive him. Blok did not succeed in saving himself—retribution came. Concealed behind the tribune's sober words is the presentiment of some future, inevitable deathly gloom. It is no wonder that in his book on Catiline, Blok speaks with such emotion about Ibsen, i.e., about himself: "An artist growing old differs from a young artist in that he withdraws and becomes immersed in himself. *An artist can never be false to himself even if he wants to be.* Of course, I do not say this to justify the artist, who needs no justification. Besides, it would be sacrilege to justify the artist in this manner, for this truth often contains within itself the roots of his *personal* tragedy."

The turn toward the already inevitable tragic denouement came at the pinnacle of Blok's maximalism and in a manner which was sudden and therefore terrifying, as tragedy demands. "Just before evening, the doorbell rang. Some young people I had never met before had come to take me to a charity function for the benefit of some very worthwhile and reputable cause. My task was to read some of my old poems, meaningful to me once, long ago—a morally questionable business." And here before Blok's troubled conscience rises the figure of Mephistopheles in the guise of a Russian dandy, of a "young man" reciting his own verse offstage: "a popular mixture of futuristic exclamations and symbolic whispers." At the end of the evening, on this dark and frosty night, a night just like the ones Blok used to depict, the young man joins him and speaks about himself, dispassionately, unmercifully and cynically as befits a Mephistopheles: "We are in the minority, but we still control the youth. We mock those who are interested in socialism, work, Revolution. We live only for poetry; in the past five years I have not missed a single new book of poems. . . It is you who are to blame for what we are. . . You poisoned us. We asked for bread and you gave us stones." And Blok admits: "I did not know how to defend myself; I did not want to, and . . . I could not."

This little story is the most frightening thing Blok ever wrote. It is not by chance that it ends with the famous word "retribution." It is the very same type of writer's confession we find in Bely. In the midst of exclamations about his grandiose future novel, Bely suddenly sees himself as the "most refined oppressor, executioner, and tyrant," and in the tyranny of Marxism, in the state monopoly of thought, he sees his own reflection: the dictator of the thought of an entire generation. Between listening to the mystical music of the Revolution and making speeches "in defense of Catiline," Blok sees with horror the "narrow and terrible well of dandyism," and at its bottom his own reflection: that of a dictator of feelings. Instead of the longed-for fusion of art, life, and politics, there was the juxtaposition of Symbolism, maximalism, and...dandyism, frightening in its "indivisibility and incompatibility."

From this moment on, Blok's will to create begins to weaken, and, by the same token, so does his will to live, because there is nothing left to support it. Again he withdraws within himself; again he starts meditating on matters of art and speaking of the necessity for a "secret freedom." His sketch "The Ghost of Rome and Monte Luca" ends with an unexpected digression *pro domo sua,* an unexpected confession: "It would be still better for me if I did not set down my recollections of this episode at all, but shared it only with my companion—she who experienced it with me; then it would not be covered with the dust of third-hand knowledge. But I did record it, and I feel the need to share it with others. Why? It is not because I want to tell others something amusing about myself or have them hear something about me that I consider lyrical, but because of something else—an intangible third force that belongs neither to me nor to others. It is this force which makes me see things the way I do and interpret all events from a particular perspective and then describe them as only I know how. This third force is art, and I am not a free man, since I serve it. *I am not a free man and although I am in government service, my position is an illegitimate one, for I am not free; I serve art, that third force which leads me from a complex of facts from the realm of life, to another complex of facts, which belongs to another realm all its own—the realm of art."*

The cycle has ended. He has rejected not only the fusion of art, life and politics, but the juxtaposition of facts as well. Art is declared a "third force," "a realm all its own." Blok also notes that he has overcome "the lyrical" in himself and thus has cleared the path for a classical art which is not bound by any "obligation" and free within its very limitations.

Yet this new path turned out to be no longer possible for Blok. The tragic denouement occurs precisely at such moments. Wallenstein exclaims:

> Can it be that I am not free in my actions?
> That I can no longer turn back?
> . . . .
> And yet even now I am still the same!

But death was already preparing its answer. Blok's essay ends on a pensive note: "Everyone now is in such a hurry..." And far in the distance resound the ominous footsteps of the Commander:

Настежь дверь. Из непромерной стужи,
Словно хриплый **бой ночных часов** —
Бой часов: —Ты звал меня на ужин.
—Я пришел. А ты готов?..

> The door opens wide. From the bitter cold,
> Like a raucous clock striking the night hours,
> Striking the hours: "You invited me to dinner.
> I have come. But are you ready?"...

Blok could no longer return to art. Speaking about Blok on the same impersonal plane (the plane of historical "retribution"), it should not be an insult to his memory to say that his last published books of poetry revealed a decline of his creative willpower, which had been strained to the breaking point by "The Twelve," whereas his Petersburg and Moscow recitals revealed a decline of his moral willpower. It is rumored that his trip to Moscow had a direct bearing on his fatal illness. These public appearances were never easy for Blok. It must have been unbearable for him to see himself merely as a modish poet sponsored by an impresario; it was unbearable and fatal to engage in the "morally questionable business" of reading some "old poems, meaningful [to him] once, long ago." Also, Mephistopheles must have tormented him too, but in a different, more terrifying way.... This was the crucifixion of self, also prophesied:

Когда в листве сырой и ржавой
Рябины заалеет гроздь, —
Когда палач рукой костлявой
Вобьет в ладонь последний гвоздь, —

Когда **над рябью рек свинцовой,**
В сырой и серой высоте,
Пред ликом родины суровой
Я закачаюсь на кресте...

> When among the damp and russet leaves
> Of the mountain ash the clusters of berries turn vermillion,
> When the executioner with his bony hand
> Drives the last nail into my palm,

When above the leaden ripple of rivers,
In the misty, gray heights,
Before the face of my austere homeland
I sway on the cross. . .

Death put an end to this crucifixion. Death itself speaks of it in Blok's lines:

Говорит *смерть:*

Когда осилила тревога,
И он в тоске обезумел,
Он разучился славить бога
И песни грешные запел.

Но, оторопью обуянный,
Он прозревал, и смутный рой
Былых видений, образ странный
Его преследовал порой.

Но он измучился—и ранний
Жар юности простыл—и вот
Тщета святых воспоминаний
Пред ним медлительно встает.

Он больше ни во что не верит,
Себя ли хочет обмануть,
А сам—к моей блаженной двери
Отыскивает вяло путь.

С него довольно славить бога—
Уж он—не голос, только—стон.
Я отворю. Пускай немного
Еще помучается он.

> *Death* **Speaks:**
>
> When anxiety overwhelmed him,
> And tedium drove him mad,
> **He forgot how to praise God**
> And started singing sinful songs.
>
> But in his state of bewilderment
> He began to see clearly, and the indistinct mass
> Of shapes from his past, that strange vision,
> Sometimes haunted him.

But he grew weary—and the first
Fires of youth grew cold—and now
The vanity of his sacred memories
Slowly looms before him.

He no longer believes in anything
And self-deception is all he seeks
As he wearily searches out the path
To my sacred door.

He praised God long enough—
He is no longer a voice, only a moan;
I will open it. Let him
Suffer a bit longer.

1910 was for Blok the year of three deaths: of Komissarzhevskaya, Vrubel, and Tolstoi.

These last years were for us years of innumerable deaths...but somewhere within them or prior to them are years of births still unknown to us.

Life goes on and with it the Retribution of History.

1921

VIKTOR ZHIRMUNSKY

Excerpts from *THE POETRY OF ALEXANDER BLOK*

I

Alexander Blok died on August 7, 1921 ...

Now, when his grave is still fresh and the pain of this sudden and very personal loss for all of us has not subsided yet, it is not the right time to speak of the poet in the objective tone of a historian. But with respect to Blok's poetry, our intimate and personal initiation into it give those of us of our generation who were raised on Blok and shared the joys and anguish of his songs, the feeling that we have a certain objective and impartial right to speak of the historical significance of his appearance among us, though our words may, by necessity, sound artificial and cold. In this respect we know more than future historians will who, approaching the lives and experiences of our contemporaries from the outside, will speak to "posterity" of the art of the last Romantic poet:

Чтобы по бледным заревам искусства
Узнали жизни гибельной пожар...

So that through the pale glow of art
They may recognize the destructive fires of life...

The new and artistic perception of life that shaped the development and writing of Blok's poetry, his life's path and poetic creativity, was his vivid awareness of the presence in the world of the infinite, divine and miraculous. This awareness colors all his poetic consciousness, giving it a new meaning, a new dimension, as it were, and an unusual, irrational and mysterious depth. It turns the poet's life into a religious tragedy in which "retribution" follows "the fall" and divine forces struggle with the demonic for the salvation of man's soul. It is from this religious perspective that Blok himself speaks about the course of his own life in the many "confessional" autobiographical poems of his last period. From the same perspective he judges, as a poet, his past and present:

Когда осилила тревога,
И он в тоске обезумел,
Он разучился славить бога
И песни грешные запел.

Но, оторопью, обуянный,
Он прозревал, и смутный рой
Былых видений, образ странный
Его преследовал порой...

С него довольно славить бога—
Уж он—не голос, только стон...

> When anxiety overwhelmed him,
> And tedium drove him mad,
> **He forgot how to praise God**
> And started singing sinful songs.

> But in his state of bewilderment
> He began to see clearly, and the indistinct mass
> Of shapes from his past, **strange visions**
> Sometimes haunted him...

> He praised God long enough—
> He is no longer a voice, only a moan...

"A poet's words are his business." For a Romantic poet who does not wish to be merely a writer of pretty verses, a "master in matters of poetics," but who in his poems either preaches or confesses, either prays or blasphemes and weeps—this statement invariably holds true. In all probability the time will come when biographers will disclose and publish the "Correspondence of Alexander Blok," the letters of this exceptionally modest poet who was highly secretive about his personal life, and some future historians will write his inner biography, the "tragedy of renunciation" of this, the last Romantic. But quite apart from that, it is perfectly clear to us even now that, without a proper understanding of Blok's early vision as a poet, his poems will seem to be only fantastic fabrications, romantic fairy tales, the pastime of a sickly and unbridled imagination. That is how at one time they impressed those early readers of his works who dismissed his poetry as "sham originality" and the "pretentiousness" of an **unintelligible** "decadent": and that is how they will impress (and probably in the not too distant future at that) the new generation of poets and readers who have overcome in themselves their own romantic mysticism. In his lyrical drama *The Unknown Lady,* **the contrast** between the poet's and the "throng's" evaluation of the phenomenon of mystical life is demonstrated by Blok with special clarity... "Gentlemen! Silence! Our wonderful poet will read to us his wonderful poem, and I hope it will again be about the beautiful lady..." "Fine, darling. I will call you Mary... There is something eccentric about you, isn't there?" This is on the plane of that everyday, real-life existence, which, however, is dismissed by the poet as "pseudo-reality," as illusory life. The main event of Blok's inner life, the only event that is truly important and genuinely real for him and by which he defines his destiny as poet and man, takes place in another reality. Of this most real reality, the poet speaks only in symbols and allegories:

—Протекали столетья, как сны.
Долго ждал я тебя на земле.

—Протекали столетья, как миги.
Я звездою в пространствах текла.

—Ты мерцала с твоей высоты
На моем голубом плаще.

—Ты гляделся в мои глаза.
Часто на небо смотришь ты?

> —The centuries were flowing by like dreams.
> Long have I waited for you on this earth."
>
> —The centuries were flowing by in a flash,
> I was floating in space like a star."
>
> —You glittered from your heights
> On my light blue cloak."
>
> —You saw your reflection in my eyes.
> Do you often look at the sky?"

And should we, in believing the reality of these poetic symbols, say to the Romantic poet (as did the simple, uncomplicated knight Bertran in *The Rose and the Cross*), "You are weaving fairy tales again," he will answer us in the words of the poet Gaetan: "And can't there be truth in fairy tales?"

Верь, мой друг, сказкам: я привык
Вникать в чудесный их язык
И постигать в обрывках слов
Туманный ход иных миров...

> Believe in fairy tales, my friend: I have grown accustomed
> To delving deep into their wondrous language,
> To catching in fragments of words
> The shadowy motion of other worlds.

Blok is the poet of love. But for him love was not merely emotional excitement, nor the natural succession of painful and joyful feelings. "Love is the knowledge of the mystery of being," "We are fully alive only when we love," says a German Romantic poet akin to Blok in spirit. And so it was in Blok's art: love was that individual emotional experience which revealed to the poet the objective, transcendent and highest mystery of life. This experience served as a springboard for mystical perception and determined the direction of the poet's life, and the content of his songs. The search for the true, the one and only love, is the goal of the Romantic lover; the poetic image of Don Juan, as interpreted by the Romantics (Hoffmann, Alfred de Musset in his poem "Namun," Alexei Tolstoi and others) is the most striking example of such a seeker. The Romantic Don Juan is not a crude sensualist who goes from one lover to another in his pursuit of pleasure; he is a young man who is romantically in love with the image of his only Love, the longed-for image, which once stirred his soul. In every woman he loves, the poet searches for this image which is always beckoning to him and is the sole object of his desires, but after each encounter he must resume his search and again be disillusioned, forever dissatisfied, forever consumed by a single, unending and unfulfillable desire. He is a faithless lover because of his own too deep and elemental loyalty to his first everlasting love. In the poem "The Footsteps of the Commander," Blok gives his interpretation of the Romantic Don Juan in the very hour when retribution is about to descend upon him for having betrayed his one true love:

> . . . Холодно и пусто в пышной спальне,
> Слуги спят, и ночь глуха.
> Из страны блаженной, незнакомой, дальней
> Слышно пенье петуха.
>
> Что изменнику блаженства звуки?
> Миги жизни сочтены.
> Донна Анна спит, скрестив на сердце руки,
> Донна Анна видит сны . . .
>
> . . . В час рассвета холодно и странно,
> В час рассвета—ночь мутна.
> Дева Света! Где ты, Донна Анна?
> Анна! Анна—Тишина. . .

> > . . . It is cold and desolate in the sumptuous bedchamber,
> > The servants are asleep, the night is deep.
> > From a blissful, unknown, distant land
> > A rooster's song is heard.

> What could these blissful sounds mean to a faithless lover?
> The minutes of his life are numbered.
> Donna Anna sleeps, her hands folded across her heart,
> Donna Anna dreams . . .
>
> . . . At the hour of dawn it is cold and strange,
> At the hour of dawn—the night is deep.
> Maid of Light! Where are you Donna Anna?
> Anna! Anna—Silence . . .

In his last poems (in volume III), Blok expressed the spirit of the Romantic Don Juan in a poetic formula:

> И в сердце первая любовь
> Жива к единственной на свете . . .
>
> And in my heart, my first love
> Responds to only one on this earth. . .

And he also defined the earthly fate of the "faithless lover," the wanderer, who is the prisoner of his unattainable dreams:

> Опять — любить Ее на небе
> И изменить Ей на земле . . .
>
> Again—to love Her in heaven
> And betray Her on earth . . .

And it is she whom he invokes at the end of his journey, speaking from the depths of "degradation," as the only bright image of his life, his sole justification as a poet, and it is to her alone that his repentant verses are addressed:

> Простишь ли мне мои мятели,
> Мой бред, поэзию и мрак?
>
> Will you forgive my storms,
> My ravings, poetry, and gloom?

In such a conception, romantic love ceases to be an isolated motif among a series of other poetic themes. It represents a basic tendency in the poet's development and becomes, by the same token, a determining factor in the history of his poetic art.

II

The poet's path unfolds before us as the path to a knowledge of life through love. The landmarks at the beginning and at the end of this path are the religious lyrics of the *Poems about the Beautiful Lady* and the gypsy themes of his last years. Hence, Vladimir Solovyov was his first teacher, and Apollon Grigoryev his companion and friend at the end of his life's journey. The succession of symbolic embodiments of his beloved in his poetry reflects the various stages of this inner experience.

Blok's youthful lyrics are full of romantic presentiments of a first, mysterious love: evening shadows, blue mists, transparent dawns, a glimpse of the celestial azure through spring clouds, and the first, indistinct summons of the infinite mysteriously stealing into his poet's soul along with the languor of spring and the anticipation of dawn (*Ante Lucem*):

Сумерки, сумерки вешние,
Хладные волны у ног,
В сердце—надежды нездешние,
Волны бегут на песок.
Отзвуки, песня далекая,
Но различить—не могу.
Плачет душа одинокая
Там на другом берегу . . .

Twilight, twilight of spring,
Cold waves at my feet,
In my heart—unearthly hopes,
Waves rushing onto the sand.
Echoes, a faraway song,
But I cannot make them out.
A lonely soul is weeping
There on the other shore . . .

His first vision of romantic love is the image of an unearthly Beloved One. She appears to the poet enveloped in a celestial, mysterious radiance: she is the "Beautiful Lady," the "Princess-Bride," "The Sunset," "The Mysterious Maiden," "Our Lady of the Universe," "The Majestic Eternal Wife." The poet calls her (always capitalizing the words) Radiant, Luminous, Bright, Goldenhaired, Unattainable, Holy. He is the knightly singer bowing in humble anticipation before the image of the Madonna and keeping "the commandment to serve the Ineffable One":

Бегут неверные дневные тени.
Высок и внятен колокольный зов.
Озарены церковные ступени,
Их камень жив—и ждет твоих шагов.

Ты здесь пройдешь, холодный камень тронешь,
Одетый страшной святостью веков,
И, может быть, **цветок** весны уронишь
Здесь в этой мгле, у строгих образов . . .

> The day's inconstant shadows are fleeting.
> The churchbells' call rings high and clear.
> The church steps glow with light,
> **Their stone is alive—and awaits your footsteps.**
>
> You'll walk through here and touch
> The cold stone cloaked in the awesome sanctity of ages,
> And perhaps you will drop a spring flower
> In this dusk by the stern-faced icons . . .

In his early poems, Blok was a disciple of Vladimir Solovyov, the poet of the "eternal feminine," the religious principle of love. A mystic feeling of expectation that the Eternal Feminine will manifest itself, that Divine Love will deign to favor him, permeates his *Poems about the Beautiful Lady.* The eschatological expectations that prompted a revival of the mystical in Russian poetry at the beginning of our century (as, for example in the poetry of Andrei Bely, Merezhkovsky and others) here assume the character of exciting **premonitions of some new and deeply personal revelation through love:**

Все виденья так мгновенны—
Буду ль верить им?
Но Владычицей вселенной,
Красотой неизреченной
Я, случайный, бедный, тленный,
Может быть, любим.

> **All visions are so ephemeral—**
> Shall I believe in them?
> But, perhaps I—accidental,
> Poor and frail—
> Am loved by One ineffably Beautiful,
> By the Sovereign Lady of the Universe.

His mystical presentiments of the manifestation of the Divine in love ("theophany") closely links Blok not only with the lyrics of Vladimir Solovyov but also—through Solovyov or perhaps, directly—with the "Hymns to the Night" of the German Romantic Novalis and with Dante's *La Vita Nuova*. But, side by side with the poet's belief in the reality of his vision, we find, already in the opening poem of his first book of verses, words which resound with doubt and fear. They are expressions of his human frailty, his impotence in the face of his wondrous gift; the possibility of his betrayal of his everlasting Love is foreshadowed, and one can also discern here the path of the poet's entire further development.

Предчувствую Тебя. Годы проходят мимо, —
Все в облике одном предчувствую Тебя.

Весь горизонт в огне — и ясен нестерпимо,
Я молча жду. — тоскуя и любя.

Весь горизонт в огне и близко появленье,
Но страшно мне: изменишь облик Ты,

И дерзкое возбудишь подозренье,
Сменив в конце привычные черты.

О, как паду — и горестно и низко,
Не одолев смертельные мечты!

Как ясен горизонт! И лучезарность близко.
Но страшно мне: изменишь облик Ты.

> I sense your approach. Years pass, but still
> My vision of You remains unchanged.
>
> The whole horizon is aflame and unbearably bright,
> Silently I wait, longing and loving.
>
> The whole horizon is aflame and the vision is near,
> And yet I fear: You'll come in another form,
>
> And will awaken in me an impudent suspicion
> By changing at the end Your familiar features.
>
> Oh, how I shall fall, so bitterly, so low,
> Without having mastered my earthly desires!
>
> How clear is the horizon! And the radiance is near,
> And yet I fear: You'll come in another form.

Unexpected Joy, Blok's second collection of poems (later included in the second volume), proceeds under the sign of this duality.

The poet finds himself "at the crossroads." The image of the heavenly Beloved has now receded into the past; it is shrouded in mist. Leaving the world of mysterious premonitions and visions, the poet enters earthly life. "Contemporary" motifs now begin to appear in his poems: the city at night flooded with electric lights, the noise of all-night restaurants and the faces of flesh and blood women. He searches for reflections of his unearthly vision in this life, dimly discerning in it the presence of another, more real reality.

В кабаках, в переулках, в извивах,
В электрическом сне наяву
Я искал бесконечно красивых,
И бессмертно влюбленных в молву.

> In taverns, in alleyways, and on street corners,
> Awake in an electric dream
> **I searched for the infinitely beautiful**
> And eternal lovers of small talk.

A woman whom he meets by chance on the street at night is transformed into the mysterious Unknown Lady and in this woman's features the poet perceives his one and only Beloved:

... И каждый вечер в час назначенный,
(Иль это только снится мне?)
Девичий стан, шелками схваченный,
В туманном движется окне.

И, медленно пройдя меж пьяными,
Всегда без спутников, одна,
Дыша духами и туманами,
Она садится у окна.

И веют древними поверьями
Ее упругие шелка,
И шляпа с траурными перьями,
И в кольцах узкая рука ...

> And every evening at the appointed hour,
> (Or is this only a dream?)
> Her girlish figure, tightly clad in silks,
> Moves across the misty windowpane.
>
> And passing slowly among the drunkards,
> Always alone, without companions,
> And breathing perfume and mists,
> She sits down by the window.
>
> And her smooth silks
> And her hat with its black **funereal feathers**
> And her slender hand adorned with rings
> Are redolent of ancient legends.

At this stage in the development of the poet's romantic consciousness, there appears for the first time that duality in his perception of life which was to be expressed in a more elaborate, finished form in the lyrical drama *The Unknown Lady*. (Compare it with the example cited above.) From now on, every poem he writes develops on two distinct planes—the first is the plane of everyday life, of actual "reality," and the second is the transcendental, and it is on this plane that spiritual events take place, events which for the poet are the only ones of importance and interest. Thus the familiar poem "In the Restaurant" tells of an accidental, and to all intents and purposes, insignificant encounter—the poet sees an unknown woman in a suburban restaurant, he sends her a rose, his eyes answer her indignant look with a bold and impudent stare, and so forth. But then, all of a sudden, this insignificant occurrence takes on a much deeper meaning when, behind the features of this unknown woman, the poet has a vision of his only Beloved, the one whom his soul had once beheld in his dreams:

> . . . Ты рванулась движеньем испуганной птицы,
> Ты прошла, словно сон мой, легла. . .
> И вздохнули духи, задремали ресницы
> Зашептались тревожно шелка . . .

> > You rushed away like a frightened bird,
> > You vanished lightly as a dream. . .
> > And perfumes sighed, eyes grew drowsy
> > And silks rustled disquietingly. . .

That is why the story of the "restaurant encounter" begins with agitated words which have the effect of emphasizing its unique significance. *"Never shall I forget* (Was there or wasn't there such an evening . . .)." And this also explains why the poet adopts a romantically heightened tone as he addresses the unknown woman:

> Я послал тебе черную розу в бокале
> Золотого, как небо, Аи . . .

> > I sent you a black rose in a goblet
> > Of champagne, as gold as the sky . . .

The romantic perception of "two realities" in the world, which is familiar to us from the fairy-tale stories of Hoffmann, has its own artistic laws. From the heights of mystical fervor, earthly reality seems illusory and unreal to the poet: romantic irony distorts this reality into hideous grotesquerie. Thus, in his description of the summer colony near St. Petersburg with which the ballad of the "Unknown Lady" opens (or of the tavern and the literary salon in the lyrical drama bearing the same title), we read:

Вдали, над пылью переулочной,
Над скукой загородных дач,
Чуть золотится крендель булочной,
И раздается детский плач.
. . . .
Над озером скрипят уключины,
И раздается женский визг,
А в небе, ко всему приученный,
Бессмысленно кривится диск.

> And far off, above the dusty side streets,
> Above the tedium of suburban *dachas,*
> A pretzel—a baker's sign—faintly glitters
> And one can hear the crying of children.
> . . . .
> Above the lake there is the squeaking of warlocks
> And shrill female voices resound,
> And in the sky, inured to everything
> The disc grimaces meaninglessly.

On the other hand, from the standpoint of day-to-day reality, the poet's own mystical insight can be doubted, and his vision of the Unknown Lady seems only a poetic illusion, a trick of the imagination, perhaps a waking dream. (See such expressions characteristic of his wavering sense of reality as "Or is this only a dream?" "You vanished lightly as a dream," "Was there or wasn't there such an evening..." and so forth.) The poet himself half gives in to the temptation of viewing his visions as daydreams or as hallucinations caused by drinking.

Из хрустального тумана,
Из невиданного сна,
Чей-то образ, чей-то странный . . .
(*В кабинете ресторана
За бутылкою вина*) . . .

> From out of a crystal fog,
> From out of a dream that was never dreamt
> Someone's image, someone's strange. . .
> (*In the booth of a restaurant
> Over a bottle of wine*) . . .

In the ballad of the "Unknown Lady" and also in the lyrical drama of the same name, the wondrous vision of the poet's only Beloved appears against the background of an all-night cabaret and this vision is explained by the gradually increasing drunkenness of the poet:

... И каждый вечер друг единственный
В моем стакане отражен
И влагой терпкой и таинственной,
Как я, смирен и оглушен ...

> And every evening I see reflected in my glass
> My one and only friend,
> And, like me, he is subdued and dazed
> **By the tart and mysterious moisture** ...

As in the tales of Hoffmann and Edgar Allan Poe, the features of the heavenly Beloved can be discerned through the poet's progressive stages of inebriation, a condition that breaks down the usual boundaries of perception:

... И перья страуса склоненные
В моем качаются мозгу,
И очи синие, бездонные
Цветут на дальнем берегу ...

> And the drooping ostrich feathers
> Sway in my brain,
> And the blue fathomless eyes
> Bloom on a distant shore ....

But for the romantic poet, intoxication has merely raised the curtain of consciousness, merely shown the path leading from the world of illusions to the world of reality:

Ты право, пьяное чудовище!
Я знаю: истина в вине ...

> You are right, you drunken monster!
> **I know: truth lies in wine** ...

From the "Unknown Lady" on, we note in Blok's poetic development some new elements which the poet himself, evaluating them from some higher point of view, regards as a cardinal sin and a defection, a betrayal of his early ideal of eternal love. But at the same time Blok's art gradually moves away from its devotional stillness and contemplative purity and is enriched by the complex, contradictory, earthly life, wretched and sinful. Significantly, his greatest poetic achievements belong to this very period. The basic themes of Blok's new poems (from the collection *Earth in Snow,* which was included in the second volume) are entry into life and a merging with life's creative, teeming, elemental forces by means of a keen and passionate experience of love:

О, весна без конца и без краю—
Без конца и без краю мечта!
Узнаю тебя, жизнь! Принимаю!
И приветствую звоном щита!

· ·

И встречаю тебя у порога-
С буйным ветром в змеиных кудрях,
С неразгаданным именем бога
На холодных и сжатых губах . . .

> O, Spring without end and without bounds,
> O endless and **boundless dream!**
> I recognize you, Life! I accept you!
> And welcome you with the clang of my shield!
>
> ·
>
> And I meet you at the threshold—
> **A wanton wind in serpentine curls,**
> **With the unfathomable name of God**
> On cold and tightly pressed lips . . .

The striving of the poet's soul remains essentially unchanged: the expectation of a miracle, the quest for the infinite, the escape from ordinary consciousness. The only change is in the direction of these romantic strivings, from a pure and sinless love for the heavenly Beloved to the caresses of a sinful and passionate worldly lover.

The image of the heavenly Beloved vanishes. The Snow Maiden, Faina, Valentina, Carmen represent the subsequent stages in the history of his romantic love.

Их было много. Но одною
Чертой соединил их я,
Одной безумной красотою,
Чье имя: страсть и жизнь моя . . .

> They were many. But one thing
> Bound them together for me—
> An irrational beauty
> Whose name is my passion and my life.

One thing links these images together: in the experience of passion, in the kisses and embraces of earthly lovers, the poet seeks moments of ecstasy, self-oblivion, ecstatic rapture. It is not the ordinary experience of love, but rather the extreme tension of passionate feelings which excites him because only they can transport him beyond the boundaries of everyday existence and into the world of inspiration and delirium—a mystical inebriation through the experience of passion.

Под ветром холодные плечи
Твои обнимать так отрадно;
Ты думаешь—нежная ласка,
Я знаю—восторг мятежа!

И теплятся очи, как свечи
Ночные, и слушаю жадно—
Шевелится страшная сказка,
И звездная дышит межа. . .

> In the wind, it is bliss
> To embrace your cold shoulders;
> You are thinking: it's a tender caress;
> I know it's the rapture of the storm.
>
> And eyes glimmer like candles in the night
> And greedily I listen:
> A frightening tale begins to stir
> And the starry vault breathes. . .

The whole "landscape of the soul" changes: instead of transparent spring dawns and gold-tinged blues, which used to accompany the apparition of the heavenly Beloved, there is a "howling" blizzard, a "gusty" wind "scorching" one's face, a "white-winged snowstorm on fire," a troika run amok, taking the poet and his lover over open "dark abysses" into the "snowy night."

И над твоим собольем мехом
Гуляет ветер голубой . . .

> Over your sable furs
> Roams a blue wind . . .

The boundlessness of an ecstatic love experience lends Blok's lyrics of this period (*The Earth in Snow, Night Hours*) a boldness and an irrationality of structure never before encountered in Russian poetry—a feeling, as it were, of the presence of an artistic primeval chaos, of unleashed cosmic forces, descending upon the poet from the "terrible" world of night and inundating the narrow region of bright daytime consciousness.

В легком сердце—страсть и беспечность,
Словно с моря мне подан знак.
Над бездонным провалом в вечность,
Задыхаясь летит рысак.

Снежный ветер, твое дыхание,
Опьяненные губы мои . . .
Валентина звезда, мечтание!
Как поют твои соловьи . . .

Страшный мир! Он для сердца тесен!
В нем—твоих поцелуев бред,
Темный морок цыганских песен,
Торопливых полет комет!

In the carefree breast—passion and light-heartedness,
As though I had been given a signal from the sea.
Across the bottomless abyss and into eternity
A breathless stallion flies.

A snowy wind, your breathing,
My drunken lips . . .
Valentina, my star, my dream!
I hear the singing of your nightingales . . .

Terrible world! It's too confining for the heart!
It holds the frenzy of your kisses,
The somber **gloom of gypsy songs**,
The hurried flight of comets!

The love lyrics of his last period lead Blok away from Vladimir Solovyov and towards **Apollon Grigoryev** and the gypsy *romans*. However, it's
clear from what was said before that what we have in Blok's art is not simply
a canonization of the gypsy song (i.e. of a secondary literary genre and its
distinctive themes which until now had remained outside the realm of lofty
poetry), but rather the complex conversion of these motifs, germane to the
poet, through the resources of romantic art and a mystic perception of life.
Blok was drawn to the gypsy *romans* by its elemental sweep of passion, by
its ecstasies and sorrows, but it was not merely its quality of abandon and
daring that drew him. He heard in them those "sounds from beyond" which
were first captured by **Apollon Grigoryev** (see his poems "**The Struggle**" and
"The Improvisation of a Wandering Romantic") and which inspired Dostoevsky to write the scene of Dmitry Karamazov's orgy with Grushenka at
Mokroe. The secret call and pull toward the passionate experience of love,
the mystical transports and flights of imagination—all these combine with a
feeling of sin and suffering, sadness and loss. But in that sin and suffering,
in the very image of the sinful beloved, there is something that calls and pulls
him, something that promises still unknown, impossible delights such as
escape from the confines of everyday life.

Неверная, лукавая,
Коварная,—пляши!
И будь навек отравою
Растраченной души.

С ума сойду, сойду с ума,
Безумствуя, **люблю,**
Что вся ты—ночь, и вся ты—тьма,
И вся ты во хмелю . . .

Что душу отняла мою,
Отравой извела,
Что о тебе, тебе пою,
И песням нет числа!

　　Unfaithful, cunning, insidious
　　Woman, dance on!
　　And be forever the poison
　　For my dissipated soul!

　　I'll lose my mind, my mind I'll lose,
　　Out of my mind I love
　　That all of you is night, that all of you is darkness,
　　That you are in a drunken haze. . .

　　That you have robbed me of my soul,
　　Poisoning it through and through,
　　That about you, about you I sing
　　And that my songs are endless!

In his last poems, which were later included in the second and in the third (posthumous) edition of his third volume, Blok is the poet of drunken, unbridled gypsy love and of a progressively heavier and more hopeless hangover. Instead of the rapturous flights of his first passionate poems there is an oppressive and increasingly stronger realization of spiritual disintegration and fall. Fall and sin open before the poet—with full clarity and in all their terrible religious significance—as "satanic depths":

Не таюсь я перед вами,
Посмотрите на меня:
Я стою перед пожарищ,
Обоженный языками,
Преисподнего огня.

> I am not hiding anything from you.
> Look at me:
> Amid charred ruins, I stand
> Burnt by the tongues
> Of an infernal fire.

Passion becomes torment and humiliation. The poet's soul seeks salvation on the "blue shores of heaven," but is unwittingly enticed back into the abyss.

> О, нет! Я не хочу, чтоб пали мы с тобой
> В объятья страстные! Чтоб долго длились муки,
> Когда—ни расплести сцепившиеся руки,
> Ни разомкнуть уста—нельзя во тьме ночной!
>
> Я слепнуть не хочу от молньи грозовой,
> Ни слушать скрипок вой (неистовые звуки!)
> Ни испытать прибой неизреченной скуки,
> Зарывшись в пепел твой горящей головой . . .
>
> . . . .
> Но ты меня зовешь! Твой ядовитый взгляд
> Иной пророчит рай! —Я уступаю, зная
> Что твой змейный рай—бездонный скуки ад.

> O, no! I do not want for you and me to fall
> Into passionate embraces, or that long drawn out torment
> When it's impossible to disentangle our entwined arms
> Or to bring apart our lips is impossible in the darkness of night.
>
> I do not want to be blinded by thunderous lightning
> Or listen to wailing violins (those frenzied sounds!)
> Or feel the pounding surf of unspoken boredom,
> Once I have buried my burning head deep into your ashes.
>
> . . . .
> But you are calling me! Your venomous glance
> Foretells a different heaven! —I give in, knowing
> That your serpentine paradise is boredom's bottomless hell.

The awareness of spiritual humiliation, of sin and fall, permeates all of Blok's later poems (e.g., especially, "Humiliation," "Black Blood," and, generally speaking, sections of "Terrible World" and "Retribution"), but in this very fall there are ecstatic flights of mystic passion, a wild intoxication with the eternal:

Даже имя твое презренно,
Но, когда ты сощуришь глаза,
Слышу—воет поток многопенный,
Из пустыни подходит гроза.

> Your very name I find despicable,
> But when your eyes flash angrily,
> I hear the howling of foaming waves,
> The approach of a storm from the desert.

But then again the image of his non-earthly Beloved returns to haunt his memory ("Do you remember your first love, and the dawns, the dawns, the dawns"), only now it reproaches the "apostate" threatening him with an imminent "retribution" or a repentance which will come too late ("The Steps of the Commander"):

. . . Что теперь твоя постылая свобода,
Страх познавший Дон Жуан?
. . . .
Что изменнику блаженства звуки?
Миги жизни сочтены . . .

> . . . What is your odious freedom,
> Now that you know fear, Don Juan?
> . . . .
> What are the sounds of bliss
> To a traitor—the seconds of his life are numbered . . .

From the depths of his fall the poet invokes once more his childlike vision of chaste and sinless love ("O, brief, tender kisses, which cannot be sold ! O, caresses of girls who cannot be bought!"). The image of the one and only Beloved rises before us in the poet's repentant, autobiographical verses:

Летели дни, крутясь проклятым роем,
Вино и страсть терзали жизнь мою . . .
И вспомнил я тебя пред аналоем,
И звал тебя, как молодость свою.

Я звал тебя, но ты не оглянулась,
Я слезы лил, но ты не снизошла.
Ты в синий плащ печально завернулась,
В сырую ночь ты из дому ушла.

> Whirling in a cursed swarm, the days were flying by,
> Wine and passion were ravaging my life . . .
> Then I remembered you before the altar
> And I called you, as if calling my youth.
>
> I called you, but you did not glance 'round,
> I shed tears, but you did not respond.
> Mournfully wrapping yourself in your blue cloak
> You left your home and stepped into the damp night . . .

But these memories belong to a distant past and can no longer serve any purpose at this time. More and more the poet speaks of life as "empty," as "lived in vain," "dull and senseless," "senseless and fathomless."

> И стало беспощадно ясно—
> Жизнь отшумела и прошла . . .
>
> And it has become mercilessly clear:
> The sounds of life have vanished . . .

Hopeless emptiness and boredom, like a heavy hangover, replace the boundless ecstasy and pain of earlier years. The "gray morning" dawns and is followed by "the cruel day, the iron day."

> О, как я был богат когда-то,
> Да все—не стоит пятака:
> Вражда, любовь, вино и злато,
> А пуще—смертная тоска . . .
>
> O, how rich I was once,
> But it was all for nought;
> Enmity, love, wine and gold,
> And above all—deadly tedium . . .

Hate for his past, hopelessness about his future, and in the present, a hopeless sorrow and ennui, that "acedia" about which the old religious writers spoke (or using newer though less significant analogies, a *Weltschmerz* or Baudelairean "spleen"), gradually possess the poet like some metaphysical "secretly and irrevocably gnawing illness" (especially in "Dances of Death" and in "Life of My Friend" in the section "Terrible World").

> Ночь, улица, фонарь, аптека,
> Бессмысленный и тусклый свет.
> Живи еще хоть четверть века—
> Все будет так. Исхода нет.

Умрешь—начнешь опять сначала,
И повторится все, как встарь:
Ночь, ледяная рябь канала,
Аптека, улица, фонарь.

> Night, a street, a lamp, a pharmacy,
> A meaningless, dull light,
> Even if you live anouther quarter-century
> Nothing will change. There is no way out.

> You'll die—you'll start again from the beginning.
> And it will all be repeated as of old:
> The night, the icy ripples on the canal
> The pharmacy, the street, the lamp.

Perhaps the most eloquent expression of this last phase in the development of the Romantic poet is found in the poem "To My Muse," a poem which significantly was assigned to the third volume. Here the Muse and the Beloved blend into one image, and the intimate and personal experience of love broadens into an impersonal interpretation of the meaning of life, as seen through love. In terms of the depth and power of his tragic perception of life, Blok's poem is very much like some of Tyutchev's more mature poems, those dedicated to his tragic "last love." Compare the verbal coincidence: Tyutchev writes: "There Are in My Painful Lethargy," and Blok:

Есть в напевах твоих сокровенных
Роковая о гибели весть,
Есть проклятье заветов священных
Поругание счастья есть.

И такая влекущая сила,
Что готов я твердить за **молвой**,
Будто ангелов ты низводила,
Соблазняя своей красотой . . .

. . . Я не знаю, зачем на рассвете,
В час, когда уже не было сил,
Не погиб я, но лик твой заметил,
И твоих утешений просил?. . .

И коварнее северной ночи,
И хмельней золотого Аи,
И любови цыганской короче
Были страшные ласки твои . . .

И была роковая отрада
В попираньи заветных святынь,
И безумная сердцу услада—
Эта горькая страсть, как полынь!

> There is in your secret melodies
> A fateful omen of doom,
> There is a curse on sacred traditions
> There is the profanation of happiness.
>
> And a power so alluring
> That I am ready to confirm the rumor
> That you made angels fall,
> Seducing them with your beauty . . .
>
> . . . And I don't know why at daybreak,
> When my strength was failing,
> I did not perish, but noticed your face
> And begged you to comfort me . . .
>
> . . . And more perfidious than a Nordic night,
> More inebriating than the golden Ai
> And briefer than gypsy love
> Were your terrifying caresses.
>
> And there was a fateful joy
> In trampling on all that was sacred,
> And this passion, bitter as wormwood,
> Was a mad delight for the heart!

What is the source of the tragic in this poem, the source of the deepest conflict and despair in the very passion of love? What is expressed in these words are not the simple, ordinary pangs of love, but infinitely deep spiritual torments, a religious illness of exceptional intensity. The "terrifying caresses" of the Beloved (let us also remember the "terrifying tale," the "terrifying world," "the terrifying embraces"), the "trampling on all that was sacred," "beauty" not as a joy but as a "curse" ("the whole curse of your beauty!") all this opens before us a whole world of emotional experiences about which Dostoevsky speaks more eloquently than anyone else:

Beauty—what a terrible and terrifying thing! It is so terrifying because it is undefinable, and it is impossible to define because God sets up nothing but riddles. Here opposite shores meet and contradictions exist side by side... Beauty! Furthermore, I cannot endure the thought that a man of lofty heart and superior intelligence may start out with the ideal of the Madonna and end with the ideal of Sodom. And what is more frightening is that with the ideal of Sodom in his soul he does not repudiate the ideal of the Madonna which burns in his heart, truly it burns, as it did when he was young and innocent. No! Man is broad, even too broad. I would have him narrow. The devil only knows what all this means! What is shameful to the mind is beauty to the heart, through and through. Can there be beauty in Sodom? Believe me, for the majority of men that's where it lies, did you know this secret or not? And what's so terrible is that beauty is not only a terrifying but a mysterious thing. Here the devil fights with God and their battlefield is the heart of man.

These words by Dostoevsky offer the most profound interpretation of Alexander Blok's tragic poetry. What is it that led the poet of the Beautiful Lady down these paths, that brought him from "the ideal of the Madonna" to the "ideal of Sodom"? A mystical yearning for infinity, the search for emotional experiences extraordinary in their intensity, for moments of ecstasy—be it in sin and suffering—which hold or promise that "taste of the infinite" *(goût de l'infini)* without which everyday life with its simple and modest sufferings and joys seems monotonous and empty. In this respect, as was already stated, the exciting premonition of the appearance of the "Tsarevna-Bride," when the poet loved purely and sinlessly, is born out of those same aspirations as the passionate and sinful predilections of his later years. "Can there be beauty in Sodom?" Both here and there the Romantic poet is the seeker of infinite happiness.

> Что счастье? Вечерние прохлады.
> В темнеющем саду, в лесной глуши?
> Иль мрачные, порочные услады,
> Вина, страстей, погибели души?

>> What is happiness? The cool of evening
>> In the darkening garden, in the thick of the forest?
>> Or the gloomy, sinful delights
>> Of wine, of passion, of the soul's doom?

This "spiritual maximalism" of the Romantic-individualist springs from a sense of the infinity of the human soul, from its incapacity to be satisfied with the finite and the limited. The soul poisoned by boundless desires seeks an infinite variety of emotional experiences which alone can satisfy its mystical hunger. Boundless demands on life, the search for the unusual and the miraculous make simple, everyday reality seem colorless. The realization of the emptiness of everyday life, the heavy hangover, the "dull, senseless boredom without a cause, and the chronic pollution of thought" inevitably follow the tormenting flights of passionate feelings.

The Romantic era at the beginning of the nineteenth century experienced this sense of the infinity of the human soul for which there is no fulfillment, these boundless demands on life, this impotence in finding answers to satisfy an awakening religious consciousness. There were many possible stages in the development of Romantic "maximalism" from theomachy, from the disillusionment and religious despair of Byron to the religious submission and morbid surrender of personal will and happiness of the German Romantics committed to the mystic worldview of the Medieval church. In the love lyrics of Alfred de Musset[2] and especially of Clemens Brentano[3] (who in many ways was closer to Blok than other contemporaries) we find, in those same familiar forms, the Romantic rift between the ideal of the Madonna and the ideal of Sodom. But it was Dostoevsky who came closer than anyone else to this problem as though anticipating in his art the emergence of Blok: in his novels, as in Blok's poems, the Russian folk element found self-expression—that "absence of measure in everything," that "maximalism of the spirit" whereby all that has limits and conditions in the course of our temporal lives is only an impediment to the unlimited and reckless yearning for creative freedom and self-affirmation. "Man is broad, even too broad. I would have him narrower. Here the devil fights with God and their battlefield is the heart of man."

1921

OSIP MANDELSTAM

THE BADGER'S DEN
(A. Blok: August 7, 1921–August 7, 1922)

The first anniversary of Blok's death should be a modest one: the seventh of August is just beginning to live in the Russian calendar. Blok's posthumous existence, his new destiny, his *Vita Nuova* is in its infancy.

The swampy vapors of Russian criticism, the heavy, noxious fog of Ivanov-Razumnik, Aikhenvald, Zorgenfrei, and others, which have thickened over this past year, have not yet lifted.

Lyrics continue to be written about lyrics. The worst kind of lyrical mating call. Conjectures. Arbitrary premises. Metaphysical puzzles. It is all flimsy, unfounded: interpretations off the top of one's head. One does not envy the reader who might want to gain an *understanding* of Blok from the critical literature of 1921–1922.

"Serious works," namely the works of Eikhenbaum and Zhirmunsky, drown in this litany, in the swampy mists of Russian criticism.

Already from the very first steps of his posthumous life we must learn to *understand* Blok, to fight the optical illusion of subjective interpretation with its inevitable coefficient of distortion. By gradually complementing our study of the poet with factual and indisputable material we clear the way for his posthumous fate.

The establishment of the literary genesis of the poet, of his literary sources, of his kinship and roots immediately brings us onto firm ground. The questions of what the poet wanted to say, the critic may or may not want to answer, but he is obliged to answer the question of where he came from . . .

As we survey the whole of Blok's poetic activity we can distinguish in it two streams, two separate beginnings: one Russian, domestic, parochial, and the other European. The eighties were Blok's cradle and it is significant that at the end of the road, in the poem "Retribution," Blok, already a mature poet, returned to his life sources, to the eighties.

The domestic and the European are two poles, not only of Blok's poetry, but of all Russian culture of the last decades. Beginning with Apollon Grigoryev it became evident that a profound spiritual schism existed in Russian society. Detachment from European interests, alienation from the unity of European culture, desertion of the hearth—an act akin to heresy and which out of shame we were afraid to admit even to ourselves—all of this was a *fait accompli*. As though anxious to rectify someone's mistake and obliterate the guilt of an inarticulate generation whose memory was short but whose love was passionate though limited, in his own name as well as in the

name of the people of the eighties, the sixties, and the forties, Blok solemnly
pledges:

Мы любим все: парижских улиц ад
И венецьянские прохлады,
Лимонных рощ далекий аромат
И Кельна дымные прохлады.

> We love everything: the hell of Paris streets
> And Venice's cool breezes,
> The distant fragrance of lemon groves
> And the smoky structures of Cologne.

But furthermore Blok loved history and maintained an historical objectivity toward that domestic period of Russian history which passed under
the banner of "intelligentsia and populism." He considered Nekrasov's heavy
ternary meter as lofty as Hesiod's *Work and Days*. The seven-string guitar,
the friend of Apollon Grigoryev, was for him no less sacred than the classical
lyre. He assimilated the gypsy *romans* and turned it into the language of
passion, understandable to all. And it seems that in the brilliant light of
Blok's perception of Russian reality, Sofia Perovskaya's[1] forehead, high
like a mathematician's, already casts forth the marble chill of true **immortality.**

One cannot stop marveling at Blok's sense of history. Long before he
urged us to listen to the music of the Revolution, he was already listening to
the underground music of Russian history, *there* where the most attentively
strained ear caught only a syncopated pause. From every line of Blok's
poetry about Russia Kostomorov,[2] Solovyov and **Klyuchevsky** stare at us;
namely **Klyuchevsky**,[3] that kind genius, the guardian spirit, the patron of
Russian culture under whose patronage one need not fear trials or tribu-
lations.

Blok was a man of the nineteenth century and he knew that the days of
his century were numbered. He greedily widened and deepened his inner
world in *time*, just as a badger burrows into the ground, preparing his den,
building two exits. The century one lives in is one's "badger's den" and to
each is apportioned a narrow, limited space in which to move about; each
frenziedly tries to expand his territory, treasuring above all else the exits from
his underground den. Moved by his badger's instinct, Blok deepened his poetic
knowledge of the nineteenth century. English and German Romanticism,
Novalis' blue flower, Heine's irony, an almost Pushkinian thirst to touch his
parched lips to the springs of European folk art—the English, French, German, all soothing in their purity and each pulsating with independent life—
long haunted Blok. Among Blok's creations are those directly inspired by the
Anglo-Saxon, the Romance, the German genius, and the immediacy of this

inspiration once more reminds one of the *Feast in Time of Plague* and of that place where "the fragrance of lemon and laurel fills the night" and of the song "I Drink To Mary." All the poetics of the nineteenth century— these are the boundaries of Blok's dominion. Here he is tsar, here his voice gains power, its movements become authoritative and its intonations compelling. The ease with which Blok uses the thematic material from these poetics makes one realize that certain subjects, until recently individual and incidental, right before our eyes have acquired equal stature with myth. Such are the themes of Carmen and Juan. Mérimée's compact and superb story met with good luck: Bizet's light, martial music, like a call to arms, spread to every remote corner the message of eternal youth and of the thirst for life of the Romance race. Blok's verses give the youngest of European myth-legends its most recent abode. But the summit of Blok's historical poetics, the triumph of the European myth, one which moves freely in traditional forms, unafraid of the anachronistic or the modern, is "The Steps of the Commander." Here strata of time lie upon one another in a freshly plowed poetic consciousness and the seeds of the old theme bear an abundance of shoots ("Quiet, black as an owl, the car . .From a blissful, unknown distant land a rooster's song is heard.").

II

In literary matters Blok was an enlightened conservative. He was exceedingly cautious with everything concerning style, metrics or imagery: not one overt break with the past. To see Blok as an innovator in literature is to picture an English lord introducing with great tact a new bill into Parliament. This conservatism of his was somehow more English than Russian, a literary revolution within the framework of tradition and irreproachable loyalty. Beginning with a direct, an almost pupil-like dependence on Vladimir Solovyov and Fet, Blok to the very end did not break any of his commitments, did not forsake a single loyalty, did not trample upon a single canon. He only complicated his poetic credo with more and more loyalties: thus, rather late in his career he introduced Nekrasov's canon into his poetry, and much later still he experienced the direct, dogmatic influence of Pushkin—a case extremely rare in Russian poetry. It was not characterlessness that affected Blok's literary susceptibility: he felt style deeply as species and that is why he perceived the development of language and literary form not as break and destruction but as interbreeding, the coupling of different species and bloods and the grafting of different fruits onto one tree.

The most startling and harshest of all Blok's works, "The Twelve," is nothing other than an application of an independent, literary form already in existence–the *chastushka*. The poem "The Twelve" is a monumental dramatic *chastushka*. The center of gravity is in the composition, in the arrangement of parts and, as a result, the transition from one *chastushka* passage to another assumes a special expressiveness and every transition in the poem is the source of discharge of fresh dramatic energy. The power of "The Twelve," however, is not only in its composition, but in its material as well, drawn directly from folklore. Here is captured and preserved the language of the street, such ephemeral slang as "She's got *Kerenki*[4] in her stocking," and it is all woven into the general texture of the poem with the most remarkable self-confidence. The value of folklore in "The Twelve" brings to mind the conversations of the minor characters in *War and Peace*. Whatever the various idle interpretations of this poem may be, "The Twelve" as folklore is immortal.

The poetry of the Symbolists was wide-ranging, rapacious: they, that is, Balmont, Bryusov, Andrei Bely, were discovering new territories for themselves, were laying them waste and, like conquerors, aimed further ahead. Blok's poetry, from beginning to end, from the poems about "The Beautiful Lady" to "The Twelve," was intensive and creative in a cultural sense. The thematic development of his poetry went from cult to cult: from "The Unknown Lady" and "The Beautiful Lady" through "The Puppet Show" and "The Snow Mask" to Russia and Russian culture and later to the Revolution as the musical climax and cataclysmic essence of culture. The spiritual makeup of the poet gravitated toward catastrophe. For both cult and culture presume a secret and protected source of energy as well as an even and expedient movement: "Love which moves the sun and the other stars." Poetic culture arises from the attempt to ward off catastrophe, to make it subject to the central sun of the entire system, be it that love of which Dante spoke, or the "music" at which Blok ultimately arrived.

Of Blok one can say that he is the poet of "The Unknown Lady" and of Russian culture; needless to say, it is absurd to assume that the Unknown Lady and the Beautiful Lady are symbols of Russian culture. It is, however, the very need for cult–the expedient discharge of poetic energy–that guided Blok's thematic creativity and found its highest gratification in the service of Russian culture and Revolution.

BORIS PASTERNAK

Excerpts from *PEOPLE AND SITUATIONS*

What is literature in the accepted and most common meaning of the word? It is the realm of eloquence, of platitudes, of well-coined phrases and venerable names of authors who, when young, had been in touch with reality, but upon achieving fame, turned to abstraction, repetition and rationalization. And when in this realm of conventional and hence imperceptible artificiality someone speaks out—not because of his penchant for the elegant phrase, but because he knows something and wants to say it—such an event creates an upheaval. It is as if it were not some individual announcing what was going on in town, but as if the town itself with a human voice were proclaiming its own presence. And that's how it was with Blok. Such was the effect and power of his word, uncorrupted like that of a child.

There was something new about the way a poem of his looked on paper. It seemed as though the words had settled down on the printed page without anyone's invitation, as though no one had composed or written the poem. It seemed that what filled the page were not verses about winds and puddles, street lamps and stars, but that the street lamps and the stars themselves were chasing their own reflection across the wind-swept rippling waters of the printed page, leaving on it their own damp, deeply informing traces.

* * *

Some of us, part of my generation, spent our youth under the influence of Blok. . . . Blok had all the attributes of a great poet: fire, gentleness, penetration, a personal worldview, a unique all-transmuting touch, a private, secret, exclusive fate. Of these traits and many others still, I will mention only what impresses me most and what, perhaps for this reason, strikes me as most characteristic of him: the typically Blokian directness, the intensity of his searching gaze, the swiftness of his observations:

Свет в окошке шатался,
В полумраке—один—
У подъезда шептался
С темнотой арлекин.

> A light was flickering in the window.
> All alone, in the twilight
> By the doorway, a harlequin
> Was speaking in whispers to the darkness.

По улицам метель метет,
Свивается, шатается,
Мне кто-то руку подает
И кто-то улыбается.

> Along the street the snowstorm sweeps
> Whirling, swirling,
> Someone extends his hand to me
> And someone smiles.

Там кто-то машет, дразнит светом.
Так зимней ночью на крыльцо
Тень чья-то глядит силуэтом
И быстро скроется лицо.

> Someone there waves, a teasing light
> So on a stoop, one wintry night
> Someone's shadow gazes in the form of a silhouette
> And a face will quickly vanish.

Adjectives without nouns, predicates without subjects, hide-and-seek games, turmoil, figures quickly flashing by, abruptness—oh, how well this style conformed to the spirit of the times: secretive, esoteric, surreptitious, a spirit barely emerged from the underground and expressing itself in the language of conspirators whose ringleader was the town and whose chief arena was the street. Blok's very being is permeated with these characteristics. It is this basic Blok who predominates in the second volume of the Alkonost edition, the Blok who wrote "The Terrible World," "The Last Day," "Deception," "A Short Novel," "The Legend," "The Meeting," "The Unknown Lady," and the poems "In the Fog above the Sparkling Dew," "In Taverns, in Alleyways, on Street Corners," "A Girl was Singing in the Church Choir."

The gust of Blok's sensitivity, like a current of fresh air, impels the shapes and features of reality to come streaming into his books—but more than that: even that which is far from reality, which might seem mystic or might be called "divine." These are not metaphysical fantasies but snatches of actual, everyday church vernacular, excerpts from litanies, quotations from the Orthodox prayers before Communion, and requiem psalms known by heart by everyone and heard over and over again at funerals.

The microcosm, the soul, the mirror of this reality was the city of Blok's poems, the main hero of his tales and his biography.

The city, this Blokian Petersburg, is the most real of all the Petersburgs depicted by artists in recent times. It exists at the same time in reality and in the imagination; it is full of that everyday prose which imbues poetry with drama and tension, and on its streets one hears the sounds of that common everyday jargon which invigorates the language of poetry. At the same time the image of this city is made up of features selected with the greatest sensitivity and so informed with spirituality that the whole image is transformed into an enticing manifestation of a most rare inner world.

* * *

. . . I introduced myself to Blok during his last visit to Moscow. It was either in the corridor or on the stairs on the evening of his reading in the auditorium of the Politechnical Museum. Blok was friendly, he said that he had heard nice things about me, complained about his health and suggested that we postpone our talk until his health improved.

That evening he was to give recitals in three places: at the Politechnical Institute, in the Press Club and at the Dante Society where his most devoted admirers had gathered to hear him read his *Italian Poems.*

Mayakovsky was at the recital at the Politechnical Institute. About the middle of the evening he told me that the benefit performance to be staged by the Press Club (under the pretext of critical integrity) was in actuality for the purpose of exposing and heckling Blok. He proposed that we both go there in order to prevent that ugly event from taking place.

We left the auditorium and walked there. Blok, however, was taken to his engagement by car and by the time we got to the Nikitsky Building where the Press Club was located, the performance had ended and Blok had already left for the Society of Friends of Italian Literature. By then the scandal which we feared had taken place after his reading; Blok had been told a pile of monstrous things and they had not been ashamed to tell him to his face that he had outlived his time and was inwardly dead—a fact with which he calmly agreed. And all this was said to him just a few months before his actual death.

BACKGROUND MATERIALS

LYUBOV MENDELEEVA-BLOK

There are many reminiscences of Blok, but few first-hand intimate accounts of his life. Until now critics have had to rely mainly on Blok's letters (not all published), his diary (much of which he destroyed), and on the interesting but biased accounts of Blok's aunt, Maria Beketova, and of Blok's once close friend and later rival, Andrei Bely. Consequently Russian and Soviet biographies, excellent works though they may be in many respects, have neglected (often for reasons beyond their control) an examination of certain less flattering aspects of Blok's personal life or have passed over them peremptorily. The critic is forced to patch together a vision of Blok's personal life from a hint here, a reference there. The manuscript of the memoirs of Lyubov Mendeleeva-Blok—unpublished in the Soviet Union, most likely because of their candor and sexual material—has been accessible only to certain Soviet critics, and those who had made use of it have carefully focused on its non-controversial sections. It is our belief that the present translation of the memoirs in full will give certain necessary, but hitherto unknown, pieces of the puzzle of Blok's personal life and will thus aid the critic in interpreting Blok's works and drawing conclusions more confidently.

Although, as the title suggests, the memoirs do much to illuminate Blok's life, it cannot be denied that large portions of the work deal solely with Mendeleeva's life. A number of things, however, is revealed about Blok through the prism of Mendeleeva' consciousness about herself—and, after all, this work is autobiography as well as biography.

I. Zilbershtein, one of the editors of *Literaturnoe nasledstvo* (Literary Heritage), relates the following anecdote. In 1936, he went to Lyubov Mendeleeva about unpublished material on Blok for a volume on Russian Symbolism that he was compiling. Expecting, like many others, to find the "Beautiful Lady," Zilbershtein was shocked and disappointed by the appearance of the woman whose beauty had once inspired two of Russia's greatest poets. Now, at fifty-four, she looked older than her years, was stout and severe. He gave her the illustrated *Literary Heritage* volume on Pushkin and recalls that upon glancing through it, she returned again and again to Gau's portrait of Natalya Pushkina and stared at it intently. A great beauty—but looks disappear—who was she as a person? What can history really know about her, except for her beauty and her role in the poet's life? And what might she have told us about the poet that the critics could not? These were the years of the beginning of Mendeleeva's memoirs about Blok and herself.

Born in 1881 into an upper-class, intellectual milieu, Lyubov belonged to the small percentage of women of her time who enjoyed the privileges of a liberal education. From her early teens, she was attracted to the theater, and her family's estate at Boblovo (adjacent to Blok's family estate at Shakhmat-ovo) was the setting for a number of amateur theatrical productions in which she performed. It was their common interest in the theater and performing that brought the young Lyubov and Blok together. Soon their relationship deepened into a courtship which observed all the formalities and the proprieties of up-per-class Russian society of the time. They married in 1903 in the ancient chapel at Tarakanovo, near Blok's family estate, in an elegant and highly formal ceremony which many writers have referred to as a fairy tale, reminis-cent of ancient aristocratic Russia.

After their marriage, which as her memoirs prove was an unconvention-al and startling one right from the beginning, Lyubov and Blok continued their studies, he at the university and she at a drama institute. This was the beginning of her acting career, a career that she would pursue throughout her married life despite Blok's frequent objections. She belonged to the Meyer-hold troupe as well as to others, and toured a great deal, which took her away from her husband for long stretches at a time. Although she was praised by the critics for some of her roles, she never rose to the prominence or to the level of artistic skill which she thought she would be able to reach. She persisted in her career because acting and establishing her identity through her craft fulfilled a deep and pressing need.

During the First World War both Blok and Lyubov were in the army, he as an administrator, she as a volunteer nurse. Interestingly enough, the nine or so months that she spent behind the front lines are not mentioned in her memoirs, but we know from Maria Beketova that Lyubov was praised for her competence and untiring devotion. Before the November Revolution she re-sumed her acting career, sometimes entertaining workers in the factories in Petrograd, sometimes on long tours.

Blok may have objected to her career, but she used her acting and de-clamatory skills to his advantange. She popularized his poems and helped establish his reputation through her readings. It is very likely that the rapid popularity of "The Twelve" was due to her frequent and critically acclaimed readings of the poem.

Although both Lyubov and Blok had welcomed the Revolution as a glorious and long-anticipated event, nevertheless the material and spiritual conditions of the post-revolutionary years were hard on both of them, par-ticularly on Blok, whose health began to fail. Blok's mother, whom Lyubov describes as "pathological" and who was Lyubov's only real lifelong rival, moved in with them early in 1920, and this caused an extremely unpleasant home environment. It was Lyubov's strength and sense of reality that sup-ported them. Her life in those days meant keeping up her home and her career and nursing Blok.

Blok died in August 1921 after a long and painful illness, and the last years of his life are uniquely illuminated by the present memoir. Liubov continued to live in the house that she had shared with Blok. In poor health in her later years, she gradually withdrew from performing, but she kept her association with the theater through teaching and coaching. Her long-standing interest in the ballet continued and she planned a biography of her favorite ballerina, Kirillova. The present work, which she herself entitled *Facts and Myths about Blok and Myself*, was begun in the late thirties, prompted by pressure from Blok's biographer Vladimir Orlov, among others. The manuscript of this work, unfinished, passed into Orlov's hands after her sudden death in 1939.

Facts and Myths about Blok and Myself served two functions for Mendeleeva: one external and the other internal. The external function was to "delineate the meaning of a life" by giving a "truthful analysis of events and motivations." With her "ruthlessness in facing the truth," this involved speaking of all that was meaningful to her, including those "things which are not 'proper' to speak of," presenting a portrait of herself with all her failings and strengths so that future readers would know who she was as a person and not who the critics depicted her as, or who Blok's contemporaries expected her to be. Since she objected so strongly to critics who gave a simplistic or sugar-coated picture of Blok, she recognized her obligation to set the record straight on him as well as on herself, and to show sides of him that only she would have known. The memoirs are her opportunity both to contribute to the literature on Blok and to be remembered accurately herself.

The memoirs serve the internal function of being the battleground upon which Lyubov attempts to liberate herself from her conflicting emotions about her past with Blok and emerge into a reconciled and dispassionate present. There is a potential tension present in the memoir as a literary form; there is a pull to relive one's past through pleasant memories and there is a pull to detach oneself from it and view one's life objectively. As Lyubov Dmitrievna writes:

> Are the points of view from which I previously looked still valid? No, they are not; they are subjective. I have been waiting for reconciliation, objectivity, historical perspective. One should not attempt to come to terms with one's own past in one's memoirs. One must already be severed from it, but such a time has not yet come for me. I am still living with my past, suffering the pain of "unforgettable wrongs" . . . .

For Mendeleeva the process of writing becomes, step by step, the process of detachment, and the search for a point of view represents the search for a unified vision of her own identity—not the identity of "The Beautiful

Lady" or the non-identity of the poet's wife. She rebelled, and the memoirs represent, in a sense, her burial of these images—both for others and, more importantly, for herself.

Incomplete as they are, the memoirs show what Vladimir Orlov calls "unquestionable literary talent." We agree with Orlov's statement but must qualify it. In the late thirties Mendeleeva's talent was still unrefined; it was not that of an experienced writer whose skills develop through criticism and the trial of repeated effort. Until *Facts and Myths about Blok and Myself* her literary experience was limited mostly to writing letters (a much underrated skill nowadays), and in this area she showed an early gift. Blok himself praised her repeatedly for the lucidity of her letters and for her "amazing" capacity to write interestingly and in a seemingly effortless manner. He recognized in her letters an embodiment of the self, her unmistakable voice, and even her "profile" and "languid movements" (Letter of May 8, 1903, *inter alia*).

In this work Mendeleeva's skills are most evident in her tone and in the narrative that engages the reader with its honesty and openness. "I am deeply convinced," she states, "that it is better not to write than to write what one does not believe in," and promises to expose "what needs to be said." She starts self-consciously, almost with painful awkwardness, as though she had difficulty placing in the proper order the many thoughts that she felt needed to be expressed before introducing the reader to the events of her life. Mendeleeva wants to be seen as a person and not as a "function" of her husband, not as the "wife of the poet," and with a minimum of words and with what she calls "ruthlessness in facing the truth," she brings us into her milieu and into her inner world. It is in her "ruthlessness in facing the truth," especially about the darker sides of herself, that her undisguised egotism, which sometimes impedes the flow of the narrative, fades into the background. We see a human being—a believable image of tormentor and tormented—and through her gain access to a private world we would not otherwise have reached.

* * *

The incomplete state of the text and the peculiarities of Mendeleeva's style present numerous problems for the translator. There is room for much interpretation. The text contains incomplete or disconnected sentences and flashes of ideas which either would have been elaborated and polished upon revision or which presuppose an intimate knowledge of allusions (particularly, but not exclusively, to Blok's poetry) which the English reader does not always possess. Thus, a slavish word-for-word translation for such passages would not convey their meaning. We have tried to translate in such a way as to show the relationship between such fragments and their immediate environment.

Certain passages, most notably those on her own folly, are informed with an irony and dark humor that are difficult to translate because they depend upon connotation and double meanings. In addition, Mendeleeva sometimes chooses words for effect from a wide range of stylistic levels—from slang to the erudite. When dealing with such subtleties we have tried to convey something of her diction and style. A comparison of some of our renderings with their Russian originals (the opening paragraph is a good example) shows how instead of adhering to the letter of the text we have often chosen to adhere to its spirit and ultimately to give the reader a translation as smooth and as easily readable as the original permits.

Lucy Vogel and *John Malnichuck*

Notes

L. D. Mendeleeva-Bloks's memoirs circulated in samizdat for years. An edition was published by Verlag K-Presse in 1977. We have used this text for our translation. The manuscript of Mendeleeva's memoirs is in the Central Government Archives of Literature and Art (TsGALI) in Moscow. The footnotes in this translation do not correspond to those found in the K-Presse edition.

1. From Blok's poem "To Friends." References to Blok's poems or prose works in this and all subsequent texts are cited from Aleksandr Blok, SOBRANIE SOCHINE-NII V VOS'MI TOMAKH (Moscow-Leningrad, 1960-1963). The volume and page number are given in parentheses in the text.

2. From Tyutchev's "Dva golosa," one of Blok's favorite poems (*viz.* VII, 99). This sentence in the Russian text is incomplete.

3. L. D. Blok refers to her love affair with one of the actors in her troupe. She discusses it later in the book.

4. Evidently L. D. Blok refers to the second part of Jules Romains' trilogy PSYCHE—LE DIEU DES CORPS, 1929. Its Russian translation appeared in 1933.

5. Anna Ivanovna Mendeleeva (Popova) (1860-1942). L. D. Blok's mother and second wife of D. I. Mendeleev. For her recollections of A. A. Blok see: VSEMIRNAIA ILLIUSTRATSIIA, XI (1923). (Cf. Blok, VII, 111-112.)

6. Maria Dmitrievna Mendeleeva (Kuzmina) (1886-1952). L. D. Blok's youngest sister. She acquired a reputation for being an expert in the breeding and training of hunting and watch dogs.

7. Serafima Dmitrievna and Lidia Dmitrievna were nieces of D. I. Mendeleev.

8. Kuzma Prutkov is a fictitous name donned by a collective of writers. Blok, in a youthful humorous poem, called himself an "admirer of Kuzma" (I, 547). The Shakhmatovo performances began with the staging of K. Prutkov plays (June 1, 1896).

9. The family of archeologist and art historian Yakov Ivanovich Smirnov (1869-1918). From 1898 he was the senior curator in the Hermitage and an expert on the Middle Ages.

10. Calderón's drama, EL MEDICO DE SU HONRA, had been translated into Russian by K. Balmont.

11. Nikolai Emmanuilovich Sum (1879-1926), a student. He later became a professor of chemistry and chemical technology.

12. L. D. Blok may be rephrasing here a line from Vladimir Solovyov's poem "Net, siloi ne podniat tiazhelogo pokrova": "Vse ta zhe vdal' tropinka vetsia snova."

13. The HAMLET performance took place in Boblovo on August 1, 1898. It is described by M. A. Beketova in ALEKSANDR BLOK (Leningrad, 1930), pp. 62-63; M. A. Rybnikova, BLOK–HAMLET (Moscow, 1923), pp. 9-14. The theme of Hamlet in Blok's early poetry is discussed by V. N. Orlov in LITERATURNOE NASLEDSTVO, 27-28, 1937.

14. In Blok's letter to L. D. Blok on June 11, 1903, one finds an explanation of the image of "the child Ophelia": "A long time ago, when we played HAMLET I was tormented by the question of what you were—a young woman or a child. In those days there was too much of both in you." (A. Blok, PIS'MA K ZHENE, LITERATURNOE NASLEDSTVO, 89, Moscow, 1978) 156.

15. The paragraphs that follow are taken from Blok's diary, *viz.* DNEVNIK AL. BLOKA, 1917-1921, ed. P. N. Medvedev (Leningrad, 1928). The choppy and fragmentary style of Blok's original has been preserved in the translation.

16. L. F. Kublitsky was the brother of Blok's stepfather.

17. DNEVNIK AL. BLOKA, pp. 122-126. Cf. VII, 339-342. L. D. Blok's observations are taken into consideration by V. N. Orlov in his comments on the text of the diary.

18. From BORIS GODUNOV.

19. Nadezhda Yakovlevna Gubkina (1855-1922), pseudonym: Kapustina. Author of SEMEINAIA KHRONIKA I VOSPOMINANIIA O MENDELEEVE (St. Petersburg, 1908). Also published in SEVERNYI VESTNIK.

20. L. D. Blok erroneously dates Blok's acquaintance with A. V. Gippius (1878-1942). Already in his letter of November 23, 1900, Blok had written: "I am in Gippius' company." PIS'MA ALEKSANDRA BLOKA K RODNYM, I (Leningrad, 1927), p. 58. A. V. Gippius, like Blok, studied law at Petersburg University.

21.The Petersburg Bestuzhev Institute for Higher Education for Women (1878-1918). One of its founders was Blok's grandfather, A. N. Beketov (VII, 7). The students were called *kursistki.*

22. M. Voloshin, "Paris," from the cycle MINUTY PROZRENII, in SEVERNYE TSVETY ASSIRSKIE, an anthology from the "Scorpion" publishing house (Moscow, 1905).

23. Ivan Dmitrievich Mendeleev (1883-1936). L. D. Blok's brother, a physicist, meteorologist and writer.

24. Compare with Blok's negative reaction to Paris on his visit in 1911 (VIII, 370).

25. Sergei Fedorovich Platonov (1860-1933). One of the most eminent historians specializing in Russian history. Professor at Petersburg University, he received the title of Academician in 1920. From 1925 to 1929 he was the Director of the Pushkin House. He died in exile.

Ilya Alexandrovich Shlyapkin (1858-1918). Literary critic and historian. Professor at Petersburg University and at the Bestuzhev Institute (1890-1913). Blok studied

Russian literature with him. See A. Gromov, "Studencheskie gody (Pamiati Bloka)" in the miscellany of the publishing house "Stozhary" (Petersburg, 1923), book 3.

Mikhail Ivanovich Rostovtsev (1870-1952). World renowned historian and archeologist. Professor at Petersburg University (1901-1918). A member of the Ivanovs' "Wednesdays." Emigrated in 1918 and from 1925 taught ancient history and classical philology at Yale University.

26. Alexander Ivanovich Vvedensky (1856-1925). Neo-Kantian philosopher. Professor at Petersburg University from 1890. Chairman of the Petersburg Philosophical Society. From 1889 he taught logic, psychology and history of philosophy at the Bestuzhev Institute.

27. Yury Erastovich Ozarovsky (1869-1927?). Famous dramatist and producer. Worked until 1915 in the Alexandrinsky Theater, from 1915 to 1918 in the Moscow Dramatic Theater and in 1918 emigrated to Paris where he started the Russian Dramatic School.

28. Vera Arkadevna Michurina-Samoilova (1866-1948), actress. She made her debut in 1886 at the Alexandrinsky Theater.

29. Maria Alexeevna Pototskaya (1861-1940), actress.

Valentina Ivanovna Kuza (1868-1910), actress.

Maria Ivanovna Dolina (Gorlenko-Dolina) (1868-1919), opera singer.

Joakin Viktorovich Tartakov (1860-1923), opera singer and producer.

30. Tomaso Salvino (1829-1916). Famous Italian dramatic actor. He appeared on the Petersburg stage in Shakespeare's KING LEAR. See Blok's diary, VII, 31.

31. The premiere of the VALKYRIE in the Marinsky Theater took place in November 1900. Brunhilde is the heroine of Wagner's RING OF THE NIBELUNGS. Blok's interest in Wagner is discussed in: S. Volkov, R. Redko, "A. Blok i nekotorye muzykal'no-esteticheskie problemy ego vremeni," BLOK I MUZYKA (Leningrad—Moscow, 1972), pp. 91-96; D. M. Magomedova, "Blok i Wagner," TVORCHESTVO A. A. BLOKA I RUSSKAIA KULTURA XX VEKA (Tartu. 1975), pp. 103-107.

32. Alexander Ivanovich Rozvadovsky (1883-1946). See Blok's letter to his mother of August 30, 1903, PIS'MA K RODNYM, I, 92-93. S.M. Solovyov, "Vospominaniia ob Aleksandre Bloke" in PIS'MA ALEKSANDRA BLOKA (Leningrad, 1925), p. 18-20.

33. Dmitry Anfimovich Shcherbinovsky (1867-1926). Teacher and artist, student of P. P. Chistyakov.

34. See R. Labry, "Alexandre Blok et Nietzsche," LA REVUE DES ETUDES SLAVES, Vol. XXVII (Paris, 1951), 201-208.

35. Mikhail Petrovich Botkin (1839-1914). Artist, genre painter, academician, famous collector. Brother of the renowned physician S. P. Botkin.

36. Cf. M. A. Beketova, ALEKSANDR BLOK (Moscow, 1922), 230.

37. Isadora Duncan (1878-1927). Toured Russia in 1904, 1907, and 1912. In 1921 she founded a ballet school in Moscow. She V. P. Verigina, VOSPOMINANIIA (Leningrad, 1974), pp. 132-134. A. Bely, NACHALO VEKA (Moscow-Leningrad, 1933), p. 439. Blok's references to Duncan in PIS'MA K RODNYM, I, 181. Irma Duncan and Allan Ross Macdougall, ISADORA DUNCAN'S RUSSIAN DAYS AND HER LAST YEAR IN FRANCE (London, 1929).

38. The first and second part of Merezhkovsky's trilogy CHRIST AND ANTICHRIST entitled SMERT' BOGOV (JULIAN OTSTUPNIK) and VOSKRESSHIE BOGI (LEONARDO DA VINCI).

39. Apparently what is meant here is not the anthology of the year 1897, as Vl. Orlov presumes in DEN' POEZII, 1965, p. 313, but D. Merezhkovsky's (1901) VECHNYE SPUTNIKI: LEV TOLSTOI I F. DOSTOEVSKII.

40. Cf. VII, 344.

41. The Russian translation appeared in 1927.

42. Blok refers here to a story by Z. Gippius (1898). A reference to it can be found in VII, 342.

43. Maria Mikhailovna Chitau-Karmina (1859-1935). Actress of the Alexandrinsky Theater and drama teacher. L. D. Blok studied with her from 1901. Blok also attended some of her classes.

44. L. D. Blok quotes the first edition of the poem written October 17, 1901. See I, 133 and 595.

45. Blok's impressions of the event are conveyed in the poem "Tam, v polumrake sobora" (I, 159).

46. Sofiya Petrovna Khitrovo (1837-1896). Devotee of Vl. Solovyov and the object of the philosopher's mystical interest.

47. Poem by Vl. Solovyov in which he speaks of his encounter with the "World Soul."

48. In the original the following lines are quoted as illustration:

. . . I k Midianke/ na koleni
Skloniaiu/ prazdnuiu/ glavu . . .

I k Midianke na koleni
Skloniaiu/ prazdnuiu glavu . . .

We have omitted them, because, of course, the point about rhythm is lost if the examples are translated.

49. The first of P. Ya. Chaadaev's (1829-1931) "Philosophical Letters" was published in the journal TELESKOP, No. 15 (1836); the sixth and seventh appeared first in the journal VOPROSY FILOSOFII I PSIKHOLOGII, books 92 and 94 (1906); the second through the fifth letters and also the eighth were discovered and published by D. I. Shakhovsky in LITERATURNOE NASLEDSTVO, 22-24, 1935.

50. Konstantin Andreevich Somov (1869-1939), artist, a contributor to MIR ISKUSSTVA, academician from 1913. In 1923 he emigrated to France. Painted the best known of Blok's portraits, a portrait which evoked many contradictory reactions. See: Blok's letter to his mother of March 12, 1908 (PIS'MA K RODNYM, I, 199); M. A. Beketova ALEKSANDR BLOK (Leningrad, 1930), p. 108; N. Lapshina MIR ISKUSSTVA: OCHERKI ISTORII I TVORCHESKOI PRAKTIKI (Moscow, 1977), pp. 249-250.

51. Vladimir Vasilevich Samus (1880-1937) (pseudonym Maximov). Well-known dramatic actor.

52. This letter was published by D. E. Maximov in UCHENYE ZAPISKI LENINGRADSKOGO GOS. PEDAGOGICHESKOGO INSTITUTA, XVIII, 5 (1956), 249-250.

53. The drafts to which L. D. Blok refers appear in ALEKSANDR BLOK: PIS'MA K ZHENE, letters 3-5.

54. Modest Ivanovich Pisarev (1844-1905), actor, teacher and friend of the dramatist A. N. Ostrovsky and competent interpreter of his works.

55. See Letter 9 in PIS'MA K ZHENE, p. 52.

56. The original note is reproduced in PIS'MA K ZHENE, p. 65.

57. See letter 12, PIS'MA K ZHENE, p. 57.

58. Aphrodite, the Greek goddess of love and beauty, whom the Romans called Venus. Evidently, L. D. Blok alludes here to her own poem "Venus ad Cometam," one line of which is quoted in II, 371.

59. Ksenia Mikhailovna Sadovskaya (1862?-1925). Blok's first "love." He met

her in 1897 in Bad Nauheim. See "Pis'ma A.A. Bloka k M. Sadovskoi," ed. L.V. Zharavina BLOKOVSKII SBORNIK, II (Tartu, 1972), pp. 309-324.

60. Lyubov Alexandrovna Delmas (1884?-1969). Opera singer, especially renowned for her role of Carmen in Bizet's opera. Blok met her in March 1914 and dedicated to her his cycle "Carmen" as well as other poems. See: Anatoly Gorelov "Aleksandr Blok i ego Karmen," GROZA NAD SOLOVYNYM SADOM: ALEKSANDR BLOK, 2nd ed. (Leningrad, 1973), pp. 556-604.

61. About the relationship between A. Bely and L. D. Blok, see: A. Bely, MEZHDU DVUKH REVOLIUTSII (Leningrad, 1933); Vl. Orlov, "Iz literaturnogo nasledstva A. Bloka," LITERATURNOE NASLEDSTVO, 27-28, 1937; Vl. Orlov, "Istoriia odnoi druzhby–vrazhdy," ALEKSANDR BLOK I ANDREI BELYI: PEREPISKA (Moscow, 1940) and in PUTI I SUD'BY (Leningrad, 1973); Bely's short story "Kust," ZOLOTOE RUNO, 1906, No. 7-9, 129-135.

62. Alexander Dmitrievich Sheremetev (1859-1919), musician, director. In 1882 he put together his own orchestra,which gave popular symphonic concerts.

63. L. Lesnaya, second-rate poet, author of the collection of poems ALLEI PRICHUD.

64. L. D. Blok uses the words "izmena," "izmenit'" (betrayal, to betray, to be untrue) with her own and Blok's deep and special meaning. For them, an extra-marital affair did not necessarily mean betrayal. The word meant a spiritual disloyalty. For their special use of certain words, see the last page of the memoirs.

65. Lev Lvovich Kobylinsky (pseudonym Ellis) (1879-1947). Minor poet and theoretician of Symbolism, friend of A. Bely.

66. V. P. Veregina, "Vospominaniia ob Aleksandre Aleksandroviche Bloke," TRUDY PO RUSSKOI I SLAVIANSKOI FILOLOGII, IV (Uchenye zapiski, TGU, 104), (Tartu, 1969), pp. 310-317 (ed. D. E. Maksimov and Z. G. Minz); VOSPOMINANIIA (Leningrad, 1974).

67. From Bely's poem "V letnem sadu" (1906).

68. G. I. Chulkov (1879-1939), poet and writer, leader of the "mystical anarchists." He commissioned Blok to write "Balaganchik." He writes of his relationship with Blok in GODY STRANSTVII. IZ KNIGI VOSPOMINANII (Moscow, 1930), pp. 121-144.

69. Page Dagobert, a character from "Zmeinookoi v nadmennom chertoge," the prologue of F. Sologub's tragedy POBEDA SMERTI, especially written for the Meyerhold–Ungern company.

70. Konstantin Eduardovich Gibshman (1884-1942?). Well-known variety actor and master of ceremonies. He began his theatrical career in 1905, worked in the theaters "Krivoe zerkalo," "Dom intermedii," "Letuchaia mysh'," "Prival komediantov."

71. Vladimir Afanas'evich Podgorny (1887-1944).Dramatic actor. Began his career in 1906 in "Teatr novoi dramy." He performed at the Komissarzhevskaya Theater, at the "Krivoe zerkalo," etc.

72. Ada Korvin (Ada Alexeevna Yushkevich) (d. 1919), ballerina and dramatic actress.

73. Compare Blok's entry in his notebook before his wedding: "If I have a child it will turn out worse than my poems..." and "It's best if the child dies." (ZAPISNYE KNIZHKI, pp. 50-51, 53).

74. Natalia Antonovna Butkevich, a dramatic actress, Baron Ungern's wife.

75. A literary-artistic group founded in 1898 by S. P. Diaghilev. See A. Benois VOZNIKNOVENIE "MIRA ISKUSSTVA" (Leningrad, 1928); N. Sokolov, MIR ISKUSSTVA (Moscow-Leningrad, 1934); A. Gusarova, MIR ISKUSSTVA (Leningrad, 1972).

76. February-March 1901. Compare with the entry in Blok's DIARY (VII,245).

Also references in I. Vinogradskaya, ZHIZN' I TVORCHESTVO K. S. STANISLAVS-KOGO: LETOPIS', Vol. I (Moscow, 1971), pp. 333-345.

77. Nikolai Ivanovich Pozdnyakov (1856-1910), poet, translator, teacher.

78. Ya. Petrovich Polonsky (1819-1898), poet.

79. See note 29.

80. Olga Nikolaevna Chyumina (1858?-1909), poet and translator. The quotattion is from her poem "U bolota" (1888).

81. Realist painters combined and organized under the name "Tvorchestvo peredvizhnykh khudozhestvennykh vystavok" in the year 1870.

82. In the 1880s, the journal RUSSKAIA MYSL' (1880-1918) was a vehicle for the Populists (Narodniks).

83. SEVERNYI VESTNIK (1885-1898), a Petersburg journal. See L. Ya. Gurevich, "Istoriia severnogo vestnika," in RUSSKAIA LITERATURA XX VEKA, 1890-1910, S. A. Vengerov (ed.), vol. I (Moscow, n.d.), pp. 235-264; V. Evgenev-Maksimov, IZ PROSHLOGO RUSSKOI ZHURNALISTIKI: STAT'I I MATERIALY (Leningrad, 1930), pp. 85-128.

84. Mikhail Alexandrovich Vrubel (1856-1910). Well-known Symbolist painter. He was related to the Mendeleevs on his mother's side through the Decembrist N. V. Basargin. In 1913, Mendeleeva-Blok took the stage pseudonym Basargina.

85. About the image of Vrubel's "Demon" in Blok's works, see S. Durylin, "Vrubel'i Lermontov," LITERATURNOE NASLEDSTVO, vol. 45-46.

86. About Artur Nikish' interpretation of Tchaikovsky's 6th Symphony, see Ferdinand Prohl, "Arthur Nikisch," LEBEN UND WIRKEN IN BEITRAGEN, H. Chevalley (ed.) (Berlin, 1922), pp. 67-69.

87. Nikolai Alexandrovich Yaroshenko (1846-1898), a realist painter; Arkhip Ivanovich Kuindzhi (1842-1910) landscape painter; Ilya Efimovich Repin (1844-1930), the most famous of the realist painters; they were all friends of the Mendeleevs' and frequent visitors at their home.

88. Dmitry Petrovich Konovalov (1856-1929), chemistry student, then colleague of D. I. Mendeleev. He became an academician in 1923.

89. Calderón's POKOLENIE KRESTU in Balmont's translation was staged by Meyerhold and performed in Vyacheslav Ivanov's Tower Theater in 1910 (see V. Ivanov's poem "Khoromnoe detstvo" and the account of the performance in the "Vstrechi" of V. Piast) and in 1912 in Terioki. L. D. Blok participated in the performance (see PIS'MA K RODNYM, II, p. 213 and Blok's comments about the performance in VII, 154-155).

90. The marriage of D. I. Mendeleev with A. I. Popova was formalized on April 22, 1882.

91. In 1896 Mendeleev's oldest son, Vladimir Dmitrievich, married Varvara Kirilovna Lemokh, the daughter of the famous artist, K. V. Lemokh (1841-1910), one of the founders of the Realist School. The conflict between the Lemokhs and the Mendeleevs occurred after Vl. Mendeleev's death in 1891 and was called forth by D. I. Mendeleev's attempt to take upon himself the bringing up of his one-year-old grandchild. See G. Smirnov, MENDELEEV (Moscow, 1974), pp. 276-277.

92. See the comparison with Siegfried in A. Bely's reminiscences of Blok: ZAPISKI MECHTATELEI (1922), No. 6, 91; EPOPEA (1923) No. 2, 275-276.

93. Olga A. Glebova-Sudeikina (d. 1945), dramatic actress.

94. "Prival komediantov" (1915-1919) was a cafe in Petrograd for artists and writers, founded by B. K. Pronin. See D. Kogan, SERGEI IUR'EVICH SUDEIKIN (Moscow, 1974); N. Evreinov, "Zhivopis' i teatr," GRANI (1959), No. 41, 182-184.

95. Compare Blok's letter to Yu. Yur'ev of November 20, 1918 in BLOKOVSKII SBORNIK (Tartu, 1964), p. 259; also see Blok's letter of March 29, 1912 to F. F. Komissarzhevsky (quoted in Vl. Orlov, PUTI I SUD'BY, p. 771).

96. D. Mendeleev apportioned the sum of 600 rubles a year for his daughter when she got married. Alexander Blok, PIS'MA K ZHENE, p. 114.

97. M. A. Beketova (1861-1938). Translator, writer of fiction and children's stories, Blok's aunt and biographer. Her diaries are preserved in Blok's archives in the Manuscript Department of IRLI (Pushkin House).

98. Lev Markovich Vasilevsky (1876-1936). Writer and theater critic.

* * *

KORNEI CHUKOVSKY
(1882-1969)

Author, literary critic, translator, writer for children. Excluded from the Royal Gymnasium in his sixth year because of his lowly origin, he began studying on his own and never stopped. He started his literary career as a journalist for the *Odessa News*. His assignment in London in 1903 as a correspondent introduced him to the English language and literature, which he came to know as well as his own native Russian. Through his long and prolific career, Chukovsky mastered many literary genres. He wrote books on literary history, *From Chekhov to Our Days* (1908), *People and Books of the Sixties* (1934); innovative works on Russian poets and writers, *The Art of Nekrasov,* for which he received the Lenin Prize in 1962, *The Book of Contemporary Writers* (1914), and many monographs and critiques on wirters such as Blok, Chekhov, Mayakovsky, Khlebnikov, and many others; he introduced British and American writers to the Russian public and for his studies on Walt Whitman and his translations into Russian of Shakespeare, Jonathan Swift, Oscar Wilde and other British classics, Oxford University awarded him in 1962 an honorary Doctor's degree. Chukovsky also wrote important works on language: *From Two to Five,* on the language of children, first published in 1925, and *Alive as Life,* an analysis of cliches popularized by the media. Chukovsky is enormoursly popular with adults and children alike for his marvelous children's poetry.

Notes

Written shortly after Blok's death, Chukovsky's essay is found in the original in ALEXANDER BLOK AS MAN AND POET (1924). The essay was later revised and reprinted in 1962 in CONTEMPORARIES. The earlier edition was chosen because it contains many interesting passages which are omitted in the Soviet edition.

Beginning with this essay all the notes which do not appear in the original will be identified as the editor's [L.V.].

1. *Raznochinets,* a term applicable to 19th century Russian intellectuals, ordinarily of liberal-radical views and non-aristocratic social origin. [L.V.]

2. V. Zorgenfrei, "Aleksandr Aleksandrovich Blok," ZAPISKI MECHTATELEI, (1922), No. 6, 149.

3. A delicacy in Russia. [L.V.]

4. M. Beketova, ALEKSANDR BLOK (Petersburg, 1922), p. 191. Beketova was Blok's maternal aunt.

5. The title of a colleciton of critical essays by D. Merezhkovsky. [L.V.]

6. The "petty demon," hero of Fyodor Sologub's famous novel, MELKII BES. [L.V.]

7. M. Beketova, p. 123.

8. If I were to try to speak of Blok in a manner unaffected by my personal emotional reactions to his poetry, I would say that even in those hatreds which molded his love for the revolution, one sensed a member of the old cultural aristocracy. His hatred for the bourgeoisie was like that of another great barin, Leo Tolstoy. Blok called the "bourgeois" monsters, swines and beasts, and dedicated to them his angry poem "The Well-Fed Ones."

He hated the intellectuals of the so-called "cultural society" with the same Tolstoyan *grand seigneur*'s hatred and contrasted their false way of life to the great truth found among the people.

His attitude toward the gentry, however, was more complex and more subtly nuanced. Like Tolstoy he hated the aristocratic "rabble" (i.e., the bureaucracy and court nobility) and called them the dregs of society. He considered the destruction of the gentry's estates the rightful revenge taken by the people for the age-old crimes commited by the nobility. But—read "Retribution"—how many compassionate, elegaic notes are sounded in that poem over the dying aristocratic way of life! Blok knew that history had justly condemned these people to extinction, but they were nonetheless very dear to him.

9. *Kosovorotka,* a kind of Russian shirt. [L.V.]

10. Cf. Pasternak's article on Blok.

11. Gastone Camillo Maspero (1846-1916), French Egyptologist. [L.V.]

12. From Blok's speech in honor of the 84th anniversary of Pushkin's death: "On the Poet's Calling" (1921). [L.V.]

13. Often Blok discovered prophesies in his poems. Leafing through his third book of verses with me, he pointed to the poem "How hard it is for a corpse to be among people..." and said to me "It turns out that I was writing about myself. When I wrote it, I had no idea that it would be prophetic." He used to say the same thing about his book GRAY MORNING: "I wrote it long ago, but only now do I understand it. It turns out to be all about our times."

14. I recorded then and there his words about "The Twelve" and I can vouch for their literal accuracy. Recently it has been reported that Blok had disavowed "The Twelve." This is nonsense. Every time he had occasion to speak about the poem to unsophisticated readers or strangers, he considered it his duty to begin by letting them know that he had not changed his views and did not regret having written it. He always loved this poem. He loved to listen to his wife, the actress Basargina, recite it on the stage. I asked him why he never recited it. He replied: "I don't know how to, but I would like to very much." If he ever regretted anything, it was his poem addressed to Zinaida Gippius which began with the words "Woman, you dreadfully proud woman." "There is one particular word in it which I now dislike," he said to me in March 1921.

15. "Here I lie at rest, I, Phillippus, a painter forever immortal. The wondrous enchantment of my brush is on everyone's lips. With my artful fingers I knew how to

breathe a soul into my colors, I knew how to confound the souls of the pious with the voice of God."

Several years before, Blok had translated this poem into Russian and included it in his Italian cycle of poems. [L.V.]

16. From a jocular poem which Blok wrote in Chukovsky's notebook, "Chuko-kala." [L.V.]

17. *Klok* means "tuft, wisp." [L.V.]

* * *

MAXIM GORKY [Alexei Maximovich Peshkov]
(1868-1936)

Novelist, playwright and essayist. He was born in Nizhny Novgorod (present-day Gorky) into a working-class family. He lost his father at the age of four and was raised by his maternal grandparents in conditions of extreme poverty and incredible cruelty: his childhood and adolescent experiences led him to choose the pseudonym of Gorky ("bitter").

As an adolescent he ran away from home and worked at many diverse jobs. Without formal education, but possessing a great love for knowledge, he read voraciously. From his experiences he acquired an intimate understanding of the social conditions of the underprivileged and a deep compassion for their plight. He first came into contact with revolutionary ideas while working in Kazan, where he had gone in the vain hope of getting into the university. He left Kazan at age 21, after a suicide attempt which permanently damaged one of his lungs. He did much wandering (often as a tramp) throughout Russia, collecting impressions which later took literary form in his writing. His first published story, "Makar Chudra," appeared in Tbilisi in 1892. Soon afterwards he landed a job as a newspaper correspondent. His literary success began with the publication of the short story "Chelkash" (1895) in a leading St. Petersburg journal. His first novel, *Foma Gordeev*, appeared in 1899 and was followed by others and by a number of plays, the most famous of which is *Lower Depths* (1902). In 1902 he was elected to the Academy of Sciences, but upon Nikolai II's orders the election was voided. While residing in Petersburg in the summer of 1905 he joined the Bolshevik party. He took active part in the 1905 Revolution and in 1906 was sent by the party to America to raise money for their cause. While abroad he wrote his most famous novel, *Mother*. Exiled from Russia, Gorky settled in Capri, and lived there until 1913, returning home only after an amnesty was declared by the Romanov regime. He continued writing and participating actively in all revolutionary activities even after his return, despite a tubercular condition. Politically Gorky was too independent to please the Party leaders, including Lenin, but nonetheless his contributions to the Revolution were accepted. In 1918-1919 he helped organize the first

Institute for the Education of Peasants and Workers and worked as an editor in Universal Literature. From 1921 to 1928 he lived abroad, most of the time in Sorrento, Italy never losing touch with his motherland and continuing to write novels, stories, critical essays, articles on various subjects. After 1928 he became highly influential in literary circles and the official literary dogmatist for newly founded Socialist Realism. He died suddenly in 1936 while under medical treatment. His death was suspect and gave rise to conjectures that Stalin himself may have been responsible for it. Among Gorky's best-known works and most praised from an artistic point of view is his autobiographical trilogy consisting of *Childhood* (1915-1916), *In the World* (1917) and *My Universities* (1932), his *Reminiscences of Tolstoy* (1919) and *Fragments from My Diary* (1924) in which his sketch on Blok appears.

Notes

1. Blok gave his talk on "The Collapse of Humanism" on April 9, 1919, and once again on November 16, 1919. The Soviet writer Konstantin Fedin left an interesting account of his impressions of Blok's reading:

It would seem that the very words "collapse" and "victim" should fill us with terror as though a fire alarm had gone off, but no one left the hall during his lecture. Blok was tall of stature, and the message of fear did not envelop him but whirled around him and under the platform he was standing on. And it was a good thing that he had taken off his coat and that his fingers were evenly turning the pages of his manuscript, and that he, as usual, stood erect and composed. He stood above all of us, who, in those terrible days, were passionately obsessed with salvation. (Blok, VI, 507) [L.V.]

2. According to Herodotus, the Scythians, a nomadic Asian tribe, invaded the Russian steppe about the seventh century B. C. and ruled it for two centuries. The Symbolists, Blok among them, felt that an invasion like that of the Scythians or even more deadly might take place in the not too distant future. It would engulf Europe as well, and signal the end of Western civilization. [L.V.]

3. By "the child question," Gorky may be referring to the problems of neglected and abandoned children. [L. V.]

* * *

ANNA AKHMATOVA [Anna Andreevna Gorenko]
(1888-1966)

Poet and one of the founders of the Acmeist movement. She was born in a suburb of Odessa and studied in Kiev and Petersburg. While attending advanced courses at the Institute of History and Letters in Petersburg, she met the poet Gumilyov, a former student of that institute, and married him in 1910. The marriage ended in divorce in 1918 and subsequently Akhmatova remarried twice. In 1910 and 1911 she visited Paris, where she met Modigliani, who drew several sketches of her. In 1912 she toured Switzerland and Italy with her husband. Her first major publication, the collection of poems, *Evening*, was under the aegis of the Acmeists' "Poets' Guild," of which her husband Gumilyov was the leader. Her second book of verses, *Rosary* (1914), established her reputation and popularity. It was followed by *White Flock* (1917), *Plaintain* (1921) and *Anno Domini* (1923). Between 1925 and 1940 none of her poetry appeared in print. Unable to subordinate her inspiration to Party dictates, she dedicated herself to the study of Pushkin. Her works on the poet were published in 1934 and 1937.

With the relative freedom of the war years, Akhmatova resumed writing poetry and publishing, but in 1946 she was censured for her "aristocratic-bourgeois" views and expelled from the Writers' Union. It was not until 1950 that she began to appear again in periodicals. Best known among her later works are the long poem "Requiem," a cry against the inhumanity of the Soviet regime and the cruel treatment of her son in prisons and concentration camps, and the "Poem without a Hero," the most complex of her works, a montage of faces and events, a grim comment on life in Russia.

Yet, despite the fact that she is regarded as the outstanding woman poet of Russia (in 1964 she was elected the President of the Writers' Union and received the Etna-Taormina prize in Italy; in 1965 she was awarded an honorary degree from Oxford), in official Soviet circles her independence of thought and courage are still not completely forgiven. The latest Soviet encyclopedia relegates her importance to her contribution to the Acmeist movement and brands her a "decadent" and an adherent to the theory of "art for art's sake."

Notes

This article appears in the journal ZVEZDA (1967), No. 12, pp. 186-187. It is the transcription of a talk Akhmatova gave on television on October 12, 1965 in Leningrad.

1. At this point Akhmatova showed her audience Blok's inscription.

2. V. M. Zhirmunsky, in his article "Anna Akhmatova i Aleksandr Blok" (RUS-SKAIA LITERATURA, 1970, No. 3, pp. 60-61), writes that Blok composed this poem the day before Akhmatova's visit and in anticipation of it.

3. *Romancero* is a kind of ballad.

4. Zhirmunsky, p. 57. He quotes Akhmatova as saying that "the only interesting thing [in her 'Reminiscences about Blok'] is the statement about Leo Tolstoi."

* * *

NIKOLAI GUMILYOV
(1886-1921)

Poet and critic, theoretician of Acmeism and one of its founders. Son of a navy doctor, he received his education in the exclusive school of Tsarskoe

Selo. In 1906 he left for Paris to study at the Sorbonne. Upon his return to Petersburg he joined the editorial staff of *Apollon*. His marriage in 1910 to A. Gorenko, the poet Akhmatova, ended in divorce in 1918. Distant, exotic places always held an attraction for Gumilyov, and he traveled extensively outside of Russian, visiting European and African countries. He fought during the First World War as a volunteer, distinguishing himself for bravery. After the Revolution he was arrested, accused of anti-Revolutionary activities and executed by a firing squad.

Gumilyov started his literary career under the influence of Symbolism. but his own tendency toward simplicity and clarity and the appeal of the exotic and heroic led him to seek new stylistic and thematic patterns. He organized the "Poets' Guild" and consequently became the main ideologist of the Acmeist movement.

Among Gumilyov's best-known works are the collections of poems *Pearls, Alien Sky,* and *Pillar of Fire.* He also wrote short stories, published posthumously under the title *Shadow from a Palm,* and critical essays, *Letters about Russian Poetry,* and did extensive translating from English and French.

Notes

This article first appeared in Gumilyov's "Pis'ma o russkoi poezii" in the journal APOLLON (1912), No. 8. pp. 60-61.

1. Pushkin's bawdy rendition of the Annunciation.

* * *

VALERY BRYUSOV
(1873-1924)

Poet, novelist, and literary critic, he was one of the most talented and influential among the writers of the first generation of Russian Symbolists. The grandson of a serf, he was born in Moscow into a well-to-do merchant family. His first literary venture was the publication of three books under the title "The Russian Symbolists." This anthology, the first of its kind, was a collection of original and translated poems and included some of Bryusov's own.

His first books, ostentatiously entitled *Chefs d'Oeuvre* (1895) and *Me Eum Esse* (1897), strongly reflect the influence of the French Symbolists, many of whose works he had translated and introduced to the Russian public. Particularly admired were his *Urbi et Orbi* (1903), a collection of original poems on city themes. The first edition of *Stefanos* (1906), another collection of poems, was immediately sold out, and firmly established his reputation as a leading literary figure. His translations from German, French,

English, and several other languages, his historical novel *The Fire Angel* (1908) and other works of fiction, his critical and biographical works on Pushkin and other Russian poets, and numerous scholarly activities (he was the chief editor of the Symbolist journal *The Balance* [1904-1908]) earned him the distinction of being the most erudite man of his generation. Bryusov is also known as a brilliant innovator and reformer in the field of Russian versification. In 1917 he accepted the Revolution and later joined the Communist Party. In 1921 he became the head of the Graduate Institute of Literature and Art which he had helped organize, and retained this post until his death.

Notes

This article appears in Bryusov's POLNOE SOBRANIE SOCHINENII, II (Moscow, 1955), pp. 283-294. Bryusov and Gumilyov's articles are the only ones in this collection which were written during Blok's lifetime.

1. The expression "in longing and in love" is taken literally from Vladimir Solovyov's poem.

2. Blok himself in his introduction to his "Lyrical Dramas " gives a different interpretation of this image, but I do not consider it incumbent upon me to accept the poet's interpretation.

3. In the text, "Aliza." This is probably an oversight on Bryusov's part. The heroine of the play is Isora; Aliza is her maid. [L.V.]

4. I have omitted the few examples of off-rhymes given by Bryusov because the point he makes is lost in translation. [L.V.]

* * *

YURY TYNYANOV
(1894-1943)

Author, critic and Formalist theoretician. The grandson of a serf, son of a doctor, he was born in Rezica, in the province of Vitebsk, and was raised in a well-to-do merchant family. In 1912 he entered the Institute of History and Philogy at the University of St. Petersburg and began his scholarly studies on Griboedov and Kyukhelbeker, which he pursued throughout his life. He graduated in 1918 and became a member of the OPOYAZ (Society for the Study of Poetic Language), a branch of the Formalist School, and soon became one of its leading scholars. In 1919 he worked as a translator-interpreter for the Komintern. From 1921 to 1930 he lectured on Russian poetry at the State Institute of the History of the Arts, one of the most active centers for literary research of the twenties. His first major critical work, *Dostoevsky and Gogol: Remarks on the Theory of Parody* (1921) is an important contribution not only from the viewpoint of literary scholarship, but also for its application of the Formalist method of literary criticism. Other important works of Formalist criticism are *The Problems of Poetic Language* (1924), in which poetry is discussed from the standpoint of rhythm and semantics and *Archaists and Innovators* (1929), a collection of essays on Russian writers. Tynyanov also distinguished himself as a historical novelist. Best known among his novels are *Kyukhlya* (1925) on the post-Decembrist Kyukelbeker and *The Death of Vazir–Mukhtar* (1927), an account of the tragic mission to Persia by the dramatist Griboyedov. Tynyanov's final years were dedicated to the writing of a monumental work on Pushkin's life and times. Unfortunately, he did not live to complete it.

Tynyanov was also most successful as a short story writer and as a translator (most notably of Heine). His contributions to the newly developed art of the cinema—he wrote theoretical and technical articles on cinematography and screenplays for various films—put him among the avant-garde of this new art form.

Notes

"Blok," first appeared in 1924 in Tynyanov's PROBLEMA STIKHOTVORNOGO IAZYKA.

1. Because of the complexity of Tynyanov's interpretation of Blok's poetry, I am supplying the volume and page number from Blok's POLNOE SOBRANIE SOCHINENII for many of his poems. Original titles or first lines of poems from other sources are given in transliteration and without English translation when such information is irrelevant to an understanding of the text.

2. Alfred de Musset (1810-1857). French poet, dramatist and novelist of the Romantic period.

Yakov Polonsky (1819-1898). Russian poet.

3. Edmund Kean (1781-1833), famous English Shakespearean actor. The epigraph to the poem "Balagan" (II, 123) is a quotation from Kean. [L.V.]

4. Tynyanov treats the quotations from III, 25 and III, 219 as though they were part of a single poem. His comments refer to the various aspects of the Russian verbs which include an unusual mixture of imperfective durative, perfective resultative, inchoative and semelfactive. [L.V.]

5. Viktor Shklovsky was the first to express the view that Blok's poetry is a canonization of the gypsy song-ballad (*romans*).

6. N. A. Apukhtin (1841-1893). A minor Russian poet, popular in his day. [L.V.]

7. The *chastushka* derives from the Russian oral tradition of folk verse. It usually consists of a simple stanza—four rhymed lines in a trochaic meter. [L.V.]

* * *

BORIS EIKHENBAUM
(1886-1950)

Writer and critic. He was one of the major representatives of the Formalist School of literature and one of its most prolific writers. He was born in the province of Smolensk, studied in Petersburg, graduating from the Institute of History and Philology in 1912. From 1918 until 1949 he taught at the university there. At first he wanted to be a musician and did not turn to scholarly writing until his late twenties. His first important article, "Karamzin," was a search for new methods of critical analysis based on philosophical principles. Many of his early works were in the field of comparative literature. In 1919 he joined the OPOYAZ (Society for the Study of Poetic Language), adopted the Formalist method and became one of its most eloquent advocates and theoreticians. His famous article, "How Gogol's Overcoat Was Made" (1909), threw a new light on literary structure; in his *Melodics of Russian Lyrical Verse* (1922), he analyzed the language of poetry, paying particular attention to rhythm and meter, and the elements of poetic instrumentation. In the twenties he continued writing critical articles on various literary subjects, but Lermontov and Tolstoi stood at the center of his creativity and remained his major interests until the end of his life. After the thirties Eikhenbaum moved away from his Formalist positions, and his criticism aimed above all at perceiving the relationship between the author and his times. His last work on Lermontov, which he started in the last year of his life but never completed, was to be entitled "Lermontov and the Russian Life of the Thirties." His best known works are: *Through Literature* (1924), *Literature* (1927), *The Young Tolstoi* (1922), *Lev Tolstoi* (two volumes, 1929-31), *Tolstoi after "War and Peace"* (1940), *Lermontov* (1924), *Lermontov, My Contemporary* (1929), *Lermontov's Literary Position* (1941), *Essay on Lermontov* (published posthumously).

There is hardly a Russian author to whose interpretation Eikhenbaum did not make a significant contribution, beginning with writers of the eighteenth century and up to his contemporaries. The bibliography of his works contains over 300 titles.

Notes

"Blok's Fate" was first given as a talk at the "Writers' Club" at an evening dedicated to Blok's memory. It was first published in the anthology O BLOKE in 1921.

1. S. Bobrov's review was published in PECHAT'I REVOLIUTSIIA, I, May-June 1921.

2. Cf. Note 2 to the Gorky selection.

3. A. Bely, "The Diary of a Writer. Why I Cannot Work in a Civilized Fashion," ZAPISKI MECHTATELEI (1921), No.2-3, p. 115.

4. Pavel Nikolaevich Milyukov (1859-1943), historian and leader of the Cadets. [L.V.]

5. Andrei Yushchinsky, a boy. He was killed in 1911 by the Black Hundreds. [L.V.]

6. Petr Arkadevich Stolypin (1862-1911), statesman and, from 1906, Minister of the Interior. He was assassinated by a Socialist Revolutionary terrorist who was also a member of the Secret Police. [L.V.]

7. Emmanuel Swedenborg (1688-1772). Swedish mystic and theologian. [L.V.]

8. From Friedrich Schiller's historical drama WALLENSTEIN. Count Albert von Wallenstein (1583-1634) was the commander of the German army during the Thirty Years War. [L.V.]

* * *

VIKTOR ZHIRMUNSKY
(1891-1971)

Formalist critic and philologist. He was born in St. Petersburg into a doctor's family, graduated in 1912 from the University of St. Petersburg, and six years later was offered a teaching post there. His scholarly works in linguistics and foreign literature (especially German) earned him international recognition and he received honorary degrees from several European universities (including Oxford and the University of Berlin) long before he was accepted as a full member of the USSR Academy of Science (1966).

Zhirmunsky first won wide recognition as a scholar with his works on German Romanticism. They were followed by studies on Symbolism ("The Poetry of Alexander Blok" among them) and on poetics (*The Composition of Lyrical Verse* [1911], *Rhythm—Its History and Theory* [1923], *Introduction to Metrics* [1925]). He joined the Society for the Study of Poetic Language (OPOYAZ) and contributed to the lively polemics of the late teens and twenties, but withdrew five years later from the Society as the result of disagreements with colleagues who took a more rigidly dogmatic view on how to apply formalist principles to literary criticism. Zhirmunsky objected to a strictly Formalist interpretation of art as "device" and stressed the importance of relating art to life—spiritual activities to social and moral phenomena, etc. Many of Zhirmunsky's works bear witness to his broad conception of art, which led him to comparative studies and to his theory of the importance of "influences" ("V. Bryusov and the Pushkin Tradition," *Byron and Pushkin* [1924], *Goethe in Russian Literature* [1937]). Zhirmunsky left hundreds of scholarly articles and over a dozen books, a document to his vast erudition and interest in many disparate literary fields. Best known among them are his works on Asian folklore, the *History of the German Language* (1963), the *Morphology of Various Types of Languages* (1963), and his important contributions to the study of Acmeism, particularly of Anna Akhmatova.

In the purges of the forties Zhirmunsky's "cosmopolitan" approach was attacked, but he survived the Stalin years and continued teaching and writing until his death.

Notes

"The Poetry of Alexander Blok" first appeared in 1921 in Petersburg in an anthology dedicated to Blok. It was reprinted in V. Zhirmunsky, VOPROSY TEORII LITERATURY in 1928. It comprises eight chapters. The first two appear here in translation.

    1. A collection of poems under the title RASPUTIA followed the POEMS ABOUT THE BEAUTIFUL LADY. [L.V.]

    2. Alfred de Musset (1810-1857), French poet and dramatist of the Romantic period.

    3. Clemens Maria Brentano (1778-1842), German Romantic poet. Compare Brentano's treatment of Manon with that of Izora in Blok's drama THE ROSE AND THE CROSS.

* * *

OSIP MANDELSTAM
(1892-1938)

    Poet, writer, critic. A leading figure in the Acmeist movement, he is considered one of the major Russian poets of the twentieth century. He was born in Warsaw, the son of a leather merchant, grew up in St. Petersburg. In 1907 he visited Paris, in the winter of 1909, studied at Heidelberg and upon his return to Russia attended the University of St. Petersburg for a time. His first poems were published in *Apollon* in 1913. They were later republished in a separate expanded edition under the title *Stone.* Although Mandelstam's beginnings as a poet were influenced by Symbolism, he soon rebelled against its mysticism, nebulousness and belief in secret truths. In his poetry he aimed at classical purity and perfection of form, which he particularly admired in ancient sculpture and architecture. His brilliant and disciplined verse reflects his extensive knowledge of the Greek and Roman cultures and his intimate knowledge of European and Russian classics. He combined brilliance and elegance of form with the difficult task of handling many levels of meaning; he stood outside his material, contemplated it with the objectivity of a demanding taskmaster. His detachment from everyday reality and his esoteric allusions gave him the reputation of being impersonal and impenetrable—a poet's poet. In 1919 he married Nadezhda Yakovlevna Khazina, a talented painter and writer who faithfully shared his tragic life and recorded it in two magnificent books after his death, *Hope Against Hope* and *Hope Abandoned.* Mandelstams's second book of poems, *Tristia,* appeared in 1923 and his third,*Poems,* in 1928. He also wrote several works of prose: *The Noise of Time,* a book of recollections, and *The Egyptian Stamp,* a lyrical novel, among others. His lack of social consciousness in prescribed terms and his indifference to the obligations imposed upon the artist by the demands of Socialist Realism made him an easy target for persecution. His epigram on Stalin, whom he called the "Kremlin mountaineer," speeded his arrest and exile in 1934. At the end of a three-year exile in Voronezh he returned to Moscow, where he was arrested for the second time in 1938. This time he was dispatched to a prison camp in Siberia where, subjected to mental and physical abuse, he died shortly thereafter.

Notes

This article is published in O. Mandelstam's SOBRANIE SOCHINENII (New York, 1955), pp. 358-362.

1. Sofiya Perovskaya, a member of the terrorist organization "The People's Will," responsible for the assassination of Alexander II in 1881. Mandelstam refers to Blok's depiction of Perovskaya in "Retribution" (III, 311-312). [L.V.]

2. Nikolai Ivanovich Kostomarov (1817-1885), Ukrainian-Russian journalist, historian, critic and writer. Representative of the Ukrainian nationalistic-religious school of historical and political thought. [L.V.]

3. Vasily Osipovich Klyuchevsky (1841-1922), one of the most respected Russian historians, a disciple of Vladimir Solovyov. [L.V.]

4. The Provisional Government headed by Kerensky was overthrown by the Bolsheviks. "Kerenki" was paper money used during his brief regime. [L.V.]

* * *

BORIS PASTERNAK
(1890-1960)

Poet, novelist and translator. Born in Moscow, he grew up in an atmosphere where love of the arts and of literature predominated: his father, the celebrated painter Leonid Pasternak, and his mother, a gifted concert pianist, counted among their friends some of the most outstanding creative personalities of that period, Leo Tolstoi, M. Vrubel, and Anton Rubinstein among others. Young Pasternak studied music under Scriabin and at first intended to make music his career, but while studying at the universities of Moscow and Marburg he turned to philosophy. His commitment to poetry grew out of his experiences as a student of neo-Kantian philosophy and his interest in the activities of the Acmeist, Symbolist and early Futurist poets. His first collection of poems, *A Twin in the Clouds,* appeared in 1914, but Pasternak did not gain the recognition of fellow poets and critics until a few years later when his more important works began to appear: *My Sister, Life* (1922), *Themes and Variations* (1923) and the long poems, *The Year 1905* and *Lieutenant Schmidt* (1927); the prose works *Tales* (1925) and the autobiographical *Safe Conduct* (1931), in which he expounded his poetic credo. Pasternak continued writing and publishing poetry until 1933, but the severity of Stalin's censorship forced him out of creative literature into the safer field of translating. Pasternak knew many languages and his trans-lations include some of the most important works of European literature: nine Shakespearean tragedies, poetry by Shelley and Keats, Goethe's *Faust*, etc. During World War II he returned to poetry. His last two collections of poems were published in 1943 and 1945. In 1956 Pasternak sent his novel, *Doctor Zhivago*, to the literary journal *New World* and to the Italian pub-lisher Feltrinelli as well. The manuscript was returned by the Russian pub-lisher but accepted abroad, gaining immediate world-wide recognition. When Pasternak won the Nobel Prize for *Doctor Zhivago* in 1958, he was forced by the Soviet authorities to decline it. A campaign of vilification was initiated against him and he was expelled from the Union of Soviet Writers. Among Pasternak's later works is his "Autobiographical Sketch," which was meant to serve as a preface to a new collection of poems to be published in 1958. But neither the new lyrics nor the "Sketch" appeared in print. A revised version of the sketch under the title "People and Situations" was published posthumously by *New World* (1967, No. 1). The present translation of Pasternak's impressions of Blok follows this version.

BIBLIOGRAPHY

This is a selected bibliography of criticism on Blok from 1960 to 1981. Included are the major publications in the USSR and the USA, but not all the voluminous critical literature in periodicals and journals that has appeared in the past two decades, particularly in the years 1979 and 1980, to commemorate Blok's centennary. My choice of articles was personal but, I trust, careful. Priority was given to literary and linguistic studies of specific aspects of Blok's art and to those critical works which have appeared in the major Slavic serials of the past two decades. I have included a limited number of "introductions" and "prefaces" to Blok's works. Selection was based on general quality and originality.

Also included in this bibliography are reprints published after 1960 of earlier critical works. Review entries are kept to a minimum, with special consideration given to cross-cultural (Soviet-American) criticism. Articles and books in languages other thanRussian or English are selectively represented. Doctoral dissertations and the respective published abstracts are included. Published dissertations are entered as books. Some of the articles, such as conference proceedings from the Soviet Union, may be difficult to obtain, but I did not feel that this fact warranted their exclusion.

One of the favorite critical themes of Blokiana has always been "The Twelve." Since a bibliography of this poem has already been complied by Dr. M. Sendich (see "Blok's 'The Twelve' "), I have limited entries on this subject to the most recent works and to those appearing in the better known Slavic publications.

I was at all times concerned with consistency and accuracy and have consulted, whenever possible, the original sources. Pagination is not always given. When this information was not provided in the source, or discrepancies arose from the collation of various sources, I chose to omit it rather than to risk possible inaccuracies.

Because our guidelines for bibliographical entries do not always fit Russian titles, the system below has been adopted for works published in the Soviet Union:

1. For books by one or more author:

Krasnova, L. POETIKA ALEKSANDRA BLOKA: OCHERKI. L'vov. 1973. (Works published in Moscow or Leningrad appear with "M." or "L."; or "M.-L.")

2. For articles dedicated to authors or subjects other than Blok, but containing specific references to him:

Belza, S. "Obraz Dante u russkikh poetov." DANTOVSKIE CHTENIIA. M., 1968, 180-181.

3. For articles in serial publications:

Kruk, I. "Blok i Belinskii." VOPROSY RUSSKOI LITERATURY, vypusk 2. L'vov, 1967. 66-72.

4. For articles in university publications specifically identified as such:

Potsepnia, D. "A Blok o khudozhestvennom slove." VLenU (SERIIA ISTORII, IAZYKA I LITERATURY) 2 (1980): 50-55.

5. For articles in anthologies dedicated to Blok:

Kotiukova, E. "Sasha Blok." A BLOK I SOVREMENNOST' (1981), 359-363. The anthology is also cited separately in full form.

6. For serials issued at regular intervals:

Chukovskii, K. "Chto ia pomniu o Bloke." NovM 2 (1967): 229-237.

It is my hope that this bibliography will serve the scholar as well as the serious student and that it may be a stepping stone to a future comprehensive bibliography of Blok.

ABBREVIATIONS

AULLA   Journal of the Australasian Universities Language and Literature Association.
BRC   Aleksandr Blok Research Conference. 3-5 April 1980. Chapel Hill, University of North Carolina. Mimeographed material.
BS I, II   Blokovskii sbornik.
IJSLP   International Journal of Slavic Linguistics and Poetics.
IZV. A. N.   Izvestiia Akademiia Nauk SSSR.
NMI   Aleksandr Blok. Novye materialy i issledovaniia.
NovM   Novyi mir.

OxSP   Oxford Slavic Papers.
RLit   Russkaia literatura.
RLT   Russian Literature Triquarterly.
RusR   Russian Review.
SEEJ   Slavic and East European Journal.
TVK II   Tezisy I vsesoiuznoi (III) konferentsii "Tvorchestvo A. A. Bloka i russkaia
            kul'tura XX veka." Tartu, 1975.
UchZ   Uchenye zapiski.
VLit   Voprosy literatury.
VLenU   Vestnik Leningradskogo universiteta.
VS I, II   Aleksandr Blok v vospominaniiakh sovremennikov.

I. Works in English

Abernathy, Robert. "A Vowel Fugue in Blok." IJSLP 7 (1963), 88-107.
———. "Blok's 'Vowel Fugue': A Suggestion for a Different Interpretation." IJSLP 11
    (1968). 150-158.
———. "The Lonely Vision of Aleksandr Blok (Blok's Vowel Fugue Revisited)." Mi-
    meographed. BRC (1980).
Annenkov, G. "The Poets and the Revolution—Blok, Maiakovskii, Esenin." RusR 2
    (1967): 120-158.
Arnesen, Hildegard Johanna. "Vozmezdie: The Concept of Retribution in the Poetry
    of Aleksandr Blok." Ph.D. dissertation, University of Washington, 1977. DAI
    37/09, 5877.
Bailey, James. "Blok and Heine: An Episode from the History of Russian Dol'niki."
    SEEJ 1 (1969), 1-22.
Banjanin, M. "The City Poetry of Baudelaire and Blok." Ph.D. dissertation. University
    of Washington, 1970. DAI 31/08, 4110.
Baran, Henryk. "Some Reminiscences in Blok: Vampirism and its Sources." BRC (1980).
Beamish-Thiriet, F. " The Myth of Women in Baudelaire and Blok." Ph.D. dissertation,
    University of Washington, 1973. DAI 34/07, 4187.
Bennett, V. THE RUSSIAN TRADITION OF NINETEENTH-CENTURY LITERARY
    MEMOIRS AND ANDREI BELYI'S 'VOSPOMINANIIA O A. A. BLOKE.'
    Ann Arbor: University Microfilms International, 1979.
"Blok, Aleksandr (1880-1921)." MODERN SLAVIC LITERATURE. RUSSIAN LIT-
    ERATURE. Vol. I. Ed. by Vasa D. Mihailovich. NY: Ungar, 1972, 48-58.
BLOK'S 'THE TWELVE': A BIBLIOGRAPHY OF CRITICISM (1918-1970)." Com-
    piled by Munir Sendich. RLT 4 (1972), 462-471. Republished with an addendum
    in TEN RUSSIAN BIBLIOGRAPHIES. Ed. by Fred Moody. Ann Arbor: Ardis,
    1977, 37-53.
Blomster, W. "A Bridge not Built: Mann and Hesse on Germany and Russia." GER-
    MANO-SLAVICA 3 (1979); 45-64.
Bowlt, J. E. "Aleksandr Blok: The Poem 'The Unknown Lady.' " TEXAS STUDIES IN
    LITERATURE AND LANGUAGE 17 (1975): 349-356.
———. "Here and There: The Question of Space in Blok's Poetry." BRC (1980).
Bowra, Sir Cecil M. "Alexander Blok." THE HERITAGE OF SYMBOLISM. NY: Schoc-
    ken Books, 1961, 143-179.
———. POETRY AND POLITICS 1900-1960. Cambridge: Cambridge UP, 1966.
Byrns, R. "Aleksandr Blok and 'Hamlet.' " CANADIAN SLAVONIC PAPERS 18
    (1976): 58-65.
———. "Novalis and Blok and the Romantic Tradition." GERMANO-SLAVICA 2, II
    (1976): 87-98.
———. "The Artistic World of Vrubel' and Blok." SEEJ 1 (1979): 38-50.
Cheron, George. "Letters of M. A. Kuzmin to A. A. Blok." WIENER SLAWISTISCHER
    ALMANAKH 5 (1980): 55-65.
Christa, B. "Metrical Innovations in Blok's Lyrical Verse." AULLA 17 (1962): 44-52.
Chukovskii, Kornei. "A. Blok." Trans. by Peter Tempest. SOVIET LITERATURE
    11 (1980): 142-149.
Cohen, J. M. "The Vision of the Apocalypse." POETRY OF THIS AGE 1908-1958.
    London: Hutchinson & Co., 1960, 87-96.
Comings, A. G. "From Lyricism to History: The Longer Poetic Form in Blok and
    Pasternak." Ph.D. dissertation. Yale University, 1973. DAI 34/05, 2615.

Crone, Anna Liza. "Blok as Don Juan in Anna Akhmatova's 'Poema bez geroia.' " BRC (1980).

Daglish, R. "Blok on the English Literary Scene: An Interview with Avril Pyman." SOVIET LITERATURE 1 (1980): 154-157.

Driver, S. "Akhmatova's 'Poema bez geroia' and Blok's 'Vozmezdie.' " BRC (1980).

Dudin, M. "Tribute to Blok." SOVIET LITERATURE 11 (1980): 97-108.

Elagin, I. "Poe in Blok's Literary Heritage." RusR 32 (1973): 403-412.

Eng, Jan van der. "Aspects of Poetic Communication: Time and Space in Four Poems by A. Blok." RUSSIAN LITERATURE 8 (1980): 377-402.

Erlich, V. "The Concept of the Poet as a Problem of Poetics." POETICS. II. Warsaw: Polish Scientific Publishers, 1966.

————. THE DOUBLE IMAGE: CONCEPTS OF THE POET IN SLAVIC LITERA-TURES. Baltimore: Johns Hopkins, 1964, 99-119.

————. "Images of the Poet and of Poetry in Slavic Romanticism and Neo-Romanticism." AMERICAN CONTRIBUTIONS TO THE FIFTH INTERNATIONAL CONGRESS OF SLAVISTS, Sofia, 1963. The Hague: Mouton, 1963, 79-113.

Feinberg, L. "The Poem as Such: Three Lyrics by Blok." IJSLP (1976), 117-130.

————. "Of Two Minds: Linear vs. Non-linear in Blok." BRC (1980).

Feinberg, L. and E. Kleinen. "Development and Stasis in Blok's 'O doblestiakh, o pod-vigakh, o slave.' " IJSLP, forthcoming.

Forsyth, James. LISTENING TO THE WIND. AN INTRODUCTION TO ALEXANDER BLOK. Oxford: Willem A. Meeuws, 1977.

————. "Prophets and Supermen. 'German' Ideological Influence on Alexandr Blok's Poetry." FORUM FOR MODERN LANGUAGE STUDIES 13, no. 1 (1977): 33-46.

Gifford, C. H. "Pasternak and the Realism of Blok." OxSP 13 (1967): 96-106.

Gippius, Zinaida. "Zinaida Gippius on Alexandr Blok." THE COMPLECTION OF RUSSIAN LIERATURE. Comp. by Andrew Field. NY: Atheneum, 1971, 191-199.

Goldman, H. "Shakespeare's 'Hamlet' in the Works of B. Pasternak and Other Modern Russian Poets (A. Blok, A. Akhmatova and M. Tsvetaeva)." Ph.D. dissertation, Indiana University, 1975. DAI 36/02: 879a.

Hackel, S. ONE, OF GREAT PRICE. London: Darton, Longman & Todd, 1965, 73-74. (Brief mention of Blok's acquaintance with Mother Maria[Kuz'mina-Karavaeva].)

————. THE POET AND THE REVOLUTION. ALEKSANDR BLOK'S "THE TWELVE." Oxford, 1975.

Hughes, R. P. "Nothing, the Cassia Flower and a 'Spirit of Music' in the Poetry of A. Blok." CALIFORNIA SLAVIC STUDIES / (1971): 49-60.

Kemball, R. ALEXANDER BLOK: A STUDY IN RHYTHM AND METRE. The Hague: Mouton, 1965.

————. "Some Metrical Problems of Russian-English Verse Translation (with special reference to Blok and Akhmatova)." SCHWEIZERISCHE BEITRAGE ZUM VIII INTERNATIONALEN SLAVISTEN-KONGRESS. Zagreb und Ljubljana, September 1978. Peter Brang, et al., eds., 128-129.

Kisch, Sir Cecil. ALEXANDER BLOK. PROPHET OF REVOLUTION. London: Weidenfeld & Nicholson, 1960.

Kleinin, F. " 'O doblestiakh, o podvigakh, o slave...' as an Introduction to the Cycle 'Vozmezdie.' "BRC (1980).

Kodjak, A. "Aleksandr Blok's Circular Structure." BRC (1980).

Kostka, E. "Blok, Schiller and the Bolshevik Revolution." REVUE DE LITTERATURE COMPAREE XXXIX Anne, 2 (1965): 255-267.

————. SCHILLER IN RUSSIAN LITERATURE. Philadelphia: Pennsylvania UP, 1965, 283-284.

Masing, I. "H. Ch. Andersen and A. Blok's Poetic Cycle 'The Snow Mask.' " AUSTRALIAN UNIVERSITIES LANGUAGE AND LITERATURE ASSOCIATION PROCEEDINGS AND PAPERS OF THE 12TH CONGRESS. University of Western Australia, 5-11 February 1969. Sidney: AULLA, 1970.

Masing-Delic, I. A. BLOK'S "THE SNOW MASK": AN INTERPRETATION. Stockholm: Almqvist & Wiksell, 1970.

————. "The Mask Motif in A. Blok's Poetry." RUSSIAN LITERATURE 5 (1973):79-101.

————. "Limitation and Pain in Briusov's and Blok's Poetry." SEEJ 4 (1975): 388-402.

————. "Three Poems at Two Meetings (Pushkin's 'K,' Tiutchev's 'K.B.,' and Blok's 'O doblestiakh...')." RUSSIAN LITERATURE 9 (1975): 37-54.

————. "Zhivago's 'Christmas Star' as Homage to Blok." BRC (1980).

————. "The Salvation Model of Blok's 'The Twelve.' " SEEJ 2 (1980): 118-132.
Muchnic, H. "Alexander Blok," FROM GORKY TO PASTERNAK. SIX MODERN RUSSIAN WRITERS. London, 1963, 104-184.
Nilsson, N. "Blok's 'Vowel Fugue': A Suggestion for a Different Interpretation." IJSLP 11 (1968): 150-158.
O'Connor, K. "Theme and Color in Blok's 'Stikhi o Prekrasnoi Dame.' " STUDIES PRESENTED TO PROFESSOR ROMAN JAKOBSON BY HIS STUDENTS. Edited by Charles E. Gribble. Columbus, Ohio: Slavica, 1968, 233-245.
Orlov, Vl. HAMAYUN: THE LIFE OF ALEKSANDR BLOK. M., 1980.
Paustovskii, K. "Aleksandr Blok." PAGES FROM TARUSA. Edited and introduced by Andrew Field. Boston: Little, Brown & Co., 1963, 354-363.
Pirog, G. "Aleksandr Blok's 'Italian Poems': A Study of Compositional Form." Ph.D. dissertation, Yale University, 1975. DAI 36/12: 8104.
————. "The City, the Woman, the Madonna: Metaphoric Inference in Blok's ITAL'IANSKIE STIKHI." FORUM AT IOWA ON RUSSIAN LITERATURE. Vol. 2, 1977, 71-86.
————. "Blok's 'Blagoveshchenie': A Study in Iconological Transformation." RUSSIAN LITERATURE 7(1979): 491-520.
————. "Blok's ITAL'IANSKIE STIKHI and the Painting of the Italian Renaissance." RUSSIAN LANGUAGE JOURNAL 1 (1980): 101-108.
————. "The Language of Love and the Limits of Language." BRC (1980).
————. "Blok's 'Ravenna': The City as Sign." RUSSIAN LITERATURE 8 (1980): 297-312.
Poggioli, R. "Aleksandr Blok." In THE POETS OF RUSSIA, 1890-1930. Cambridge: Harvard University Press, 1960, 179-211.
Putnam, G. "Aleksandr Blok and the Russian Intelligentsia." SEEJ 9 (1965): 29-46.
Pyman, A. ALEXANDER BLOK. SELECTED POEMS. Introduction, commentaries, bibliography. Oxford: Pergamon Press, 1972.
————. "Survey." SLAVIC AND EAST EUROPEAN REVIEW (London), Vol. LIV, 4 (1976): 602-607.
————. THE LIFE OF ALEKSANDR BLOK. Vol. I: THE DISTANT THUNDER, 1880-1908. Oxford: Oxford University Press, 1979.
————. THE LIFE OF ALEXANDER BLOK. Vol. II: THE RELEASE OF HARMONY, 1908-1921. Oxford: Oxford University Press, 1980.
————."Aleksandr Blok and the Merezhkovskiis." BRC (1980).
Reeve, F. D. ALEKSANDR BLOK. BETWEEN IMAGE AND IDEA. NY: Columbia University Press, 1962. Reviewed by Z. Mints and I. Chernov in RLit 3 (1963): 213-217; by R. Kemball in RusR 2 (1962): 203-205; by Z. Iur'eva in NOVYI ZHURNAL 71 (1963): 276-281.
————. "A Geometry of Prose." KENYON REVIEW 25 (1963): 9-25.
Rosenthal, B. Glatzer. "Eschatology and the Appeal of Revolution: Merezhkovsky, Bely, Blok." CALIFORNIA SLAVIC STUDIES 11 (1980): 105-139.
Rougle, Ch. THREE RUSSIANS CONSIDER AMERICA. AMERICA IN THE WORKS OF MAKSIM GORKIJ, ALEKSANDR BLOK, AND VLADIMIR MAJAKOVSKIJ. Stockholm Studies in Russian Literature. Stockholm, 1976, 59-96.
Sagatov, Bogdan. "Individuation in Blok's 'Nochnaia Fialka.' " BRC (1980).
Sendich, Munir. BLOK'S 'THE TWELVE': A BIBLIOGRAPHY OF CRITICISM (1918-1970)."RLT 4 (1972), 462-471. Republished with an addendum in TEN RUSSIAN BIBLIOGRAPHIES. Edited by Fred Moody. Ann Arbor: Ardis, 1977.
Shklovskii, V. A SENTIMENTAL JOURNEY. MEMOIRS 1917-1922. Trans. Richard Sheldon. Ithaca: Cornell UP, 1970, 238-242.
Schoolbraid, G. "Blok's 'Neznakomka': A Note." RUSSIAN LANGUAGE JOURNAL 89 (1970): 22-32.
Sloane, D. "Aleksandr Blok's Lyric Cycle 'Strashnyi Mir': An Interpretative Analysis." Ph.D. dissertation, Harvard University, 1979.
————. "The Cyclical Dynamics of Blok's 'Zhizn' moego priatelia.' " BRC (1980).
Stankiewicz, Edward. "The Polyphonic Structure of Blok's 'Dvenadtsat'.'"BRC (1980).
Taranovskii, K. "Certain Aspects of Blok's Symbolism." STUDIES IN SLAVIC LINGUISTICS AND POETICS IN HONOR OF BORIS O. UNBEGAUN. Edited by R. Magidoff, et al. NY: New York University Press, 1968, 249-260.
Thompson, E. "The Development of Aleksandr Blok as a Dramatist." SEEJ 14 (1970): 341-351.
Thomson, R. D. B. "Blok and the October Revolution." CO-EXISTENCE, Vol. IV, 2 (July 1967): 221-228.
————. "The Non-Literary Sources of 'The Rose and the Cross.' " SLAVONIC AND EAST EUROPEAN JOURNAL, Vol. XLV, no. 105 (July 1967): 292-307.

Todd, A. "The Spiritual in Recent Soviet Literature." SURVEY 66 (January 1968): 92-107.
Vickery, W. "Comments on Blok's 'Solov'inyi sad.' " BRC (1980).
Vogel, L. " Blok in the Land of Dante." RusR 26 (1967): 251-263.
———. "A Symbolist's Inferno: Blok and Dante." RusR 29 (1970): 38-51.
———. "Lightning Flashes of Art." ITALIAN QUARTERLY, vol. XX (Summer-Fall 1976): 19-30.
———. ALEKSANDR BLOK: THE JOURNEY TO ITALY. Ithaca: Cornell University Press, 1973.
———. "Masks and Doubles in Blok's Early Poetry." RUSSIAN LANGUAGE JOURNAL 30, 105 (1976): 60-76.
———. "Blok, Alexandr." ENCYCLOPEDIA OF WORLD LITERATURE IN THE 20TH CENTURY. Vol. I, 2nd ed. NY: Ungar, 1981.
Wainwright, J. "Poetry and Revolution: Aleksandr Blok and Osip Mandel'shtam." AGENDA 12, 4-13 (1975): 53-64.
Weidle, V. "The Poison of Modernism." RUSSIAN MODERNISM. Eds. G. Gibian and H. N. Tjalsma. Ithaca: Cornell University Press, 1976, 18-30.
White, D. "The Figurative Language and the Fiction in the Poetry of Aleksandr Blok." Ph.D. dissertation, University of Michigan, 1971. DAI 32/11: 6462.
Woodward, James B., ed. & introduction. SELECTED POEMS OF ALEKSANDR BLOK. Oxford: Oxford University Press, 1968, 1-32.
———. "Rhythmic Modulations in the 'dol'nik' trimeter of Blok." SEEJ 12 (1968): 297-310.
Zhirmunskii, V. "Two Tendencies of Contemporary Lyric Poetry: Blok and Akhmatova." Trans. John Glad. RLT 4 (Fall 1972): 157-180.
———. "On Classical and Romantic Poetry." Trans. P. Frantz and R. Parrott. RLT 10 (1974): 193-196.
———. "The Passion of Aleksandr Blok." TWENTIETH CENTURY RUSSIAN LITERARY CRITICISM, ed. V. Erlich. New Haven: Yale University Press, 1975.
———. THE POETRY OF ALEKSANDR BLOK. Letchworth: Prideaux Press, 1975.
Zil'bershtein, I. "Alexandr Blok and Vladimir Mayakovsky." SOVIET LITERATURE 7 (1973): 156-157.

II. Works in Russian

A. BLOK I SOVREMENNOST'. Ed. S. Lesnevskii. M., 1981.
Abramovich, S. "Kontseptsiia slavianstva v stikhotvorneii A. Bloka 'Skify' i poema Ia. Ivashkevicha 'Aziaty.' " OCHERKI PO ISTORII SLAVIANSKIKH LITERATURNYCH SVIAZEI. Lvov, 1978, 101-119.
Adamovich, G. "Nasledstvo Bloka." KOMENTARII. Washington: Victor Kamkin, 1967. 147-165.
Adel'geim, E. "Garmoniia i algebra poezii." RADUGA 11 (1966): 173-174. [About the poem "Khudozhnik.]
Akhmatova, A. "Vospominaniia o Bloke: Vystuplenie po leningr. televideniiu 12 oktiabria 1965 goda." Afterword by D. Maksimov. ZVEZDA 12 (1967): 186-191.
———. "O Bloke." VS II (1980), 94-96.
ALEKSANDR BLOK. PIS'MA K ZHENE. LITERATURNOE NASLEDSTVO, 89 (1978).
ALEKSANDR BLOK. NOVYE MATERIALY I ISSLEDOVANIIA. Vol. I. LITERATURNOE NASLEDSTVO 92 (1980). [Referred to as NMI in bibliography.]
ALEKSANDR BLOK V PORTRETAKH, ILLUSTRATSIIAKH I DOKUMENTAKH. L., 1972.
ALEKSANDR BLOK V VOSPOMINANIIAKH SOVREMENNIKOV. 2 vols. M., 1980.
Aleksandrov, A. "Veter vremeni: Khronika zhizni Aleksandra Bloka." ZVEZDA 10 (1980): 120-158.
Aleneva, K. "Vospominaniia ob A. A. Bloke." NEVA 11 (1980): 193-194.
Al'fonsov, V. "K kharakteristike obshchestvennykh motivov v lirike A. A. Bloka 1911-1914 godov." UchZ LENINGRADSKOGO PEDAGOGICHESKOGO INSTITUTA IM. GERTSENA, vol. 208, part 2 (1960): 41-68.
———. "Zametiki o poeticheskom svoeobrazii." UchZ LENINGRADSKOGO PEDAGOGICHESKOGO INSTITUTA IM. GERTSENA, vol. 271 (1965): 3-28.
———. "Blok i Vrubel' " and "V mire obrazov Vozrozhdeniia." In his SLOVA I KRASKI. M.-L., 1966.

Alianskii, S. "Vstrechi s Blokom." NovM 6 (1967): 159-206.
―――. VSTRECHI S BLOKOM. M., 1969.
―――. "Vstrechi s Aleksandrom Blokom." VS II (1980): 259-325.
Aliger, M. "V polednii raz." MOSKVA 12 (1974): 158, 170-172. [On Blok and Akhmatova.]
Al'tman, M. "Iz besed s poetom Viacheslavom Ivanovichem Ivanovym (Baku, 1921)."
TRUDY PO RUSSKOI I SLAVIANSKOI FILOLOGII. XI, vyp. 209. Tartu, 1968.
305, 306, 310.
―――. "Pushkinskie reministsentsii u Bloka." PHILOLOGIA. L., 1973, 344-355.
Al'tschuler, A. "Nenavidiashchaia liubov': Zametki o 'Skifakh' A. Bloka." VLit 2 (1972):
68-78.
Anichkov, E. "Rodnoe: Aleksandr Blok i Andrei Belyi." In his NOVAIA RUSSKAIA
POEZIIA. Berlin, 1923; rpt. The Hague: Mouton, 1969, 90-108.
Annenkov, Iu. DNEVNIK MOIKH VSTRECH. Vol. I. NY: Inter-Language Associates,
1966, 59-96.
Anpetkova-Sharova, G. and K. Grigor'ian. "Studencheskie raboty Bloka ob antichnykh
avtorakh." RLit 3 (1980): 200-214.
Antiukhin, G. "Blok i V. Briusov v 'Sirene'." SOBESEDNIK. Voronezh, 1973, 213-215.
Antokol'skii, P. "Aleksandr Blok." In his PUTI POETOV. M., 1965, 223-280.
―――. "Aleksandr Blok." SMENA 24 (1970): 24-26.
―――. "Prikliucheniia metafory." VLit 1 (1977): 170, 178.
―――. "Iz ocherka 'Aleksandr Blok'," VS II (1980), 135-140.
Arel'skii, G. "Iz vospominanii o Bloke." VS II (1980), 91-93.
Arev, Andrei. "Zemnoe serdtse: khudozhestvennoe samosoznanie poeta." ZVEZDA
10 (1980): 112-119.
Arsen'eva, K. "Vospominaniia o Bloke." VS II (1980): 97-98.
Artiushkov, I. "Prervannye predlozheniia. (Na materiale poezii Bloka.)" RUSSKII
IAZYK V SHKOLE 4 (1981): 83-87.
Assev, N. SOBRANIE SOCHINENII. Vol. 5. M., 1964, 389-390, 482, 486-488, 497-
498, 501.
―――. "O poslednikh stikhakh Aleksandra Bloka." RLit 1 (1971): 134-137.
Asmus, V. "Filosofiia i estetika russkogo simvolizma." VOPROSY TEORII I ISTORII
ESTETIKI. M., 1968, 531-535, 548, 550, 596-609.
Averintsev, S. "Struktura otnosheniia k poeticheskomu slovu v tvorchestve Viacheslava
Ivanova." TVK III (1975): 152-155. [About the phonetic structure of Blok's
verse.]
Avramenko, A. "Traditsii A. Feta v rannei poezii A. Bloka." VESTNIK MOSKOV-
SKOGO UNIVERSITETA. Seriia VII. (Filologiia. Zhurnalistika) 6 (1980): 61-
70.
Azadovskii, K. "Blok i A. M. Dobroliubov." TVK III (1975): 96-102.
Babenchikov, M. "Otvazhnaia krasota." VS II (1980), 146-178. [Also in ZVEZDA
3 (1968):186-200.]
Baevskii, V. "K evoliutsii liricheskogo stikha Bloka." In his STIKH RUSSKOI SOVET-
SKOI POEZII. Smolensk, 1972, 44-56.
―――. "Stikhi Bloka kak tekst i podtekst." TVK III (1975): 63-68.
Bakhtin, V. ALEKSANDR PROKOF'EV. L., 1963, 216-219. [About the Italian poems.]
Bakina, M. " 'Oplech' u Al. Bloka." RUSSKAIA RECH' 4 (1969): 101-102.
Balashova, T. "Aleksandr Blok i Frantsiia." RLit 2 (1974): 74-82. Enlarged and revised
in V MIRE BLOKA (1980), 517-534.
―――. "Mnogoznachnost' simvola: interpretatsiia poezii A. Bloka frantsuzskoi kriti-
koi." IDEINO-ESTETICHESKIE PROBLEMY. M., 1975, 119-136.
Barabash, Iu. VOPROSY ESTETIKI I POETIKI. 2nd rev. ed. M., 1977, 288-290.
Baranov, V. "Zagadka odnogo prototipa: Bessonov-Blok." ZVEZDA 10 (1980): 210-
215.
―――. "Po sledam dnevnikovykh zapisei A. Bloka: Esenin i Blok." V MIRE BLOKA
(1981), 383-415.
Baranova, Z. "Mestoimeniia v rechi V. Maiakovskogo i A. Bloka." UchZ TASHKENT-
SKOGO PEDAGOGICHESKOGO INSTITUTA, vol. 101 (1972): 32-41.
Bazanov, V. "Gremel moi praded Avvakum." KUL'TURNOE NASLEDIE DREVNEI
RUSI. M., 1976. [On Avvakum, Kliuev and Blok.]
―――. "Olonetskii krest'ianin i peterburgskii poet." SEVER 9 (1978): 91-110. [On
Blok and Kliuev.]
―――. "Razrushenie legendy." RLit 3 (1980): 92-114.
―――. "K tvorcheskim iskaniiam Bloka." A. BLOK I SOVREMENNOST' (1981), 200-
226.

Beketova, M. ALEKSANDR BLOK: BIOGRAFICHESKII OCHERK. The Hague: Mouton, 1970. [Reprint of the 1922 edition.]
————. "Aleksandr Blok i ego mat'." VS I (1980), 39-69.
————. "Veselost' i iumor Bloka." A. BLOK I SOVREMENNOST' (1981), 317-324.
Bel'kind, E. "Blok i Viacheslav Ivanov." BS II (1972), 365-384.
Belov, S. MASTER KNIGI. OCHERK ZHIZNI I DEIATEL'NOSTI S. M. ALIANSKOGO. L., 1979. [Dedicates an important segment to the relationship between Blok, Alianskii and Annenkov.]
Bel'skaia, L. "Rol' A. Bloka v stanovlenii poetiki rannego Esenina." RLit 4 (1968): 120-130.
Belyi, A. "Iz knigi 'Nachalo veka.' " VLit 6 (1974): 214-245.
————. "Vospominaniia ob Aleksandre Bloke." VS I (1980), 204-324.
Belza, S. "Obraz Dante u russkikh poetov." DANTOVSKIE CHTENIIA. M., 1968, 180-181.
————. "Don Kikhot v russkoi poezii." SERVANTES I VSEMIRNAIA LITERATURA. M., 1969, 229.
Berestov, V. "Vechnyi iunosha." NovM 11 (1980): 226-229.
Berezark, I. "Otets A. Bloka." RLit 3 (1977): 188-191. [Translated into English in SOVIET STUDIES IN LITERATURE 3 (1978): 87-95.
Berezneva, A. RUSSKAIA ROMANTICHESKAIA POEMA: LERMONTOV, NEKRASOV, BLOK. K PROBLEME EVOLIUTSII ZHANRA. Saratov, 1976, 2-15; 71-96. [About "Nightingale Garden."]
Bernshtein, S. "Moi vstrechi s A. A. Blokom." DEN' POEZII (1965): 167-186. Also in VS I (1980), 352-360.
————. "Khudozhestvennaia struktura stikhotvoreniia Bloka 'Pliaski osennie.' " TRUDY PO ZNAKOVYM SISTEMAM. UchZ TARTUSKOGO UN-TA, vup. 308 (1973): 521-545.
Bezzubov, V. "Aleksandr Blok i Leonid Andreev." BS I (1964), 226-320.
Bezzubov, V. and S. Isakova, eds. "Blok uchastnik studencheskogo sbornika." BS II (1972), 325-332.
Blagoi, D. OT KANTEMIRA DO NASHIKH DNEI. 2 vols. M., 1973. Vol. I pp. 190-191; 193-194; 198-199, 200-202; 208-233; 235-241; 502-530. Vol. II 443-445; 459-460.
Blium, A. "Pod sudom 'pedagogicheskoi tsenzury.' " ZVEZDA 10 (1980): 184-185.
Blok, G. "Iz ocherka 'Geroi Vozmezdiia' " and "Iz ocherka 'Iz semeinykh vospominanii.' " VS I (1980), 96-105, 105-109.
————. "Iz semeinykh vospominanii." NEVA 11 (1980): 181-184.
BLOK I MUZYKA. Edited by M. Elik. L.—M., 1972.
Blok, L. D. (Mendeleeva). I BYL' I NEBELITSY O BLOKE I O SEBE. Bremen: Studien und Texte, 1977. Also in VS I (1980), 134-187. Excerpts in DEN' POEZII (1965), 306-320.
BLOKOVSKII SBORNIK I. Trudy nauchnoi konferentsii, posviashchennoi izucheniiu zhizni i tvorchestva A. A. Bloka, mai 1962 goda. Eds. V. Adams et al. Tartu, 1964.
BLOKOVSKII SBORNIK II. Trudy nauchnoi konferentsii, posviashchennoi izucheniiu zhizni i tvorchestva A. A. Bloka. Eds. Z. G. Mints et al. Tartu, 1972.
Bobrov, E. "Iz vospominanii ob A. Bloke." NMI (1980), 299-302.
Bogat, E. "Istoriia odnoi liubvi: Iz pisem E. Iu. Kuz'minoi-Karavaevoi A. Bloku (1912-1917)." LITERATURNAIA GAZETA. 14 September 1977, 6.
————. CHTO DVIZHET SOLNTSE I SVETILA: LIUBOV' V PIS'MAKH VYDAIUSHCHIKHSIA LIUDEI. M., 1978, 194-216. [Included are some of Kuz'mina-Karavaeva's letters to Blok.]
Boleslavskaia, T. "Poeziia Bloka v romanakh N. Ia. Miaskovskogo i V. V. Shcherbacheva." BLOK I MUZYKA (1972), 153-177.
Borisov, L. "Vstrecha s Blokom." In his RODITELI, NASTAVNIKI, POETY: KNIGA V MOEI ZHIZNI. 2nd expanded edition. M., 1969, 95-100, 9, 36, 78-79, 146.
————. ZA KRUGLYM STOLOM PROSHLOGO: VOSPOMINANIIA. L., 1971, 3-20, 24-25, 97-98, 101, 119, 122-123, 135, 153-154, 158-159.
————. "O Bloke." VS II (1980), 252-258.
Borisova, M. "Strogaia strannost'." ZVEZDA 10 (1980): 160.
Borovoi, L. PUT' SLOVA: STAROE I NOVOE V IAZYKE RUSSKOI SOVREMENNOI LITERATURY. 2nd rev. ed. M., 1963, 52-54, 68-69, 401-402, 577, 612-613, 633-634.
————. PUT' SLOVA: OCHERKI I RAZYSKANIIA. M., 1974. [Numerous references to Blok throughout.]
Botner, V. "Blok i russkaia dramaturgiia." VOPROSY LITERATURY: METOD, STIL'. POETIKA. Kiev, 1973, 92-107.

————. "O khudozhestvennom metode dramy A. Bloka 'Roza i krest.' " VOPROSY LITERATURY: METOD, STIL'. Kiev, 1975, 57-72.

Brazhnin, I. SUMKA VOLSHEBNIKA. L., 1968, 294-302. [About Blok's poem "Neznakomka."]

Broitman, S. "Stanovlenie zhanra poemy v tvorchestve A. Bloka." TVK III (1975), 28-42.

Budnikova, L. "Traditsii N. A. Nekrasova v poezii A. A. Bloka." PROBLEMY SOVETSKOI POEZII, vyp. 2. Cheliabinsk, 1974, 54-71.

Burago, S. "Valerii Briusov v literaturno-esteticheskoi otsenke Bloka." RUSSKAIA LITERATURA XX VEKA: DOOKT. PERIOD, Vol. 3. Kaluga, 1971, 91-108.

Buznik, V. et al. Foreword to "Perepiska Bloka s A. V. Gippiusom (1900-1915)." NMI (1980), 414-415.

Cherepin, L. "Aleksandr Blok i istoriia." VOPROSY ISTORII 1 (1967): 37-59.

————. "Russkaia revoliutsiia i A. A. Blok kak istorik." ISTORICHESKIE VZGLIADY KLASSIKOV RUSSKOI LITERATURY. M., 1968.

Chernov, I. "A. Blok i knigoizdatel'stvo 'Alkonost.' " BS I (1964), 530-538.

Cherniavskii, V. "Vstrechi s Eseninym." NovM 10 (1965): 189-201.

Chernyi, K. "Chuvstvo puti." ZNAMIA II (1970): 227-240. .

Chertkov, L. "V. A. Zorgenfrei-sputnik Bloka." RUSSKAIA FILOLOGIIA: SBORNIK STUDENCHESKIKH NAUCHNYKH RABOT, vyp. 2. Tartu, 1967, 113-139.

Chikovani, S. "A. Blok." In his MYSLI. VPECHATLENIIA. VOSPOMINANIIA. M., 1968, 39-40, 47-51.

Chudakova, M. "Po strogim zakonam nauki." NovM 10 (1965): 249. [About memoir literature on Blok and the 1964 Tartu conference.]

Chukovskaia, E. "Iz dnevnika (1919-1921)." VLit 10 (1980): 284-313.

Chukovskii, K. "A. Blok." LIUDI I KNIGI. M., 1960.

————. "A. Blok." SOVREMENNIKI. M., 1962.

————. SOBRANIE SOCHINENII. 6 vols. M., 1965-1969. [For references to Blok see indexes in vols. 2, 4, 5, 6.]

————. Introduction to A.BLOK. STIKHOTVORENIIA. M., 1968, 5-44.

————. "Blok v Chukkolade.' " BS II (1972), 424-429.

————. KNIGA OB ALEKSANDRE BLOKE. Paris: YMCA, 1976.

————. "A. Blok." Introduction to A. BLOK. IZBRANNOE. M., 1978, 3-26.

————. "Iz dnevnika (1919-1921)." VLit 10 (1980): 284-313.

————. "A. Blok." VS II (1980): 219-251.

Chukovskii, N. "Chto ia pomniu o Bloke." NovM 2 (1967—: 229-237.

Chulkov, G. "A. Blok i ego vremia." VS I (1980): 343-363.

Chulkova, N. "Vospominaniia o Bloke." NEVA 11 (1980): 186-188.

————. "Vospominaniia o Bloke." A. BLOK I SOVREMENNOST'. (1981), 337-343.

Chumakov, Iu. "Kompozitsiia odnogo stikhotvoreniia: 'Ia prigvozhden k traktirnoi stoike...' " TRUDY PRZHV. PEDAGOGICHESKOGO INSTITUTA 16 (1970): 137-144.

————. "Al. Blok i Iu. Polonskii: 'Vozmezdie' i 'Svezhee predan'e.' " TVK III (1975), 112-116.

Daniel, S. "Zamechaniia k odnoi stat'e Aleksandra Bloka." TVK III (1975), 79-80.

Daskalova, E. "Aleksandr Blok i bolgarskaia literatura posle oktiabr'skoi revoliutsii." RLit 3 (1966): 50-64.

————. "Aleksandr Blok i bolgarskaia literatura." SOVETSKOE SLAVIANOVEDENIE 2 (1966): 14-20.

————. " Blok i Bolgariia." NEVA 8 (1971): 184-193.

————. "Revoliutsionnaia poeziia Aleksandra Bloka i bolgarskaia literatura." RUSSKO-BOLGARSKIE FOLKLORNYE I LITERATURNYE SVIAZI, vol. 2. L., 1977, 217-245.

————. "Bolgariia v tvorcheskom soznanii Bloka: Osvoboditel'naia epopeia 1877-1878 godov v poeme 'Vozmezdie.' RLit 2 (1980): 196-200.

————. Aleksandr Blok i teatral'noe iskusstvo Bolgarii." NEVA 11 (1980): 206-210.

Davydov, Iu. "Blok i Maiakovskii: Nekotorye sotsial'no-esteticheskie aspekty problemy 'Iskusstvo i revoliutsiia.' " VOPROSY ESTETIKI, vyp. 9 (1971): 5-62.

Del'mas, L. " 'Moi golos dlia tebia....' Vospominaniia." Ed. I. Fashchevskaia. AVRORA 1 (1971): 66-72.

Dement'ev, V. "O, Rus' moia!...." A. BLOK I SOVREMENNOST'. (1981), 82-118.

Deich, A. "Vspominaia minuvshee." ZVEZDA 5 (1966): 163-166, 171-173. [About the staging of "Balaganchik" and "Neznakomka."]

————. GOLOS PAMIATI: TEATRALNYE VPECHATLENIIA I VSTRECHI. M., 1966, 51, 57-67, 70, 75-77, 83-88.

————. "Nemnogoe, chto pamiat' sokhranila..." VSTRECHI S MEIERKHOLDOM. M., 1967, 61-66.
————. "Vse ostan'sia v pamiati krylatoi..." ALEKSANDR PROKOF'EV: VSPOMINA-IUT DRUZ'IA. M., 1977, 280-281.
D'iakonov, A. "A. Blok v teatre Komissarzhevskoi." O KOMISSARZHEVSKOI: ZA-BYTOE I NOVOE. VOSPOMINANIIA. STATI'I. PIS'MA. M., 1965, 81-116.
Dikman, M. "Detskii zhurnal Bloka 'Vestnik.' " NMI (1980), 203-221.
Dobin, E. "Siuzhetnoe masterstvo kritika." NovM 3 (1970): 224-225, 235-236. [About Chukovskii's book on Blok.]
Dolgopolov, L. POEMY BLOKA I RUSSKAIA POEMA KONTSA XIX—NACHALA XX VEKOV. M., 1964.
————. "Tiutchev i Blok." RLit 2 (1967): 59-80.
————. "Poeziia russkogo simvolizma." ISTORIIA RUSSKOI POEZII. Vol. 2. L., 1969, 308-329.
————. ed. "Aleksandr Blok v poslednie gody zhizni." BELYE NOCHI: O TEKH, KTO PROSLAVIL GOROD NA NEVE. OCHERKI, ZARISOVKI, DOKUMENTY, VOSPOMINANIIA. L., 1973, 125-145.
————. "Problema lichnosti i 'vodovorot' istorii: A. Blok i Tiutchev." In his NA RUBE-ZHE VEKOV: O RUSSKOI LITERATURE KONTSA XIX—NACHALA XX VEKOV. L., 1977, 123-157. Other references to Blok on pp. 119-122, 197-204.
————. ALEKSANDR BLOK. LICHNOST' I TVORCHESTVO. L., 1978.
————. "Dostoevskii i Blok v 'Poeme bez geroia' Anny Akhmatovoi." V MIRE BLOKA (1981), 454-480.
Dolgopolov, L. and O. Miller. "Imia' ili 'Slovo'?" RLit 3 (1980): 219.
Dongarov, R. "Blok—redaktor Bal'monta." BS II (1972), 416-423.
Druzin, V. "Poet, uslyshavshii revoliutsiiu." OKTIABR' 11 (1980): 202-206.
Dudin, M. "Veter vremeni i poet." A. BLOK I SOVREMENNOST' (1981), 32-49.
Dunaevskii, M. "Kontury muzykal'noi Blokiany." BLOK I MUZYKA (1972), 115-136.
Efimov, V. "Aleksandr Blok v otsenke A. V. Lunacharskogo." TRUDY PRZHEV. PEDAGOGICHESKOGO INSTITUTA 12 (1965): 42-68.
Efron, A. "Stranitsy vospominanii." ZVEZDA 3 (1973): 175-178. [On Blok and Tsveta-eva.]
Eikhenbaum, B. "Sud'ba Bloka." SKVOZ' LITERATURU. The Hague: Mouton, 1962, 215-252. [Reprint of the 1924 Leningrad edition.]
————. O POEZII. M., 1969, 76, 79-80, 107, 308-309, 514, 520.
Ekimov, A. "D. I. Mendeleev v zhizni i tvrochestve Aleksandra Bloka." RLit 1 (1960): 156-160.
Elik, M. "Notografiia proizvedenii na stikhi i siuzhety A. Bloka." BLOK I MUZYKA (1972), 246-279.
Elshina, T. "Printsipy organizatsii istoricheskogo, publitsisticheskogo i literaturnogo materiala v ocherke Bloka 'Katilina.' " PROBLEMY SOVETSKOI LITERA-TURY, vyp. 1. M., 1978.
Elzon, M. "Drug Bloka: S. V. Belov, master knigi." NEVA 12 (1979): 190.
Emel'anova, V. and A. Stiunekova. "Vash obraz, dorogoi navek..." A. BLOK I SOVRE-MENNOST' (1981), 265-289.
Enisherlov, V. "Na druzheskoi noge...s Blokom." LITERATURNAIA GAZETA. 18 March, 1970.
————. "Moskovskie vstrechi Aleksandra Bloka. Materialy k biografii poeta." TVER-SKOI BUL'VAR, 25. STUDENCHESKII ALMANAKH LITERATURNOGO INSTITUTA IMENI GOR'KOGO 12 (1972): 205-216.
————. " A. Blok i ego neizdannye pis'ma." NovM 4 (1979):113-126.
————. "S. Gorodetskii—A. A. Blok." NovM (1980): 266-267.
————. "Sud'ba ottsa: Iz biograficheskikh motiviv 'Vozmezdiia.' " VLit 10 (1980.   .:
————. "V pamiati sovremennikov." A. BLOK I SOVREMENNOST' (1981), 314-316.
————. "Aleksandr Blok—kritik." V MIRE BLOKA (1981), 291-332.
————. "Aleksandr Blok: Strikhi sud'by." SOVREMENNIK, forthcoming.
Eremina, I. "Poetika kontrasta: Lingvisticheskii analiz teksta stikhotvoreniia A. Bloka 'Na zheleznoi doroge.' " RUSSKII IAZYK V SHKOLE 5 (1972): 20-24.
————. " 'Sedoe utro' A. Bloka." OBRAZNOE SLOVO A. BLOKA (1980), 132-160.
————. "Tekst i slovo v poetike A. Bloka." OBRAZNOE SLOVO A. BLOKA (1980), 5-55.
————. "K istolkovaniiu finala poemy A. A. Bloka 'Dvenadtsat',' "FILOLOGICHESKIE NAUKI 6 (1980): 3-9.
Erenburg, I. SOBRANIE SOCHINENII. 9 vols. M., 1962-1967. [Numerous references to Blok throughout.]

————. "Aleksandr Aleksandrovich Blok." In his PORTRETY. Munchen: Wilhelm Fink Verlag, pp. 36-39.

Ermakova, O. "Opyt lingvisticheskogo tolkovaniia stikhotvoreniia A. Bloka 'Net, nikogda moei, i ty nichei ne budesh.' " OBRAZNOE SLOVO A. BLOKA (1980), 122-131.

Ermilova, E. "K prirode simvola v poezii Bloka." A. BLOK I SOVREMENNOST' (1981), 241-264.

Ershov, F. "Simvolicheskaia lirika na stsene: 'Balaganchik' A. Bloka." NOVYI ZHURNAL 67 (1962): 98-117.

Eterlei, E. "Barometr mirooshchushcheniia: O iazyke Aleksandra Bloka." RUSSKAIA RECH' 5 (1980): 20-26; 6 (1980): 15-20.

Etkind, E. "Ten' Danta...: Tri stikhotvoreniia iz ital'ianskogo tsikla Bloka." VLit 9 (1970): 88-106.

————. " 'Karmen' Aleksandra Bloka: Liricheskaia poema kak anti-roman." BRC (1980).

Evreinova, N. "Tsikl stikhov A. Bloka 'Na pole Kulikovom' i ego istochniki v drevnei russkoi literature." RUSSKAIA SOVETSKAIA POEZIIA I STIKHOVEDENIE. M., 1969, 151-172.

Farber, L. "Perepiska iz dvukh mirov." NEVA 8 (1971): 184-187.

Fatiushchenko, V. "Poeticheskii simvol u Aleksandra Bloka." VESTNIK MOSKOVSKOGO UNIVERSITETA. Seriia VII. (Filologiia. Zhurnalistika.) 6 (1980): 25-33.

Fedin, K. "Aleksandr Blok." PISATEL'. ISKUSSTVO. VREMIA. M., 1961, 37-47.

————. "Gor'kii sredi nas." SOBRANIE SOCHINENII. Vol. 10. M., 1973, 21, 31-32, 37-40, 72-73, 98-100.

————. "Aleksandr Blok." VS II (1980), 412-422.

Fedorov, A. "Dramaturgiia Bloka." VLit 11 (1970): 67-87.

————. TEATR A. BLOKA I DRAMATURGIIA EGO VREMENI. L., 1972.

————. "Vokrug dramy 'Roza i krest.' " PHILOLOGIA. L., 1973, 344-349.

————. "Proza A. Bloka i 'Knigi otrazhenii' I. Annenskogo." TVK III (1975), 90-95.

————. "Blok—prozaik i Geine." SRAVNITEL'NOE IZUCHENIE LITERATUR: SBORNIK STATEI K 80-LETIIU AKADEMIKA M. P. ALEKSEEVA. L., 1976, 533-540.

————. "Pamflet A. Bloka: Sograzhdane. Opyt stilisticheskoi interpretatsii satiry." VLenU (SERIIA ISTORII, IAZYKA I LITERATURY) 2 (1980): 44-50.

————. "Al. Blok—dramaturg." (USSR). Forthcoming.

Filippova, L. "Substatsivatsiia imen prilagatel'nykh v poezii A. A. Bloka." ISSLEDOVANIE IAZYKA KHUDOZHESTVENNYKH PROIZVEDENII. Kuibyshev, 1975. 29-33, 124-127.

Finkel, A. "Opyt lingvisticheskogo analiza stikhotvoreniia A. Bloka 'Neznakomka.' " SBORNIK NAUCHNYKH TRUDOV. MOSKOVSKII PEDAGOGICHESKII INSTITUT INOSTRANNYKH IAZYKOV, vyp. 73 (1975): 314-326.

Florenskii, S. "O Bloke." VESTNIK RUSSKOGO KHRISTIANSKOGO DVIZHENIIA (Paris) 4, no. 114 (1974): 169-197.

Foogd-Stoianova, T. "Stikhotvorenie Aleksandra Bloka 'Bolotnyi popik.' " DUTCH CONTRIBUTIONS TO THE EIGHTH INTERNATIONAL CONGRESS OF SLAVISTS (Zagreb, Ljubljana, Sept. 3-9, 1978). Jan Meijer, ed. Amsterdam: Benjamins, 1979, 383-395.

Frumkina, L. and L. Fleishman. "A. A. Blok mezhdu 'Musagetom' i 'Sirinom." BS II (1972), 385-397.

Gagen-Torn, M. "Vospominaniia ob Aleksandre Bloke." BS II (1972), 444-446.

Gaidarov, V. "A. A. Blok. Vospominaniia." RLit 4 (1964): 209-214.

————. V TEATRE I V KINO. L.-M., 1966, 72-81.

Galis, A. "Vosemnadtsat' dnei Aleksandra Bloka v Varshave." Translated from Polish. ZVEZDA 4 (1978): 187-201.

Gal'perin, I. "Glubina poeticheskogo teksta: Na materiale odnogo stikhotvoreniia A. Bloka (Byla ty vsekh iarche, vernei i prelestnei...)." TEORIIA IAZYKA. ANGLISTIKA. KELTOLOGIIA. M., 1976, 31-40.

Gasparov, M. "Tsennye strofy v russkoi poezii nachala XX veka." RUSSKAIA SOVETSKAIA POEZIIA I STIKHOVEDENIE. M., 1969, 252.

————. "Rifma Bloka." TVK III (1975), 74-75.

Gasparov, B. and Iu. Lotman. "Igrovye motivy v poeme 'Dvenadtsat'.' " TVK III (1975). 53-63.

Gerasimov, Iu. "Teatr i drama v kritike A. Bloka v period pervoi russkoi revoliutsii." VLenU (SERIIA ISTORII, IAZYKA I LITERATURY) 20 (1962): 73-85.

————. "Stanislavskii i Blok." NEVA 2 (1963): 166-169.

————. " 'Roza i krest' v Moskovskom khudozhestvennom teatre." BS I (1964), 522-523. [Followed by several unpublished letters by Blok.]

————. Aleksandr Blok i sovetskii teatr pervykh let revoliutsii." BS I (1964), 321-343.
————. "Ob okruzhenii Aleksandra Bloka vo vremia pervoi russkoi revoliutsii." BS I (1964), 539-544.
Gertsog, E. "Otets poeta Bloka." NMI (1980), 302-307.
Ginsburg, L. "O prozaizmakh v lirike Bloka." BS I (1964), 157-171.
————. O LIRIKE. 2nd rev. ed. L., 1974.
Gippius, V. "Vstrechi s Blokom." OT PUSHKINA DO BLOKA. M.-L., 1966, 331-340. Also in VS II (1980), 76-85.
Gippius, Z. ZHIVYE LITSA. Munchen: Fink, 1971. [Reprint of the Prague 1925 edition.]
Girshman, M. "Tri chudnykh mgnoveniia." RUSSKAIA RECH' 1 (1969): 11-18.
Glazunov, I. "Tam gde zhil Blok. Zametki khudozhnika." LITERATURNAIA GAZETA. 6 April, 1965. [About Shakhmatovo.]
Glebov, I. "Videnie mira v dukhe muzyki: Poeziia A. Bloka." BLOK I MUZYKA (1972), 8-57.
Glushkova, T. "Obraz Rossii v lirike Bloka." DAUGAVA 11 (1980): 80-87.
Golenishchev-Kutuzov, I. TVORCHESTVO DANTE I MIROVAIA KUL'TURA. M., 1971, 470-483.
Golitsina, V. "Pushkin i Blok." PUSHKINSKII SBORNIK. Pskov, 1962, 57-73.
————. "K voprosu ob esteticheskikh vzgliadiakh A. Bloka (Dookt. period)." UchZ LENINGRADSKOGO PED. IN-TA, vol. 306 (1966): 101-127.
————. "Tsvetaeva o Bloke." TVK III (1975), 135-140.
Golovanova, G. "Nasledie Lermontova v poezii XX veka." RUSSKAIA SOVETSKAIA POEZIIA: TRADITSII I NOVATORSTVO. 1917-1945. L., 1972, 92-100.
Golovashenko, Iu. "Aleksandr Blok v Bol'shom dramaticheskom teatre: K 90-letiiu so dnia rozhdeniia poeta." NEVA 11 (1970): 202-208.
Golub, I. "Simvolika zvukov." RUSSKAIA RECH' 6 (1980): 30-36.
Golubkov, D. "Ital'ianskaia tema v tvorchestve Aleksandra Bloka." PROBLEMY ITAL'-IANSKOI ISTORII. M., 1972, 296-306.
Gomberg, E. and D. Maksimov, eds. "Vospominaniia i zapiski Evgeniia Ivanova ob A. Bloke." With an introduction by D. Maksimov. BS I (1964), 344-436.
Gopshtein, N. "Tvardovskii i A. Blok." UchZ TASHKENTSKOGO PED. IN-TA, vol. 44, vyp. 3 (1963): 213-247.
Gorbovskii, G. "Vstrecha s Blokom." ZVEZDA 10 (1980): 159. [Poem]
Gordin, A. "Risuet Aleksandr Blok." NEVA 8 (1971): 188-190.
Gordin, M. "Istoriia—eto vozmezdie." ZVEZDA 10 (1980): 87-102.
Gorelov, A. "Skvoz' v'iugi: A. A. Blok." OCHERKI O RUSSKIKH PISATELIAKH. L., 1964, 657-740.
————. "Tsikl 'Karmen' Al. Bloka." ZVEZDA 11 (1969): 190-199.
————. "Vysokoe naznachenie poeta." ZVEZDA 11 (1970): 177-189. [On Blok's letters to L. A. Delmas.]
————. "Aleksandr Blok i ego Karmen." AVRORA 1 (1971): 66-72.
————. GROZA NAD SOLOV'INYM SADOM. 2d. ed. L., 1973.
Gor'kii, M. "A. A. Blok." VS II (1980), 326-333.
Gorodetskii, S. "Vospominaniia ob Aleksandre Bloke." RUSSKIE PORTRETY: VOS-POMINANIIA O BLOKE, ESENINE, LIADOVE. M., 1978, 6-19. Also in VS I (1980), 325-342.
Grechishkin, S. and A. Lavrov. "A. A. Blok: Pis'ma k Zorgenfreiu." RLit 4 (1979): 128-138. [18 letters included.]
————. "...Sovremennaia russkaia zhizn' est' revoliutsionnaia stikhiia." NovM 11 (1980): 256-257.
Grechnev, V. ZHANR LITERATURNOGO PORTRETA V TVORCHESTVE M. GOR'-KOGO. M.-L., 1964, 113-130. [About Gor'kii and Chukovskii's literary portraits of Blok.]
Gribovskaia, M. "Vospominaniia ob Aleksandre Bloke." VS I (1980), 81.
Grigor'ev, N. "Zabytye stroki Bloka." NEVA 2 (1969): 207-208.
Grigor'ev. A. "Russkii modernizm v zarubezhnom literaturovedenii." RLit 3 (1968): 201, 203-206, 214.
————. RUSSKAIA LITERATURA V ZARUBEZHNOM LITERATUROVEDENII. L., 1977.
Grigor'an, K. "Perevody Bloka iz liriki Isaakiana." RLit 1 (1981): 189-196.
Gromov, P. GEROI I VREMIA. L., 1961, 385-578. [On Blok's lyrical dramas.]
————. BLOK, EGO PREDSHESTVENNIKI I SOVREMENNIKI. M.-L., 1966.
————. "V studencheskie gody." VS I (1980), 402-409.
Gukovskii, G. "K voprosu o tvorcheskom metode Bloka." NMI (1980), 63-84.

Gusev, V. "Kontseptsiia romantizma v stat'iakh A. A. Bloka." LITERATURNYE NA-PRAVLENIIA I STILI. M., 1976, 298-309.
————. "...Chto gumanizmom my zovem." V MIRE BLOKA (1981), 135-163.
Gutman, D. "Genrikh Ibsen v vospriiatii i istolkovanii A. Bloka." PISATEL' I VREMIA, vyp. 1. Ul'ianovsk, 1975, 167-169.
Guzhieva, N. "Dlia nastoiashchikh knig vsegda zhdu nesuetnykh chasov." V MIRE BLOKA (1981), 481-502.
Gzovskaia, O. "A. A. Blok v Moskovskom Khudozhestvennom teatre." RLit 3 (1961): 197-205. Also in VS II (1980), 115-134.
————. "A. A. Blok." PUTI I PEREPUT'IA. M., 1976, 243-256. [Numerous references to Blok throughout.]
Iakobson SEE Jakobson
Il'ev, S. "Leonid Andreev i simvolisty." RUSSKAIA LITERATURA XX VEKA: DOOK. PERIOD, Vol. 2,Kaluga, 1970, 202=216.
Il'in, N. and S. Nebol'sin. "Predki Bloka: Semeinye predaniia i dokumenty." IZV. AN SSSR. SERIIA LITERATURY I IAZYKA, vol. 34, no. 5 (1975): 450-455.
Iurchuk, T. "Soznatel'nye nepravil'nosti: Udarenie v poezii Bloka." RUSSKAIA RECH' 4 (1972): 24-30.
Ivanov, Viacheslav. SOBRANIE SOCHINENII. 2 vols. Brussels: Foyer Oriental Chretien, 1971. Vol. 1, 161-165. [On Ivanov's relationship with Blok.]
————. "Struktura stikhotvoreniia Bloka 'Shagi komandora.' " TVK III (1975), 33-38.
Ivanov, Vsevolod. "Iz ocherka 'Istoriia moikh knig.' " VS II (1980), 401-404.
Ivanov-Razumnik, V. A. BLOK. A. BELYI. Letchworth: Hertz, 1971.
Ivask, Iu. " 'Venetsiia' Mandel'shtama i Bloka." NOVYI ZHURNAL 122 (1976): 113-126.
————. "Epokha Bloka i Mandel'shtama: O novoi russkoi poezii." MOSTY 13-14 (1967-1968), 209-227.
Jakobson, A. KONETS TRAGEDII. NY: Chekhov Publishing, 1973, 9-195.
Jakobson, R. "Devushka pela: nabliudeniia nad iazykovym stroem stansov A. A. Bloka." ORBIS SCRIPTUS. Munchen: Fink Verlag, 1966, 385-401.
Jur'eva, Z. "Vvedenie." LUG ZELENYI. NY: Johnson Reprint Co., 1967, v-xiv.
————. "Mif ob Orfee v tvorchestve Andreia Belogo, Aleksandra Bloka i Viacheslava Ivanova." AMERICAN CONTRIBUTIONS TO THE 8TH INTERNATIONAL CONGRESS OF SLAVISTS (Zagreb, Ljubljana, Sept. 3-9, 1978). V. Terras, ed. Vol. 2.
Kachaeva, L. "Glagol kak izobrazitel'noe sredstvo." RUSSKAIA RECH' 5 (1975): 102. [On "Greshit' besstydno, neprobudno..."]
Kaidalova, N. " Moskovskaia Blokiana." A. BLOK I SOVREMENNOST' (1981), 290-311.
Kamianov, V. "Po zakonam poezii." VLit 1 (1978): 132-133.
Karpov, A. "Poema Bloka 'Solov'inyi sad': Problemy zhanra." RUSSKAIA LITERA-TURA XX VEKA: DOOK. PERIOD, vol. 2. Kaluga, 1970, 262-275.
————. PRODIKTOVANO VREMENEM. Tula, 1974, 4-32, 49-50, 57, 78-79. [Comments on "Solov'inyi sad," "Dvenadtsat' " and "Vozmezdie."]
Kazanovich, E. "Kak bylo napisano A. Blokom stikhotvorenie 'Pushkinskomu Domu.' " ZVEZDA 10 (1977): 199-201.
Kazarkin, A. "Khudozhestvennaia perspektiva v tsikle A. Bloka 'Na pole Kulikovom.' " KHUDOZHESTVENNOE TVORCHESTVO I LITERATURNYI PROTSESS, vyp. 1. Tomsk, 1976, 79-90.
Khlodovskii, R. "Pesn' ada: Zametki k teme 'Blok i Dante.' " FILOLOGICHESKIE NAUKI 4 (1965): 58-65.
————. "Blok i Dante." DANTE I VSEMIRNAIA LITERATURA. M., 1967, 176-248.
Khmara, G. "Aleksandr Blok v khudozhestvennom teatre." NEVA 11 (1980): 190-191.
Khodasevich, Vl. "Gumilev i Blok." NEKROPOL'. Paris: YMCA, 1976, 118-140.
Kholodilova, L. "Iz opyta analiza iazyka stikhotvornogo teksta: A. Blok, 'O ia khochu bezumno zhit'...' " ISSLEDOVANIE IAZYKA KHUDOZHESTVENNYKH PROIZVEDENII. Kuibyshev, 1975, 29-33, 124-127.
Kholopova, V. "Portret M. Gor'kogo 'A. A. Blok.' " VOPROSY LITERATURY I STILIA. Samarkand, 1969, 39-47.
Khoprova, T. MUZYKA V ZHIZNI I TVORCHESTVE BLOKA. L., 1974.
Kireeva, A. "A. Blok i S. Esenin (K problemu literaturnoi preemstvennosti)." TRUDY KAFEDRY SOV. LIT. SARAT. PED. IN-TA. Vyp. 2 (1975): 108-140.
Kirpotin, V. "Polemicheskii podtekst 'Solov'inogo sada.' " PAFOS BUDUSHCHEGO. M., 1963.

Knipovich, E. "Ob Aleksandre Bloke." VLit 10 (1980): 105-156.

Kochetov, V. "Put' poeta." NASH SOVREMENNIK 11 (1980): 169-174.

Kolobaeva, L. "Vstrecha vremen: Khudozhestvennoe vremia v tsikle 'Rodina' A. Bloka." VESTNIK MOSKOVSKOGO UNIVERSITETA. Seria VII. (Filologiia. Zhurnalistika.) 6 (1980): 25-33.

Komarovskaia, N. VIDENNOE I PEREZHITOE. IZ VOSPOMINANII AKTRISY. M.-L., 1965, 76-77, 127, 132-134, 136, 141-157, 159, 169, 171, 232.

————. "Aleksandr Blok v Bol'shom dramaticheskom teatre." VS II (1980), 334-351.

Kondarov, G. "Garmoniia kontrasta: Antonim, epitety A. Bloka." RUSSKAIA RECH' 1 (1971): 13-18.

Konopatskaia, T. N. Introduction and notes to "Pis'ma ottsa k Bloku: 1892-1908." NMI (1980), 249-274.

Koonen, A. "Stranitsy zhizni. Vospominaniia." TEATR 7 (1966): 116. [On her two meetings with Blok.]

Korzhavin, N. "Igra s d'iavolom. Po povodu stikhotvoreniia Aleksandra Bloka 'K muze.'" GRANI 95 (1975): 76-107.

Koshkarev, K. "Romantizm Aleksandra Bloka." RUSSKII ROMANTIZM. M., 1974, 195-209.

Kosolapov, R. "Tol'ko ob odnoi zvezde." V MIRE BLOKA (1981), 54-84.

Kotiukova, E. "Sasha Blok." A. BLOK I SOVREMENNOST' (1981), 359-363.

Kotrelev, N. "Neizvestnye avtografy rannikh stikhotvorenii Bloka." NMI (1980), 222-248.

Kotrelev, N. and A. Lavrov. Introduction to "Perepiska Bloka s S. M. Solov'evym (1896-1915)." NMI (1980), 308-324.

Kozhin, A. "Leksicheskii povtor v stikhotvornykh tekstakh A. Bloka." OBRAZNOE SLOVO A. BLOKA. (1980), 56-88.

Kozhinov, V. "Sud'ba poeta i liricheskoe tvorchestvo: Blok i Esenin." KAK PISHUT STIKHI. M., 1970, 159, 163, 180-182, 189-238.

Kovalevskaia, V. "Kompozitsiia fonologicheskoi sistemy v lirike A. A. Bloka: 'K muze.'" VOPROSY SIUZHETOSLOZHENIIA. Riga, 1976, 130-146.

Koz'min, M. "Velikii poet Rossii." VLit 10 (1980): 3-23.

Koziakina, N. "Liricheskie dramy Aleksandra Bloka i teatr." NEVA 11 (1980): 196-205.

Krasnova, L. "Poeticheskii stroi 'Skifov' A. Bloka." VOPROSY LITERATURY, vyp, 2, L'vov, 1968: 104-110.

————. "Iz nabliudenii nad simvolikoi krasnogo tsveta v poetike A. Bloka." VOPROSY RUSSKOI LITERATURY, vyp. 3, L'vov, 1969: 49-56.

————. "Ob odnoi osobennosti poeticheskogo sintaksisa A. Bloka." VOPROSY RUSSKOI LITERATURY, vyp. 1. L'vov, 1971: 78-86.

————. POETIKA ALEKSANDRA BLOKA: OCHERKI. L'vov, 1973.

————. "Simvolika chernogo i belogo tsvetov v poetike A. Bloka." NAUCHNYE DOKLADY VYSSHEI SHKOLY. FILOLOGICHESKIE NAUKI 4 (1976): 3-13.

Kriukova, A. "K istorii otnoshenii Gor'kogo i Bloka." VLit 10 (1980): 197-227.

Kruk, I. "Blok i Gogol'."RLit 1 (1961): 85-103.

————. "Pometki A. Bloka na sochineniiakh V. S. Belinskogo." VOPROSY RUSSKOI LITERATURY, vyp. 1, L'vov, 1966, 21-27.

————."Blok i Belinskii." VOPROSY RUSSKOI LITERATURY, vyp. 2, L'vov, 1967: 66-72.

————. "Obraz demona v poezii Bloka: K evoliutsii romantizma." RUSSKAIA LITERATURA XX VEKA: DOOKT. PERIOD, vol. 2. Kaluga, 1968, 212-226.

————. "Metodika analiza stikhotvorenii A. Bloka: Tsikl 'Iamby.'" METODIKA PREPODAVANIIA RUSSKOGO IAZYKA I LITERATURY (Kiev), no. 4 (1969): 54-70.

————. "Poet i deistvitel'nost': Cherty mirovozreniia i tvorchestva A. Bloka v svete literaturnoi traditsii i problem epokhi." Doctoral dissertation, Kiev, 1969.

————. POEZIIA ALEKSANDRA BLOKA. M., 1970.

————. "K voprosu o mistitsizme i 'fantasticheskom realizme' A. Bloka." RUSSKAIA LITERATURA XX VEKA: DOOK. PERIOD, vol. 2. Kaluga, 1970, 230-241.

————. "A. A. Blok." RUSSKAIA LITERATURA XX VEKA: DOOKT. PERIOD. Kiev, 1970, 312-358.

————. "Realizm i obshchestvenno-esteticheskie iskaniia A. Bloka." VOPROSY RUSSKOI LITERATURY, vyp. 3, L'vov, 1971: 15-22.

————. "Blok ob obshchestvennom naznachenii iskusstva: K voprosu o sviaziakh poeta c russ. estetikoi XIX veka." RUSSKAIA LITERATURA XX VEKA: DOOKT. PERIOD, vol. 3. Kaluga, 1971, 16-30.

————. "Muzyka nas ne pokinet...: Ob odnoi osobennosti tvorchestva A. Bloka." RUSSKAIA LITERATURA XX VEKA: DOOKT. PERIOD, vol. 7. Tula, 1975.
————. PROBLEMY EVOLIUTSII TVORCHESTVA BLOKA, "SOKROVENNYI DVI-GATEL' EGO..." Kiev, 1980.
Krutikova, N. V NACHALE VEKA: GOR'KII I SIMVOLISTY. Kiev, 1978, 124, 211, 270, 277-278, 280-290, 294-295.
Kublitskii, F. "Sasha Blok: Iz vospominaniia detstva i iunosti." VS I (1980), 82-90.
Kublitskii-Piottukh, F. "Chastitsa ego liubvi k Rossii." SMENA 15 (1972): 14-15.
Kudasova, V. "Blok i Ap. Grigor'ev. Tvorcheskie paralleli." VOPROSY LITERATURY: KHUDOZH. METOD—KHUDOZH. SVOEOBRAZIE, vol 9. Vladimir, 1975, 86-99.
————. "Liricheskoe tvorchestvo Ap. Grigor'eva i poeziia Al. Bloka." Doctoral dissertation, Leningrad Pedagogical Institute, 1977.
Kudriavtseva, T. "Aleksandr Blok—akter." TEATR 3 (1967): 77-78.
Kuliukin, A. "Novoobrazovaniia v proizvedeniiakh Bloka." RUSSKAIA RECH' 4 (1976): 38-41.
Kupiaev, Stanislav. "V dospekhakh prostogo voina." A. BLOK I SOVREMENNOST' (1981), 60-70.
Kupriianovskii, P. 'Aleksandr Blok i poety akmeisty." SKVOZ' VREMIA. Iaroslav, 1972, 37-73.
Kurysheva, T. "Blokovskii tsikl D. Shostakovicha." BLOK I MUZYKA (1972), 214-228.
Kuskov, V. "Osmyslenie poeticheskikh obrazov drevnerusskoi literatury v tysikle stikho-tvorenii A. Bloka 'Na pole Kulikovym.' " VESTNIK MOSKOVSKOGO UNI-VERSITETA. Seriia VII. 6 (1980): 12-17.
Kuziakina, N. "Liricheskie dramy Aleksandra Bloka i teatr." NEVA 11 (1980): 196-205.
Kuz'min, B. A. "O Bloke." O GOLDSMITE, O BAIRONE, O BLOKE. M., 1977, 302-309.
Kuz'mina, N. "Traditsionno-poeticheskaia frazeologiia v lirike Bloka." RUSSKAIA RECH' 4 (1976): 32-47.
Kuz'mina-Karavaeva, E. "Vstrechi s Blokom." TRUDY PO RUSSKOI I SLAVIANSKOI FILOLOGII XI (LITERATUROVEDENIE), vyp. 209. Tartu, 1968, 257-278. Also in VS II (1980), 58-75.
Lagunov, A. "A. Fet v tvorchestve rannego Aleksandra Bloka." RUSSKAIA LITERA-TURA XX VEKA. Stavropol', 1973, 45-85.
Landa, E. "A. Blok i perevody iz Geine." MASTERSTVO PEREVODA. M., 1964, 292-328.
————. "Blok—redaktor Geine." REDAKTOR I PEREVOD. M., 1965, 72-107.
Laputina, A. "Svidetel'stvo sovremennitsy." RADUGA 4 (1971): 174-178.
Lavrov, A. and V. Przdpelskii (Iurii Tumanov). "Blok na fronte." RLit 4 (1980): 151-159.
Lavut, P. MAIAKOVSKII EDET PO SOIUZU: VOSPOMINANIIA. 2d rev. ed. M., 1969, 86, 99-100.
Lazarevskii, I. "Progulka pod parusami." DEN' POEZII. L., 1968, 203-205. Also in: NEVA 11 (1980): 188-189.
Lebedev-Polianskii, P. "Iz vstrechi s A. Blokom." VS II (1980), 181-185.
Lekh, V. "Blok v Parokhonske." VS II (1980), 141-144.
Lenchik, L. "Drama A. Bloka 'Neznakomka' v vyskazyvaniiakh sovremennykh literaturo-vedov." NAUCHNYE TRUDY NOVOSIB. PED. INST., vyp. 65, 1971.
————. "Simvolika siuzhetno-obraznykh sviazei v drame A. Bloka 'Korol' na ploshcha-di.' " BS II (1972), 206-217.
————. "Simvolicheskii stroi dramy A. Bloka 'Neznakomka.' " TVK (1975), 24-28.
Lesnevskii, S. "Shakhmatovo: Semeinaia khronika (Neopublikovannye vospominaniia M. Beketovoi)." VLit 11 (1970): 107-121.
————. PUT' OKKRYTYI VZORAM. MOSKOVSKAIA ZELMIA V ZHIZNI ALEK-SANDRA BLOKA. M., 1980.
————. "Problizhaetsia zvuk..." V MIRE BLOKA (1981), 164-171.
————. "Chitatel' Nekrasova." A. BLOK I SOVREMENNOST' (1981), 188-198.
Levina, M. "Semantika prilagatel'nykh so znacheniem tsveta v poeticheskikh tekstakh (na materiale stikhov A. A. Akhmatovoi i A. Bloka)." MATERIALY XXVI NAUCH. STUD. KONF. Tartu, 1971.
Levinton, G. "Dve zametki o Bloke." TVK (1975), 69-73.
Levinton, G. and I. Smirnov. "Na pole Kulikovym Bloka i pamiatniki Kulikovskogo tsikla." TRUDY OTDELA DREVNERUSSKOI LITERATURY 34 (1979): 72-95.
Libedinskaia, L. ZHIZN' I STIKHI. M., 1970.
Likhachev, D. S. "Iz kommentarii k stikhotvoreniiu A. Bloka 'Noch', ulitsa, fonar', apteka.' " RLit 1 (1978): 186-188.

Liubareva, E. "Prodolzhateli: Traditsii A. Bloka v sovetskoi poezii 20-kh godov." VLit 10 (1980): 157-170.

Liubomudrov, M. "Rezhisserskie iskaniia Bol'shogo dramaticheskogo teatra (1919-1926)." TEATR I DRAMATURGIIA, vyp. 4. L., 1974, 97-131.

————. "Teatral'naia programma Aleksandra Bloka." ZVEZDA 10 (1980): 103-111.

Liushkin, Iu. " 'Rozhdestvo golubogo ruch'ia...'(O poetike A. A. Bloka)." RUSSKA-IA RECH' 5 (1972): 44-46.

Lobanov, M. "Kul'tura dukha." MUZHESTVO CHELOVECHNOSTI. M., 1969, 239-265.

Lokshina, B. POEZIIA A. BLOKA I S. ESENINA V SHKOL'NOM IZUCHENII. L., 1978.

Loman, A., I. Loman. "Tovarishchi po chustvam, po peru..." NEVA 10 (1970): 199-200.

Loshchinskaia, N. "Blok i ego rodnye. Poslednye gody. Po arkhivnym materialam." NovM 11 (1980): 246-255.

Losinskaia, A. "V te dalekie gody." A. BLOK I SOVREMENNOST' (1981), 325-326.

Lotman, Iu. and Z. Mints. " 'Chelovek prirody' v russkoi literature XIX veka i tsyganskaia tema u Bloka." BS I (1964), 98-156.

————. ANALIZ POETICHESKOGO TEKSTA: STRUKTURA STIKHA. L., 1972, 223-234. Also pp. 74, 99. 213, 236, 237.

————. "Ob odnoi tsitate u Bloka. (K probleme: ' Blok i dekabristy')." TVK III (1975), 102-103.

Lugovtsov, A. TVORCHESTVO OL'GI FORSH. L., 1964, 14-16, 78, 81. [On Forsh's portrayal of Blok in SUMASSHEDSHII KORABL'.]

Lunacharskii, A. "Aleksandr Blok." SOBRANIE SOCHINENII. 8 vols. Vol. 1. M., 1963, 464-496; 430-431, 436.

————. "Blok i revoliutsiia." STAT'I O SOVETSKOI LITERATURE. 2nd rev. ed. M., 1971, 121-122.

Magomedova, D. "O genezise i znachenii simvola, 'mirovogo orkestra' v tvorchestve A. Bloka." VESTNIK MOSKOVSKOGO UNIVERSITETA. FILOLOGIIA. No. 5 (1974): 10-19.

————. "Kontseptsiia 'muzyki' v rannem tvorchestve Bloka." FILOLOGICHESKIE NAUKI 4 (1975): 13-23.

————. "Kontseptsiia 'muzyki' v mirovozrenii i tvorchestve A. Bloka." Doctoral dissertation, Moscow University, 1975.

————. "O zarozhdenii kontseptsii 'muzyki' v mirovozrenii A. Bloka." RUSSKAIA LITERATURA XX VEKA: DOOKT. PERIOD, vol. 7. Tula, 1975.

————. "Blok i Vagner." TVK III (1975), 103-107.

————. "Blok i antichnost': K postanovke voprosa." VESTNIK MOSKOVSKOGO UNIVERSITETA. SERIIA VII. (FILOLOGIIA. ZHURNALISTIKA.) 6 (1980): 42-49.

————. "A. Blok.: Perevod 'AMORES III,' 5 Ovidiia." VESTNIK MOSKOVSKOGO UNIVERSITETA. SERIIA VII. (FILOLOGIIA. ZHURNALISTIKA.) 6 (1980): 50-51.

Maiakovskii, Vl. "Umer Aleksandr Blok." VS II (1980), 179-180.

Makovskii, S. "Aleksandr Blok." NA PARNASE 'SEREBRIANNOGO VEKA.' Munich: Tsope, 1962, 143-175.

————. "Eshche o Bloke." RUSSKAIA MYSL'. 15 March 1962.

Maksimov, D. "Lermontov i Blok." POEZIIA LERMONTOVA. M.-L., 1964, 247-265.

————. "Kriticheskaia proza Bloka." BS I (1964), 28-97.

————. "Akhmatova o Bloke." ZVEZDA 12 (1967): 187-191.

————. "Ideaia puti v poeticheskom soznanii Al. Bloka." BS II (1972), 25-121.

————. "A. Blok. 'Dvoinik.' " In his POETICHESKII STROI RUSSKOI LIRIKI. L., 1973, 211-235.

————. POEZIIA I PROZA AL. BLOKA. L., 1975.

————. "O spiraleobraznykh formakh razvitiia literatury: K voprosu ob evoliutsii A. Bloka." KUL'TURNOE NASLEDIE DREVNEI RUSI: ISTOKI. STANOVLENIE. TRADITSII. M., 1976.

Maksimov, D. and Z. Mints. "Vospominaniia o Bloke E. E. Iu. Kuz'minoi-Karavaevoi." TRUDY PO RUSSKOI I SLAVIANSKOI FILOLOGII. XI. LITERATUROVEDENIE. Tartu, 1968, 257-264.

Malinin, A. "Tvorchestvo Bloka v otsenke A. B. Lunacharskogo." OKTIABR' I KHUDOZHESTVENNAIA LITERATURA. Minsk, 1968, 123-137.

Maliukova, L. "Blok i Esenin: K voprosam o sviaziakh i vliianiiakh." VOPROSY ISTORII I TEORII LITERATURY, no. 9/10. Cheliabinsk, 1972, 72-85.

Mal'ts, A. and Iu. Lotman. "Stikhotvorenie Bloka 'Anne Akhmatovoi' v perevode Debory Vaarandi: K probleme sopostavitel'nogo analiza." BS II (1972), 4-24.

Mandel'shtam, O. RAZGOVOR O DANTE. M., 1966, 22.

Marshak, S. "Molodym poetam." NovM 9 (1965): 233-235. [On the influence of Pushkin and Nekrasov on Blok.]

Mashbits-Verov, I. RUSSKII SIMVOLIZM I PUT' ALEKSANDRA BLOKA. Kuibyshev, 1969.

Medianskii, S. "Perifrazy v poezii A. Bloka." TRUDY VORONEZHSKOGO UNIVERSITETA (Voronezh), no. 4 (1969): 80-83.

Medvedev, P. "Dramy i poemy Al. Bloka: Iz istorii ikh sozdaniia." In his V LABORATORII PISATELIA. L., 1971, 173-294.

Meierkhol'd, V. STATI'I, PIS'MA, RECHI, BESEDY. 2 vols. M., 1968. [Numerous references to Blok. See index in Part 2.]

Mendeleeva, A. "A. A. Blok." VS I (1980), 70-80.

Mendeleeva-Blok, L. D. SEE Blok, L. D.

Mgebrov, A. "Iz knigi 'Zhizn' v teatre.' " VS II (1980), 99-100.

Mikeshin, A. "O blokovskoi kontseptsii romantizma: Po stat'iam i vystupleniiam 1917-1921 godov." LITERATURA PRAVDY I MECHTY. Kemerovo, 1966, 21-72.

———. " 'Solov'inyi sad' A. Bloka kak romanticheskaia poema." PROBLEMY IZUCHENIIA KHUDOZHESTVENNOGO PROIZVEDENIIA (METODOLOGIIA, POETIKA, METODIKA). Part 2. M., 44-46.

———. " 'Neznakomka' v tvorcheskoi evoliutsii A. Bloka." RUSSKAIA LITERATURA XX VEKA: DOOKT. PERIOD, vol. 1. Kaluga, 1968, 190-211.

———. " 'Solov'inyi sad' v tvorcheskoi evoliutsii A. Bloka." RUSSKAIA LITERATURA XX VEKA: DOOKT. PERIOD, vol. 2. Kaulga, 1970, 242-261.

Michurin, G. GORIACHIE DNI AKTERSKOI ZHIZNI. L., 1972. 51-52, 54-56, 60, 62, 64, 71-73, 82, 86-87, 94, 103, 110, 114, 118-119, 123-124, 129-134, 135, 140.

Mikhailov, A. "Chuvstvo puti." OKTIABR' 11 (1980): 201-212.

———. "Poeticheskii mir Bloka." V MIRE BLOKA (1981), 135-163.

Mikhailova, M. "Zhanrovo-kompozitsionnye osobennosti retsenzii A. Bloka: Teatral'nye retsenzii." VESTNIK MOSKOVSKOGO UNIVERSITETA. SERIIA VII. (FILOLOGIIA. ZHURNALISTIKA.). 6 (1980): 52-60.

Mikhailovskii, B. IZBRANNYE STAT'I O LITERATURE I ISKUSSTVE. M., 1969, 390, 394, 395-396, 401, 403, 404, 407, 409, 415, 421, 428, 429, 432, 433-434, 441-442, 445-447, 452-453, 458-459, 461, 464-466, 473, 475-477, 485-486, 488, 500-501, 504.

Mikhalkov, S. "Aleksandr Blok." In his MOIA PROFESSIIA. M., 1974, 162-169.

———. "Nash sovremennik." A. BLOK I SOVREMENNOST' (1981), 15-19.

Miller, O. "Pomety Aleksandra Bloka na polnom sobranii sochinenii M. Iu. Lermontova." RLit 3 (1975): 212-219. Also in V MIRE BLOKA (1981), 503-516.

Minakova, A. "K probleme liricheskoi dramy XX veka: Blok, Maiakovskii, Esenin." PROBLEMY SOVETSKOI LITERATURY. SBORNIK TRUDOV, vyp. 1. M., 1978.

Mindlin, E. NEOBYKNOVENNYE SOBESEDNIKI. M., 1968, 18, 71. [Blok and M. Tsvetaeva.]

———. "Zvezdnyi chas poeta." NAUKA I RELIGIIA 6 (1968): 40-46. [On Blok relinquishing his religious and mystic outlook.]

Mints, Z. "Poeticheskii ideal molodogo Bloka." BS I (1962), 172-225.

———. "Al. Blok i L. N. Tolstoi." TRUDY PO RUSSKOI I SLAVIANSKOI FILOLOGII V. UchZ TART. UNIV., no. 119 (1962): 232-278.

———. "Poema Bloka 'Ee pribytie' i revoliutsiia 1905 goda." TRUDY PO RUSSKOI I SLAVIANSKOI FILOLOGII VI. UchZ TART. UNIV. (Tartu), no. 139 (1963): 164-180.

———. "Ob odnom sposobe obrazovaniia slov v proizvedenii iskusstva: Ironicheskoe i poeticheskoe v stikhotvorenii Al. Bloka 'Neznakomka.' " TRUDY PO ZNAKOVYM SISTEMAM II. UchZ TART. UNIV. (Tartu), no. 181 (1965): 330-380.

———. LIRIKA ALEKSANDRA BLOKA 1907-1911. Tartu, 1969.

———. "Struktura 'khudozhestvennogo prostranstva' v lirike A. Bloka." TRUDY PO RUSSKOI I SLAVIANSKOI FILOLOGII XV. UchZ. TART. UNIV. (Tartu), no. 251 (1970): 203-293.

————. "K genezisu komicheskogo u Bloka: Vl. Solov'ev i A. Blok." TRUDY PO RUSSKOI I SLAVIANSKOI FILOLOGII XVIII. UchZ Tart. Univ. (Tartu), no. 266 (1971).
————. "Blok i Dostoevskii." DOSTOEVSKII I EGO VREMIA. L., 1971, 217-247.
————. "Blok i Gogol'." BS II (1972), 122-205.
————. "Al. Blok i russkaia realisticheskaia literatura XIX veka." Doctoral dissertation, Tartu, 1972.
————. LIRIKA ALEKSANDRA BLOKA 1898-1916. 3rd. ed., Tartu, 1973.
————. "Blok i Pushkin." TRUDY PO RUSSKOI I SLAVIANSKOI FILOLOGII XXI. UchZ TART. UNIV. (TARTU), no. 306 (1973): 135-296.
————. "Funktsiia reministsentsii v poetike A. Bloka." TRUDY PO ZNAKOVYM SISTEMAM VI. UchZ TART. UNIV. (Tartu), no. 308 (1973): 387-417.
————. LIRIKA ALEKSANDRA BLOKA. ALEKSANDR BLOK I TRADITSIIA RUSSKOI DEMOKRATICHESKOI LITERATURY XIX V., vyp. 3. Tartu, 1973.
————. "Stroenie 'khudozhestvennogo mira' i semantika slovesnogo obraza v tvorchestve Al. Bloka 1910-kh godov." TVK III (1975), 43-47.
————. LIRIKA ALEKSANDRA BLOKA. 1910-e gody. vyp. 4. Tartu, 1975.
————. "Iz poeticheskoi mifologii 'tret'ego toma.' " TVK III (1975), 47-53.
————. "A. Blok—A. Remizov." NovM 11 (1980): 260-262. [Introduction to the Blok—Remizov correspondence.]
————. "Blok i russkii simvolizm." NMI (1980), 98-172.
————. "Simvol u A. Bloka." V MIRE BLOKA (1981), 172-208.
Mints. Z. et al. "Chastotnyi slovar' 'Stikhov o Prekrasnoi Dame' A. Bloka i nekotorye zamechaniia o strukture tsikla." TRUDY PO ZNAKOVYM SISTEMAM III. UchZ TART. UNIV. (TARTU), no. 198 (1967): 209-316.
————. Introduction to "Perepiska Bloka s V. Ia. Briusovym (1903-1919)." NMI (1980), 466-485.
Mirza-Avakyan, M. "A. Blok i russkii dramaticheskii teatr nachala XX veka." NAUCHNYE TRUDY EREVANSKOGO UNIVERSITETA, vol. 7, no. 7, part 1, 1960, 157-181.
Mokul'skii, S. O TEATRE. M., 1963.
Moldavskii, Dm. "Uroki Aleksandra Bloka." ZVEZDA 10 (1980): 206-209.
Murashov, M. "A. Blok i S. Esenin. (Stranitsy iz vospominanii)." VS II (1980). 111-114.
Muratova, K. GOR'KII NA KAPRI. L., 1971, 147-149, 158, 266. [On Blok and Italy.]
Murav'ev, Vl. "Bloku—ver'te." A. BLOK. IZBRANNOE. M., 1980, 5-38.
Mushina, I. "Blok i Zhukovskii." ZVEZDA 10 (1980): 216-222.
Nadirov, S. S. "Tsvetovye prilagatel'nye v stikhotvoreniiakh Aleksandra Bloka." RUSSKII IAZYK V SHKOLE 6 (1970): 3-6.
Nagapetan, A. "Metafora Aleksandra Bloka." Doctoral dissertation, Moscow Pedagogical Institute, 1974.
Nappel'baum, Ida. "Listki vospominanii." A. BLOK I SOVREMENNOST' (1981), 344-346.
Narovchatov, S. "Slovo o Bloke," in his TRI SLOVA. M., 1972. Also in NMI (1980), 9-15.
————. "Uroki Aleksandra Bloka." In his ATLANTIDA RIADOM S TOBOI. M., 1972, 87-100. Other references on pp. 302-302, 306, 307, 315, 316.
————. "Pamiatnye uroki." A. BLOK I SOVREMENNOST' (1981), 20-31.
Nartsissov, B. "Simvolika tsveta u Bloka." NOVOE RUSSKOE SLOVO, 23 Nov. 1980, 5,7.
Nazarenko, V. "Istoriia odnoi vstrechi." MOSKVA 6 (1967): 212-217. [Blok and Stanislavskii.]
Nebol'sin, S. "Aleksandr Blok v sovremennon zapadnom literaturovedenii." VLit 9 (1968): 189-196.
————. "Aleksandr Blok i sovremennoe zapadnoe literaturovedenie." RUSSKAIA LITERATURA I EE ZARUBEZHNYE KRITIKI. M., 1974, 302-342.
————. "O 'ravnodushnoi prirode' i soprotivlenii 'stikhiiam': Pushkin i Blok." PUSHKIN I LITERATURA NARODOV SOVETSKOGO SOIUZA. Erevan, 1975, 159-178.
————. "Mne meshaet pisat' Lev Tolstoi: Chernoviki A. Bloka." LITERATURNAIA UCHEBA 4 (1978): 189-198.
————. "Istoriia dvukh sovpadenii (v tvorchestve Bloka s A. Grigor'evym i Eseninym)." LITERATURNAIA UCHEBA 3 (1978): 224-226.

————. "Ob odnom sobytii v lirike A. Bloka." REVOLIUTSIIA 1905-1907 GODOV I LITERATURA. M., 1978, 99-115. [On Blok and Rilke.]
————. "Blok i Oktiabr'." VLit 10 (1980): 76-104.
————. "V pervykh stolknoveniiakh s dekadentami: Iz proizvedenii iunogo Bloka." IZV. AN SSSR (SERIIA LITERATURY I IAZYKA) 39 (1980): 492-498.
————. "V pervykh stolknoveniiakh s dekadentami." A. BLOK I SOVREMENNOST' (1981), 227-240.
Nekrasova, E. "Vidy ekspressivnoi tonal'nosti v stikhotvornykh proizvedeniiakh A. Bloka." OBRAZNOE SLOVO A. BLOKA (1980), 89-121.
Nikitina, E. "Rozhdenie zhanra." VOPROSY SLAVIANSKOI FILOLOGII. Saratov, 1963, 146-165. [On "Vozmezdie."]
————. RUSSKAIA POEZIIA NA RUBEZHE DVUKH EPOKH. Part I. Saratov, 1970. [Numerous references to Blok.]
Nikol'skaia, L. "Bairon v perevodakh." VOPROSY LINGVOSTILISTIKI ROMANO-GERMANSKIKH IAZYKOV. Smolensk, 1975, 25-41.
Nikulin, L. "Aleksandr Blok." LIUDI I STRANSTVIIA. VOPSPOMINANIIA I VSTRECHI. M., 1962, 76-82. Also in VS II (1980), 388-394.
Nolle-Kogan, N. "Iz vospominanii." VS II (1980), 361-378.
OBRAZNOE SLOVO A. BLOKA. Ed. A. N. Kozhin. M., 1980.
Odoevskaia, I. NA BEREGAKH NEVY. Washington: Victor Kamkin, Inc., 1967, 252-319.
Ognev, V. "Etiud o Bloke." In his STANOVLENIE TALANTA. M., 1972, 185-192.
Ogenva, E. " 'Roza i krest' Aleksandra Bloka: Avtobiograficheskaia osnova." RLit 2 (1976): 136-143.
Orlov, Vl. "Tri ocherka ob Aleksandre Bloka." PUTI I SUD'BY, M.-L., 1963, 1971. ["Vechnyi boi," "Istoriia odnoi 'druzhby—vrazhdy,' " "Istoriia odnoi liubvi."]
————. "Nekotorye itogi i zadachi sovetskogo blokovedeniia." BS I (1964), 507-521.
————. "Poet i ego sovremenniki." ZVEZDA 3 (1968)' 171-182.
————. "Zhizn', strast', dolg. Uroki Bloka." In his PEREPUT'IA. IZ ISTORII RUSSKOI POEZII NACHALA XX VEKA. M., 1976, 313-366.
————. "Sny i iav." A. BLOK. PIS'MA K ZHENE. LITERATURNOE NASLEDSTVO 89 (1978), 11-32.
————. GAMAIUN. ZHIZN' ALEKSANDRA BLOKA. L., 1980. [English translation: HAMAYUN: THE LIFE OF ALEKSANDR BLOK. M., 1980.]
————. "Neizvestnyi Blok." LITERATURNAIA GAZETA, 19 Nov. 1980, p. 6.
————. "Aleksandr Blok v pamiati sovremennikov." VS I (1980), 7-36.
————. "Poet i gorod (Aleksandr Blok i Peterburg)." ZVEZDA 10 (1980): 4-86.
Otsup, N. "Litso Bloka." LITERATURNYE OCHERKI. Paris, 1961, 55-77.
Ozerov, L. "Dver' v masterskuiu." VLit 6 (1968): 173-179.
————. "Chitaia Bloka o Bloke." NovM 11 (1971): 273-277.
————. "Odukhotvorennost'...." MASTERSTVO I VOLSHEBSTVO. M., 1976, 205-236.
————. "Nachala i kontsy." V MIRE BLOKA (1981), 441-453.
Papaian, P. "K voprosu o sootnoshenii stikhotvornykh razmerov i intensivnosti tropov v lirike A. Bloka." BS II (1972), 268-290.
————. "K dinamike ritma chetyrekhstopnogo iamba liriki A. Bloka." TVK III (1975), 75-78.
Papernyi, Z. "Blok i revoliutsiia." SAMOE TRUDNOE. M., 1963, 66-99;
————. "Negotovymi dorogami." VLit 11 (1964): 46-63. Also in his MAIAKOVSKII I PROBLEMY NOVATORSTVA. M., 1965, 171-210. [A comparison of Blok's, Esenin's, and Maiakovskii's poetry.]
————. " 'Vishnevyi sad' Chekhova i 'Solov'inyi sad' Bloka." TVK III (1975), 116-117.
————. "Blok i 'Proiskhozhdenie tragedii' Nitsshe. (K probleme 'Blok i Nitsshe')." TVK III (1975), 107-112.
Pasternak B. "Veter. (Chetyre otryvka o Bloke)." STIKHOTVORENIIA I POEMY. M.-L., 1965, 464-466.
————. "Liudi i polozheniia." NovM 1 (1967): 213-214, 216.
————. "Iz ocherka 'Liudi i polozheniia.' " VS II (1980), 405,
Pasternak, E. "Pasternak o Bloke." BS II (1972), 447-450.
Paustovskii, K. "Aleksandr Blok." TARUSSKIE STRANITSY, Kaluga, 1961, 37-41. Also in BLIZKIE I DALEKIE. M., 1967, 277-285, and NAEDINE S OSEN'IU. M., 1967, 102-109. [Translated into English in PAGES FROM TARUSA. Ed. and intro. Andrew Field. Boston: Little, Brown, 1963, 354-363.]

Pavlovich, N. "Vospominaniia ob Aleksandre Bloke." Introduction by Z. Mints. BS I (1964), 446-506. Also in: PROMETEI, vol. 2. M., 1977, 219-253.
————. "Vospominaniia ob Aleksandre Bloke. Poema." In her DUMY I VOSPOMI-NANIIA. 2nd rev. ed. M., 1966, 7-40.
————. "Iz vospominaniia ob Aleksandre Bloke." VS II (1980), 395-400.
————. "Pis'mo P. A. Pavlovich k B. I. Solov'evu." ZVEZDA 10 (1980): 176-178. [About his book POET I EGO PODVIG.]
Pereleshin, V. " 'Solov'inyi sad' Aleksandra Bloka." GRANI 68 (1968): 132-136.
Pertsov, P. "Rannii Blok." VS I (1980), 195-203.
————. "V sinem vorotnike." NEVA 11 (1980): 184-185. Also in A. BLOK I SOV-REMENNOST' (1981), 334-336.
Pertsov, V. "O putiakh sovremennoi poezii." VLit 10 (1962): 43-44, 47, 51-55.
————. "O khudozhestvennom mnogobrazii." MOSKVA 10 (1967): 202-207.
————. POETY I PROZAIKI VELIKIKH LET. 2nd rev. and enlarged ed. M., 1974, 103-104, 108-110, 113, 117-120, 165, 167, 239-242.
"Pesnia buri: K 100-letiiu so dnia rozhdeniia A. A. Bloka." RUSSKII IAZYK ZA RU-BEZHOM 5 (1980): 97-99.
Petrosov, K. " 'Ia' i 'my' v poeme Maiakovskogo 'Oblaka v shtanakh' i tvorchestve proletarskikh poetov: (O kharaktere liricheskogo geroia Bloka)." RUSSKAIA LITERATURA XX VEKA: DOOKT. PERIOD, vol. 3, Kaluga, 1971, 287-288.
————. "O romanticheskom dvoemirii v russkoi poezii nachala XX veka: (A. Blok, A. Belyi, rannii Maiakovskii)." IZ ISTORII RUSSKOGO ROMANTIZMA, no. 1, Kemerovo, 1971.
Petrova, I. "Blok i Tiutchev," VOPROSY ISTORII I TEORII LITERATURY, no. 4. Cheliabinsk, 1968, 76-101.
P'ianykh, M. "Rol' poeticheskikh traditsii Nekrasova v razvitii liriki russkikh simvolis-tov." NEKRASOVSKII SBORNIK IV. L., 1967, 158-169.
————. "Zhizn' i poeticheskaia sud'ba Aleksandra Bloka." NEVA 1 (1979): 193-194.
————. "Blok i russkaia sovetskaia poeziia." NMI (1980), 173-200.
————. "Vozvrashchenie Aleksandra Bloka." ZVEZDA 10 (1980): 190-205.
————. " 'Russkii stroi dushi' v revoliutsionnuiu epokhu: ('Dvenadtsat' ' i 'Skify' A. Bloka)." V MIRE BLOKA (1981), 245-290.
Piast, Vl. "Vospominaniia o Bloke." VS I (1980), 364-397.
————. "Dva slova o chtenii Blokom stikhov." VS I (1980), 397-401.
Pliukhanova, M. Foreword to "Blok v perepiske Blokov i Kachalovykh." NMI (1980)' 275-278.
Polonskaia, B. "Vstrechi." NEVA 1 (1966): 188-189. [About an unpublished article by Zoshchenko on Blok.]
Pomirchii, R. "Literaturnye istochniki dramy." VLit 11 (1965): 194-197. [On Zhir-munskii's study of THE ROSE AND THE CROSS.]
————. "Materialy k bibliografii A. Bloka za 1958-1970 gody." BS II (1972), 528-589.
Potsepnia, D. "Epitet 'pevuchii' v poezii Bloka." VOPROSY TEORII I ISTORII IAZY-KA. L., 1969, 75-84.
————. "O edinstve esteticheskikh svoistv slova v poezii i proze A. Bloka." VOPROSY STILISTIKI (Saratov), vyp. 4 (1972); 74-84.
————. "O slovesnom voploshchenii khudozhestvennoi idei. (Po proze A. Bloka)." VLUn. Seriia 14, vyp. 3 (1972): 114-121.
————. "O iazyke prozy A. Bloka." Doctoral dissertation, Leningrad University, 1973.
————. "Proza A. Bloka. STILISTICHESKIE PROBLEMY. L., 1976. [Reviewed by G. Pirog in SEEJ 2 (1979): 279-280.
————. "A. Blok o khudozhestvennom slove." VLenU (SERIIA ISTORII, IAZYKA I LITERATURY) 2 (1980): 50-55.
Pradivlianyi, G. "Problema romanticheskogo geroia v poeme A. Bloka 'Vozmezdie.' " UchZ TOMSKOGO INST. 83 (1973): 101-108.
————. "Poema A. Bloka 'Solov'inyi sad.' " PROBLEMY METODA I ZHANRA. (Tomsk) vyp. 2 (1974): 42-51.
Pravdina, I. "Iz istorii formirovaniia 'tret'ego toma' liriki A. Bloka." TVK III (1975), 38-43.
————. "Istoriia formirovaniia tsikla 'Strashnyi mir.' " V MIRE BLOKA (1981), 209-244.
Primochkina, N. "Problema gumanizma v esteticheskikh vozreniiakh A. Bloka (1917-1921)." FILOLOGICHESKIE NAUKI 2 (1978): 3-12.
————. "A. Blok i problema 'mekhanizatsii' kul'tury (1918-1919 godov)." IZV. AN SSSR (SERIIA LITERATURY I IAZYKA), vol. 37, no. 2 (1978): 157-167.

Prokushev, Iu. "Delo dlia menia ochen' vazhnoe..." OGONEK 40 (1970): 24-26. [About Blok and Esenin.]
——. "Ot dushi." A. BLOK I SOVREMENNOST' (1981), 119-141.
PROMETEI. No. 14, forthcoming. Dedicated to Blok.
Pyman, A. "Aleksandr Blok v Anglii." RLit (1961): 214-220.
——. "Ob angliiskikh perevodakh stikhotvorenii Bloka." MEZHDUNARODNYE SVIAZI RUSSKOI LITERATURY. M.-L., 1963, 417-433.
——. "Materialy k bibliografii Aleksandra Bloka (Zarubezhnaia literatura)." BS I (1964), 557-573.
Rachkov, D. "N. Aseev ob Aleksandre Bloke." RLit 2 (1970); 192-193.
Rassadin, S. "Iskusstvo byt' samim soboi." NovM 7 (1967): 207-209, 214-217, 220. [About K. Chukovskii on Blok.]
Remizov, A. "Iz ognennoi Rossii (Pamiati Bloka)." VS II (1980), 406-411.
Rerikh, N. "Blok i Vrubel'." IZ LITERATURNOGO NASLEDIIA . M., 1974, 105-106.
Rezvina, O. "Grammaticheskie oshibki Bloka." SBORNIK STATEI PO VTORICHNYM MODELIRUIUSHCHIM SISTEMAM. Tartu, 1973, 157-162.
Rez, Z. LIRIKA AL. BLOKA V SHKOL'NOM IZUCHENII. L., 1975.
Rodina, T. ALEKSANDR BLOK I RUSSKII TEATR NACHALA XX VEKA. M., 1972.
Rodnianskaia, I. "Muza Aleksandra Bloka." NovM 11 (1980): 230-245.
Roitershtein, M., "Muzykal'nye struktury v poezii A. Bloka." O MUZYKE: PROBLEMY ANALIZA. M., 1974, 323-343.
Rostotskii, B. "Modernizm v teatre." RUSSKAIA KHUDOZHESTVENNAIA KUL'-TURA KONTSA XIX NACHALA XX VEKA (1895-1907), vol. 1. M., 1968, 207-217. [See also R's index.]
Rozanov, I. "Ob Aleksandre Bloke. Iz vospominanii." VS II (1980), 379-387.
Rozenblium, L. "Pis'ma Aleksandra Bloka k zhene: Literaturnoe nasledstvo 89." VEST-NIK AKADEMII NAUK 4 (1978): 118-129.
Rozhdestvenskii, V. "Litso v griadushchee." ZVEZDA 11 (1960): 189-198.
——. "Aleksandr Blok." In his STRANITSY ZHIZNI. M., 1974, 195-219. Also 102, 106-107, 124, 126, 156-160, 177, 223, 252-255, 355.
——. "Zapiski, 1974-1975-1976-1977." NEVA 12 (1978): 126. [About a meeting with Delmas.]
——. "Iz knigi STRANITSY ZHIZNI." VS II (1980), 108-110. [Esenin's version of his meeting with Blok.]
Rubtsov, A. DRAMATURGIIA ALEKSANDRA BLOKA. Minsk, 1968.
Rudnev, P. "Metrika Aleksandra Bloka." Doctoral dissertation, Tartu, 1969.
——. "O stile dramy A. Bloka 'Roza i krest.' " TRUDY PO RUSSKOI I SLAVIAN-SKOI FILOLOGII. XV (Tartu) UchZ TAR. UNIV., no. 251 (1970): 294-334.
——. " Stikhotvorenie A. Bloka 'Vse tikho na svetlom litse....' " POETIKA I STILI-STIKA RUSSKOI LITERATURY. L., 1971, 450-455.
——. "Metricheskii repertuar A. Bloka." BS II (1974), 218-267.
RUSSKAIA MYSL', no. 2860, 16 September 1971. [Dedicated to Blok.]
Rybin, M. "Iz nabliudenii nad poetikoi rannego Bloka." NEKOTORYE VOPROSY RUSSKOI LITERATURY XX VEKA. M., 1973, 20-38.
——. "U istokov: Filos.-estet. aspekty rannei liriki A. Bloka." PROBLEMY REAL-IZMA RUSSKOI LITERATURY NACHALA XX VEKA. M., 1976, 38-53.
Rybnikova, M. "Blok v roli Gamleta i Don Zhuana." VS I (1980), 128-133.
Rylenkov, N. "Aleksandr Blok." In his DUSHA POEZII. M., 1969, 99-108.
Ryl'skii, M. "Aleksandr Blok." In his O POEZII. M., 1974, 265-270.
Saakiants, A. "Trud etot nelegkii..." VLit 1 (1978): 260-261. [About Tsvetaeva's "Stikhi k Bloku."]
——. "Marina Tsvetaeva ob Aleksandre Bloke." V MIRE BLOKA (1981), 119-141.
Sadovskoi, B. "Vstrechi." ZVEZDA 3 (1968); 182-186.
——. "Vstrechi s Blokom." VS II (1980), 47-57.
Sagatov, Bogdan. "Individuation in Blok's 'Nochnaia fialka.' " BRC (1980).
Samarina, O. "Sashura Blok." NEVA 11 (1980): 178-181. [Also in A. BLOK I SOVRE-MENNOST' (1981), 327-333.
Samoilov, D. "O perevodakh Aleksandra Bloka," in A. Blok, NA DOL'NEM GORI-ZONTE: STIKHI I DRAMY ZARUBEZHNYKH POETOV V PEREVODE A. BLOKA. M., 1970, 6-16.
——. "Rifma Bloka," KNIGA O RUSSKOI RIFME. M., 1973, 214-224.
Sapogov, V. "O nekotorykh strukturnykh osobennostiakh liricheskogo tsikla A. Bloka." IAZYK I STIL' KHUDOZHESTVENNOGO PROIZVEDENIIA. M., 1966, 88-89, 90-91.
——. " 'Snezhnaia maska' Aleksandra Bloka." UchZ MOSK. PED. INSTIT. IMENI

LENINA no. 255 (1966): 5-23.
————. "O poniatii tsvetoobraza v lirike A. Bloka." PROBLEMY MASTERSTVA V IZUCHENII I PREPODAVANII KHUDOZHESTVENNOI LITERATURY. M., 1967, 243-245.
————. "Liricheskii tsikl i liricheskaia poema v tvorchestve A. Bloka." RUSSKAIA LITERATURA XX VEKA: DOOKT. PERIOD, vol. 1. Kaluga, 1968, 174-189.
Savushkina, N. RUSSKAIA SOVETSKAIA POEZIIA XX GODOV I FOL'KLOR. M., 1971, 26-35, 56-66. [On the influence of folklore in Blok's poetry.]
Sazhin, V. "Pamiat'." ZVEZDA 10 (1980): 186-189.
Sedykh, A. "Dnevniki." NOVOE RUSSKOE SLOVO, 23 November 1980, 5, 7. [On Blok's diaries, especially those written after the Revolution.]
Senderovich, Marena. "Sdvig funktsii opredeleniia v knige vtoroi Bloka." BRC (1980).
Senderovich, Savelii. "Semioticheskii radikal blokovskoi semantiki." BRC (1980).
Serbin, P. IZUCHENIE TVORCHESTVA A. BLOKA. Kiev, 1980.
Shaginian, M. "Chelovek i vremia: Vospominaniia." NovM (1978): 204-214.
Shakhovskoi, Archbishop Ioann. "O Bloke." NOVOE RUSSKOE SLOVO, 10 December 1961.
Shanskii, M. "Ob odnom mnogoznachnom slove u Pushkina, Lermontova I Bloka." RUSSKII IAZYK V SHKOLE 3 (1974): 8-10.
Shapovalov, L. "Ob odnom lermontovskom obraze u Aleksandra Bloka." M. IU. LER- MONTOV. ISSLEDOVANIIA I MATERIALY. Voronezh, 1964, 221-235. [The demonic theme in Lermontov and Blok.]
————. "Pochemu ne okoncheno 'Vozmezdie' A. Bloka?" VOPROSY LITERATURY I FOL'KLORA. Voronezh, 1969, 42-56.
Sharlaimova, L. "Obraz dvoinika v tsikle stikhov Bloka 'Strashnyi mir.' " NAUCHNYE TRUDY NOVOSIBIRSKOGO PED. INST., n. 65 (1971).
————. "Tema dvoinika v poezii russkogo simvolizma: Blok i Briusov." NAUCHNYE TRUDY BARNAUL. PED. INSTITUTA, vol. 20 (1972), 57-69.
Sharypkin, D. "Blok i Strindberg." VLenU, no. 2, vyp. 1 (1963): 82-91.
————. "Blok i Ibsen." SKANDINAVSKII SBORNIK 6 (1963), 159-176.
————. "Pervonachanl'naia redaktsiia stati'i Bloka 'Pamiati Avgusta Strindberga.' " BS I (1964), 552-556.
————. "Avgust Strindberg i russkaia literatura." Doctoral dissertation, Institute of Russian Literature, L., 1968.
Shcheglov, M. "Spor ob A. Bloke." in his LITERATURNO-KRITICHESKIE STAT'I. M., 1965, 201-206. [Also in his LITERATURNAIA KRITIKA. M., 1971, 414- 418. About Orlov's ALEKSANDR BLOK. M., 1956.]
Shefner, V. "Kto Blok dlia menia." ZVEZDA 10 (1980): 161.
Shilov, L. "Karmen. Po stranitsam blokovskikh dnevnikov i pisem." IUNOST' 10 (1980: 92-99.
Shiriaev, B. "Predchustvie vozmezdiia. " RELIGIOZNYE MOTIVY V RUSSKOI PO- EZII. Brussels: Zhizn' s Bogom, 1960.
Shklovskii, V. ZHILI, BYLI... M., 1966. [Numerous references to Blok.]
Shmakov, G. "Blok i Kuzmin." BS II (1972), 341-364.
Sholomova, S. "A. Blok i L. Reisner." TVK III (1975), 127-128.
————. "Za strochkami pisem—sud'ba. (Iz perepiski A. A. Bloka s G. P. Blokom). ZVEZDA 10 (1980): 178-183.
Shomrakov, I. "Aleksandr Blok kak chitatel': Iz chteniia peredovoi russkoi intelli- gentsii nachala XX veka." TRUDY LEN. INST. KUL'TURY, vol. 25, 1 (1973): 124-140.
Shtein, S. "Vospominaniia ob Aleksandre Bloke." VS I (1980), 188-194.
Sidorov, V. "Na vershinakh: Tvorcheskaia biografiia Rerikha, rasskazana im samim i ego sovremennikami." MOLODAIA GVARDIIA 10 (1974): 218-219. [Blok and Rerikh.]
Silov, L. "Kak chital svoi stikhi Aleksandr Blok." RUSSKII IAZYK ZA RUBEZHOM 5 (1980): 100-103.
Simonov, K. "Vstrecha s Blokom." PRAVDA, 11 August 1970.
Siniavskii, A. "Poetika Pasternaka." B. Pasternak, STIKHOTVORENIIA I POEMY. M.-L., 1965, 26-27, 43. [On Blok as interpreted by Pasternak.]
Skatov, N. N. "Rossiia u Aleksandra Bloka i poeticheskaia traditsiia Nekrasova." RLit 3 (1970): 37-56. [Also in V MIRE BLOKA (1981), 85-114.]
————. "K teme 'Strashnogo mira' u Nekrasova i Bloka. (Ob odnom 'blokovskom stikhotvorenii Nekrasova)." METOD I MASTERSTVO. RUSSKAIA LITERA- TURA, vyp. 1, Vologda, 1970, 194-206.
————. "Nekrasov v poeticheskom mire Aleksandra Bloka i Andreia Belogo." In N. Nekrasov, SOVREMENNIKI I PRODOLZHATELI. L., 1973, 210-312.

Skopenko, L. "Aleksandr Blok o nemetskikh romantikakh." IZ ISTORII RUSSKOGO ROMANTIZMA. Kemerovo, 1971.

Skvoznikov, V. "Blok protiv dekadenstva." SOVREMENNYE PROBLEMY REALIZMA I MODERNIZMA. M., 1965, 214-254.

———. "Blok i simvolizm." VOPROSY FILOSOFII 5 (1965): 95-106.

Slonimskii, M. "...Liubov'iu svoei k rodnomu narodu." ZVEZDA 10 (1980): 174-175.

Sokolov, Vl. "I s mirom utverdilas' sviaz'..." A. BLOK I SOVREMENNOST' (1981), 52-60.

Sokolova, L. "Neopredelenno-sub'ektnye predlozheniia v russkom iazyke i poetike Bloka." OBRAZNOE SLOVA A. BLOKA (1980), 161-214.

———. "Anglo-amerikanskaia burzhuaznaia kritika o tvorcheskom nasledii Bloka i nekotorye ee problemy v izuchenii sovetskoi literatury." PROBLEMY ANGLIISKOI LITERATURY XIX-XX VV. M., 1974, 220-242.

Sokol'skii, A. "Poet i revoliutsiia." NOVOE RUSSKOE SLOVO, 23 November, 1980, 5, 7.

Soloukhin, V. "Bol'shoe Shakhmatovo." MOSKVA 1 (1979): 196-206; MOSKVA 2 (1979): 183-200.

Solov'ev, B. "Predvestnik luchshego." MOSKVA 11 (1970): 200-202.

———. "Blok i Dostoevskii." DOSTOEVSKII I RUSSKIE PISATELI. Ed. V. Kirpotin. M., 1971, 246-322. Also in his OT ISTORII K SOVREMENNOSTI. 2nd ed. M., 1976, 73-139.

———. POET I EGO PODVIG: TVORCHESKII PUT' ALEKSANDRA BLOKA. M., 1973.

Solov'ev. S. "Vospominaniia ob Aleksandre Bloke." VS I (1980), 110-127.

SOVETSKII TEATR: DOKUMENTY I MATERIALY 1917-1921. L., 1968. [Numerous references to Blok.]

Stankeeva, Z. "O nekrasovskikh traditsiiakh v poetike Bloka." UchZ PERM. UNIV., no. 241 (1970): 215-229.

Stepanov, G. "Vstrecha s Blokom." In his DEN' IZ ZHIZNI PISATELIA. Riga, 1961, 295-305. [First meeting of Blok and Esenin.]

———. "Istoriosofskoe i politicheskoe mirosozertsanie Aleksandra Bloka." VOZDUSHNYE PUTI 4 (1965): 241-255.

Storitsyn, P. "Moia vstrecha s Blokom." NEVA 11 (1980): 195.

Storozhev, A. "Satira v poeme A. Bloka 'Vozmezdie.' " MATERIALY XXXIV NAUCH. KONF. URAL. PED. INSTIT. Ural'sk, 1970, 71-81.

Stratievskii, A. "Kantata Slonimskogo. 'Goloz iz khora.' " BLOK I MUZYKA (1972), 229-245.

Strazhev, V. "Vospominaniia o Bloke." BS I (1964), 427-436. Also in VS II (1980), 40-46.

Struve, G. O CHETYREKH POETAKH. BLOK, SOLOGUB, GUMILEV, MANDEL'-SHTAM. SBORNIK STATEI. London: Overseas Publications, 1981.

Sukhotin, P. "Pamiati A. A. Bloka." VS II (1980), 86-90.

Sumarokov, A. "Moia vstrecha s A. Blokom." VS II (1980), 186-195.

Suvorova, K. "Arkhivist ishchet datu: K izuchenii arkhiva A. A. Bloka." VSTRECHI S PROSHLYM, vyp. 2. M., 1976, 118-123.

———. "Rukoi Aleksandra Bloka: Nabliudeniia arkhivista; VSTRECHI S PROSHLYM, vyp. 3. M., 1978.

———. Introduction to "Perepiska Bloka s S. A. Sokolovym (1903-1910)." NMI (1980), 527-528.

Taborisskaia, E. "A. Blok. Shagi komandora:Opyt monogr. prochteniia." LIRICHESKAIA I EPICHESKAIA POEZIIA XIX VEKA. L., 1976, 27-43.

Taganov, L. "Molodoi Blok chitaet Dostoevskogo." RUSSKAIA LITERATURA XX VEKA: DOOKT. PERIOD. Sbornik 6. Tula, 1974, 220-242.

Tager, E. "Blok v 1915 godu." VS II (1980), 101-107.

———. "Zhanr literaturnogo portreta v tvorchestve Gor'kogo." O KHUDOZHESTVENNOM MASTERSTVE GOR'KOGO. M., 1960, 412-414.

———. "Motivy 'Vozmezdiia' i 'strashnogo mira' v lirike Bloka." NMI (1980), 85-97.

Taranovskii, K. "Zelenye zvezdy i poiushchie vody v lirike Bloka." RUSSIAN LITERATURE 8 (1980): 363-376.

Tarasenkov, S. "A. Blok—redaktor svoikh stikhov." TRUDY KRASNODARSKOGO PED. INSTIT., vyp. 36 (1963): 105-122.

———. "A. Blok o lirike." TRUDY KRASNODARSKOGO PED. INSTIT., vyp, 83, (1966): 122-134.

———. "Satira Bloka i ego svoeobrazie: 'Strashnyi mir.' " OT PUSHKINA DO BLOKA. Krasnodar, 1968, 268-288.

————. "Blok i Maiakovskii: Problemy preemstvennosti." SOVETSKAIA LITERA-
TURA: TRADITSIIA I NOVATORSTVO, no. 1. L., 1976, 23-43.
Tarkhov, A. "Ob Aleksandre Bloke: Tri etiuda." A. Blok, STIKHOTVORENIIA. PO-
EMY. ROZA I KREST. M., 1974, 3-24.
Terapiano, Iu. "Aleksandr Blok." SOVREMENNIK (Canada) 4 (1961): 54-58.
TEZISY I VSESOIUZNOI (III) KONFERENTSII "TVORCHESTVO A. A. BLOKA I
RUSSKAIA KUL'TURA XX VEKA." Tartu, 1975. [TVK III, 1975]
Timenchik, R. "Printsipy tsitirovaniia u Akhmatovoi v sopostavlenii s Blokom." TVK
III (1975), 124-127.
Timenchik, R. et al. "Sny Bloka i 'Peterburgskii tekst' nachala XX veka." TVK III
(1975), 129-135.
Timofeev, L. "Poetika kontrasta v poezii Aleksandra Bloka." RLit 2 (1961): 98-107.
————. TVORCHESTVO ALEKSANDRA BLOKA. M., 1963.
————. "O poetike Bloka." SOVETSKAIA LITERATURA: METOD, STIL', POETIKA.
M., 1964, 476-522.
————. "O poezii Aleksandra Bloka." LITERATURA V SHKOLE 5 (1968): 21-26.
————. "Dve neznakomki: (K voprosu o gumanizme v tvorchestve A. Bloka)." TVK III
(1975), 19-23.
————. "Nasledie poeta." VLit 10 (9180): 51-75.
————. "Nasledie poeta." NMI (1980), 47-62.
————. "O gumanizme v tvorchestve Bloka." V MIRE BLOKA (1981), 115-123.
Tolstoi, A. N. "Padshii angel. Aleksandr Blok." DON 3 (1966): 173-180.
————. "Iz stat'i 'Padshii angel.' "VS II (1980), 145.
Tolstoi, D. "Nachalo zhizni." NEVA 1 (1971): 124-126. [About Blok and A. Tolstoi.]
Toporov, V. "Blok i Zhukovskii: k probleme reministsentii." TVK III (1975), 83-89.
————. "Ob odnom aspekte 'ispanskoi' temy u Bloka." TVK III (1975), 118-123.
Trifonov, N. "Lunacharskii i Aleksandr Blok." PROSTOR 12 (1970), 115-121.
Trofimov, I. "A. A. Blok i A. A. Grigor'ev." III MEZHDOVUZ. STUD. NAUCH. FIL-
OLOG. KONF: KRATKOE SODERZHANIE DOKLADOV. L., 1970, 88-89.
Tsshokher, A. "Iz vospominanii ob Aleksandre Bloke." NEVA 11 (1980): 191-192.
Tsvetaeva, M., "Stikhi o Bloke." IZBRANNYE PROIZVEDENIIA. M.-L., 1965, 92-102.
————. "Plennyi dukh: Moia vstrecha s A. Belym." MOSKVA 4 (1967). [References
to Blok on pp. 113, 117, 124-127, 139, 140.]
Tsybin, Vl. "Mir vokrug chelovecheksogo serdtsa." A. BLOK I SOVREMENNOST'
(1981), 181-187.
Trukov, A. "Tvorcheskie sny." NEDELIA, 4-10 August 1969, p. 6. [About the cycle
"Karmen."]
————. ALEKSANDR BLOK. M., 1969, 1976.
————. "Novyi zvuk: K istorii odnogo stikhotvoreniia 'Aviator.' " NAUKA I ZHIZN'
2 (1970): 66-67.
————. "Sred' bushuiushchikh sozvuchii...." MUZYKAL'NAIA ZHIZN' 23 (1970):
18-20. [About Blok and music.]
————. "Uznaiu tebe zhizn'! Prinimaiu!" and "Sred' bushuiushchikh sozvuchii..."
OTKRYTOE VREMIA. M., 1975, 9-36.
————. "Ia idu." In his VYSOKOE NEBO. CHETYRE PORTRETA. PUSHKIN, GO-
GOL', CHEKHOV, BLOK. M., 1977, 147-172.
Tutolmina, S. "Moi vospominaniia ob Aleksandre Bloke." VS I (1980), 91-95.
————. "Aleksandr Blok v vospominaniiakh." NMI (1980), 293-296.
Tvardovskii, A. "O Bloke." A. BLOK I SOVREMENNOST', (1981), 12-14.
Tynianov, Iu. "Blok." In his PROBLEMA STIKHOTVORNOGO IAZYKA. M., 1965,
248-258. References to Blok on pp. 123-125, 135-136, 261.
Ushakov, N. "A. A. Blok." In his SOSTIAZANIE V POEZII. Kiev, 1969, 57-61.
Usok, I. "Lermontov i Blok." LERMONTOV I LITERATURA NARODOV SOVET-
SKOGO SOIUZA. Erevan, 1974, 192-211.
V MIRE BLOKA. SBORNIK STATEI. Compiled by A. Mikhailov and St. Lesnevskii.
M., 1981.
Vainberg, I. "Blok i Gor'kii." V MIRE BLOKA (1981), 333-382.
Valentinov, N. (Vol'skii). "Chrevoveshchatel' nevmiatits." NOVOE RUSSKOI SLOVO,
4, 5, 6 July 1961.
————. DVA GODA S SIMVOLISTAMI. Ed. and intro. Gleb Struve. Stanford: The
Hoover Institution, 1969.
Valgina, N. " 'Ni moria net glubzhe, ni bezdny temnei': O punktuatsii A. Bloka." RUS-
SKAIA RECH' 6 (1980): 21-29.
Vasil'eva, S. "Poeticheskaia simfoniia A. Bloka ('Roza i Krest')." TEATR 1 (1974):
55-61.
Vasina-Grossman, V. "O poezii Bloka, Esenina i Maiakovskogo v sovetskoi muzyke."

Scha: ₃en zur Wirkung Bloks
en 20er Jahre." ZEIT-

Stell₁ ₃rs.' " ZEITSCHRIFT

Trior SE ET SOVIETIQUE,

AVES, vol. 38 (1961):

Worn ₃S LIED DES SCHICK-